THE POLITICAL EDUCATION
OF HENRY ADAMS

THE
POLITICAL EDUCATION
OF
HENRY ADAMS

BROOKS D. SIMPSON

UNIVERSITY OF SOUTH CAROLINA

© 1996 by the University of South Carolina

Published in Columbia, South Carolina, by the
University of South Carolina Press

Manufactured in the United States of America

Library of Congress Cataloging-in-Publication Data

Simpson, Brooks D.
    The political education of Henry Adams / Brooks D. Simpson.
        p.   cm.
    Includes bibliographical references and index.
    ISBN 1-57003-053-7
    1. Adams, Henry, 1838-1918—Career in politics. 2. Historians—
United States—Biography. 3. United States—Politics and
government—1865-1900. I. Title.
    E175.5.A2S56 1996
    973'.07202—dc20   95-4371

To the Berlins
Chet, Anne, Doug, Alex, and Gordon
and the Simpsons
John, Adeliade, and Joy
and
Jean, Rebecca, and Emily

CONTENTS

PREFACE

No one can ever write a biography about me because I wrote the *Education* to forestall it.

Henry Adams

Henry Adams was an embittered man in his old age. He looked back upon his life as a failure. As historian, journalist, political gadfly, and husband, he had fallen far short of the goals he had set for himself. He spent much of his life grasping for power and influence, but found himself clutching at straws. Whatever others might think of his life's work, he knew he had failed in his effort to shape American politics, intellect, and culture according to his own standards. More than mere position or office, Henry Adams craved to possess influence. He remained convinced that he had never attained it. As he sadly concluded, "We leave no followers, no school, no tradition."[1]

Adams knew who was to blame—the Hero of Appomattox, the savior of the Union, Ulysses S. Grant. "I have always considered that Grant wrecked my own life, and the last hope or chance of lifting society back to a reasonably high plane," he told his brother and close confidante Charles. "Grant's administration is to me the dividing line between what we hoped, and what we have got." He had a score to settle with that silent, puzzling man. And Adams did more than settle it: in *The Education of Henry Adams*, published after his death in 1918, he issues a scathing indictment of the eighteenth president of the United States: "He had no right to exist."[2]

It is one of the ironies of Henry Adams's life that we today regard his celebration of failure as his greatest success. A man who assiduously courted unpopularity, Adams would take small satisfaction in learning that he has become a cult figure among historians and intellectuals, many of whom share his sense of alienation from the world. His vitriolic account of Grant's first years in the White House has contributed greatly to the popular historical stereotype of the president, giving rise to yet another interpretation of Grant's malleable first two initials: "uniquely stupid." The *Education* has also exercised a profound influence upon subsequent scholarship on Gilded

Age politics, appearing to confirm the impression that the era was rife with corruption and incompetence in high places.

But *The Education of Henry Adams* is neither objective history nor autobiography. It is part personal recollection, part polemic, and part philosophy. In addition to the unconscious warping of the past in his memory, Adams consciously distorted his life story both to illustrate larger themes and to explain the reasons for his failure. He admitted the deception to Henry James, explaining, "The volume is a mere shield of protection in the grave. I advise you to take your own life in the same way, in order to prevent biographers from taking it in theirs."[3] To be sure, several scholars have expressed doubts as to the accuracy of labeling the *Education* an autobiography. They question whether Henry Adams was in fact a failure. As a historian, Adams continues to hold a high place in the annals of the profession; his attention to history as a literary art is still well worth emulating. The *Education* is a compelling work of literature that has received high acclaim from most critics. But it is not an objective account of Adams's life.

Controversy surrounds Adams's account of his career in politics. Many scholars, while admitting that Adams failed in political life, argue that his failure was due to the moral and intellectual bankruptcy of national politics, not to any major shortcomings on his part. Among them is Ernest Samuels, Adams's most prominent biographer, who said that the *Education* "not only distorts and suppresses many of the facts of his life, but . . . often falls into plain factual error." Samuels described the *Education* as a "strangely blighting shadow" over its subject's life, and sought to illuminate the dark corners. But in his account of Adams's political career in Grant's Washington, Samuels adopted Adams's point of view unquestioningly. The only errors that Samuels appeared interested in correcting concerned those which cast Adams in a bad light. He did not consider whether Adams's view of events was also clouded, flawed, or self-serving.[4]

Other biographers of Adams followed Samuels's lead. According to Richard P. Blackmur, "The question was perhaps not initially of Adams's failure but of society's failure to make use of him: its inability to furnish a free field for intelligent political action." Adams's talents were wasted, Blackmur continued, "because talent has never been given a chance without being at the same moment brutally hamstrung." In their analyses of Adams's works, Earl N. Harbert and John J. Conder never paused to examine whether his writings accurately depict what they purport to describe. Awed by Adams's formidable intellect as displayed in his later writings, these critics forgot Adams's own admonition that in 1870 he was a "strangely different being" from what he was after 1890. In the first two volumes of his trilogy, Edward Chalfant came close to confusing biography with hagiography in discussing his subject's career in politics.[5]

Historians of Gilded Age reform offered a contrasting perspective. Arguing that the self-professed disinterestedness of Adams and his fellow reformers masked their personal ambition, these historians suggested that Adams's failure in politics was no great tragedy. Ari Hoogenboom attributed Adams's hostility toward Grant to his failure to secure political office. John G. Sproat portrayed Adams as part of a liberal reform movement which was nostalgic, unrealistic, narrow-minded, and self-serving, deserving scorn, not sympathy. The Henry Adams that emerged from these accounts was a selfish, ambitious hypocrite who pompously promoted reform because he had been denied political position.[6]

A third group of scholars, who emphasized Adams's achievements as a historian, saw his political career as simply a wrong turn. "From the first Adams should have followed the course he finally took," claimed William Jordy. "He should have ignored reform to hitch his talents to the star of scholarship and literature." According to Jordy, "the vanity of heritage and ambition . . . forced Adams in directions unsuitable for his talents." Adams "never seriously tried to follow the brilliant precedents" of his family, although he felt guilty over his decision.[7] William Dusinberre carried Jordy's argument several steps further, asserting that Adams's real ambitions in life were literary, not political, and that he intended the *Education* to draw attention away from what he thought was his literary failure by making it appear as if political failure had been his major disappointment. Such cleverness is worthy of Adams himself; however, it is riddled by hindsight. The question is not what Henry Adams should have done with his life, but what he actually did and why.[8]

This study, while drawing on the insights offered by the scholars cited above, offers a different perspective on Henry Adams as political reformer. I agree that Adams's political career was a failure. The nature of that failure is to be understood not by explicating the *Education* but by examining the Henry Adams of 1870—a young, brash reformer, infused with energy, excitement, ambition, and desire, determined to make a mark for himself in American politics as he walked the streets of Ulysses S. Grant's Washington. Several elements are crucial to understanding Adams's political career. There is the ever-present fact that he was an Adams, heir to a family tradition of public service, a heritage that was both a blessing and a burden. Being an Adams conferred status, wealth, and opportunity on family members; it also meant great pressures on them to succeed. The family disseminated a set of values to each of its members: the values could lend stability and structure to one's life or stifle attempts to break free of the family mold. To understand Henry Adams, one must first understand what being an Adams meant.

Henry Adams struggled to come to terms with his heritage, to discover an identity and a role which satisfied the demands of family as well as of self. Unable to shake the influences of his background, he sought to fuse them with his own interests, which tended to the analytical and literary, and his desire to educate others. However, the legacy of being an Adams predisposed him to look for intellectual and emotional sustenance in the familiar fields of politics, literature, and philosophy. During the decade following his graduation from Harvard in 1858, Adams undertook the difficult task of trying to find out who he was and what he wanted to do. Slowly, influenced by political theorists John Stuart Mill and Alexis de Tocqueville and by his personal experiences in London during the American Civil War, Adams crafted a career as a political journalist and critic, a member of an educated elite guiding governance and shaping public opinion.

These insights into Adams's early life suggest that previous explanations of his political career fall short of providing a complete picture. Adams was no disinterested reformer with nothing to gain from politics personally. His choice of a political career reflected his own ambitions and interests, and his vision of an elite directing American democracy included a place for himself. However, he did not enter politics simply to gain office. Although he would have accepted political appointment, he wanted to be an influential political critic and adviser, a "stable-companion to statesmen, whether they liked it or not," as he put it.[9] An office might bolster, but would not fulfill, this ambition to be influential, and it is Adams's failure to gain influence, not office, that is at the core of this inquiry.

Henry Adams sincerely believed that his ambitions would serve the public good and improve the American polity. Historians need not argue that ideas and interests are mutually exclusive in discussing motivation. We will understand Adams better if we accept the view that both ideas and interests played their part in shaping his decisions. Such an interpretation rejects the notion that Adams had no political ambitions, or that he did not regard the frustrations of these ambitions as a failure. Politics *was* an integral part of Adams's concept of a national elite, for the elite had to control the governing process in order to exert its influence.

The explanation for Adams's failure lies elsewhere. Part of his disappointment can be attributed to unrealistically high expectations. The world expected great things from an Adams; it was satisfied with no less. Henry Adams had shared these expectations even as a child, causing the family gardener to snap, "You'll be thinkin' you'll be President, too!"[10] When he had not achieved political success by his fortieth birthday, he dismissed the whole concern as a failure, at a time when most of his contemporaries were just setting out to build a political reputation.

Adams needed only to look in the mirror to see one cause of his failure. His personality hindered his quest for influence. His arrogance and derogatory attitude toward those with whom he disagreed limited his effectiveness. His biting satirical portraiture of public figures, more akin to political doggerel than penetrating analysis, may have amused his readers but alienated his subjects, offending the very people he desired to influence. Lacking commitment to reform beyond his personal involvement, he measured the importance of the reform movement according to his importance in it.

Another reason for Adams's failure is attributable to the nature of the reform movement and its advocates. Reformers were far more influential as critics than they were as proponents of new policies and principles. Their lengthy and scholarly expositions on free trade, political corruption, and specie resumption often appeared in esoteric journals read only by fellow reformers and today's historians. Beyond these issues, they had little to offer in terms of specific policy recommendations—although to criticize them for failing to anticipate the twentieth century state is to go too far, for they thought deeply about the problems of governance, even if their solutions were limited and a tad self-serving. Rather than outlining fundamental systemic reform, they called upon the American people to allow an educated and virtuous elite—meaning themselves—to govern and to guide. Few among them realized that they were merely enlistees in a continuing struggle to shore up the rapidly crumbling walls of an ordered, deferential, and stable society, a war which they had been losing for over two centuries. They saw the American Civil War as presenting a new opportunity for them to assume power. Unwilling to engage in the rough-and-tumble of politics to attain their ends—indeed, protesting the means as well as the ends of American politics—they struggled for control of the polity with professional politicians and power brokers. Eventually, the contours of the American state and the forms of American governance did change, sometimes along lines the reformers advocated, but the reformers failed to control the process or reap the fruits of what victories they did achieve. Rather, politicians adopted their principles and policies when to do so served their ends.

If Adams failed with his peers, he seems to have had more success with historians, many of whom accept in varying degrees the image of Gilded Age politics presented in the *Education*. If handled with care, the *Education* can prove revealing about Henry Adams's years in Washington, but, like any form of historical evidence, it must be viewed critically, and its assumptions deserve scrutiny. Too often, historians and other scholars mistake Adams's wit for insight, and delight in quoting Adams without assessing his accuracy. They let Adams's righteous rhetoric and searing sarcasm obscure the fact that what appears to be a question of right versus wrong, of good versus evil, of intelligence versus stupidity, is in reality a difference of opinion over the way presidential power is to be used and the purposes toward which it is to be directed. For Henry Adams's portrayal of the Grant administration was shaped far more by his personal prejudices than by an attempt to analyze the performance of President Grant. Adams deemed Grant incompetent because Grant rejected his outdated theory of presidential power, one framed in terms of classical republicanism more appropriate to the founding period. Adams urged Grant to ignore both partisan considerations and the interests of Congress in asserting the independence of the executive branch. Grant chose to work within the existing political structure, using patronage to build alliances in Congress and elsewhere to engender support for policy. According to Adams, this practice was inherently corrupt, for it violated the republican ideal. It was in this sense, not in the sense of the scandals which plagued Grant's second term, that Adams used the word "corruption." In many ways, Henry Adams was one of the last defenders of the republican ideal in its original form.

Henry Adams's encounter with American politics was a dual failure. He was unable to convince most people of the need to return to the pristine constitutional order endorsed by his fathers, yet his obsession with attempting to do so left him unable to respond creatively to the problems of his time. He withdrew to history as a means of understanding why the old order had fallen by the wayside. For the rest of his life, until his death in 1918, he contemplated the relationship between knowledge and power, and pondered man's control over his own fate. His conclusion in both the *History* and the *Education*—that societies were shaped, defined, and developed by forces beyond human control—was foreshadowed by his failure to influence his own time.

ACKNOWLEDGMENTS

Henry Adams considered biography an act of murder. It is only fair that I make the public (and the authorities) aware of my accomplices in committing this dastardly deed. Robert J. Brugger, now with the Johns Hopkins University Press, introduced me to Adams during my first year at the University of Virginia and helped me to develop my notions about the nature of biography. Several scholars at the University of Wisconsin-Madison took time off from their own endeavors to read, criticize, and improve my work. Allan G. Bogue and John Milton Cooper, Jr., contributed their extensive knowledge of politics during Adams's time, while Paul S. Boyer lent his understanding of the intellectual atmosphere in which Adams moved. Christopher Berkeley shared with me his thoughts on Adams and the *Education* on countless occasions, while remaining properly humble about Boston Bruin defeats and New York Islander victories during the dynasty years. I owe my greatest debt to Richard H. Sewell, who scrutinized the manuscript for clumsy prose and cloudy logic while pushing me onwards.

Several people proved essential in turning this manuscript into a book. Alice Valenzuela helped with the typing and preparation of the manuscript when other responsibilities proved pressing. Department chairs Robert Trennert and Retha Warnicke have been supportive of me and my work as I adjusted to life at Arizona State. Charles Dellheim read the manuscript and offered his thoughts as well as his friendship in an effort to save me from myself—a thankless endeavor. I promise to do the same for him. Geoffrey Blodgett, John Sproat, Charles Calhoun, and especially Gerald MacFarland and Mark Summers commented on various drafts. Each will recognize where I heeded his counsel; even in cases where I believed these readers to be dead wrong, their queries forced me to strengthen or recast arguments to prove how wrong they were. Warren Slesinger has encouraged me along the way with patience and good humor. I deeply appreciate his support.

My thanks go to the Massachusetts Historical Society for allowing me to quote from the Adams Family Papers. Thanks also go to Gore Vidal, for whenever I want to see how Henry Adams would fare in today's world, his spiritual heir is always there to show me.

Any book about a member of the Adams family is in part a book about the impact of family upon its members; writing this book has caused me to recall and rethink some things about family. Doubtless Chet Berlin will overlook the fact that this is not a book about Winston Churchill, while Anne Berlin will welcome the chance to explore the practice of political journalism before the advent of *The Washington Post*—although I suspect that Henry Adams would have been far more at home on *The McLaughlin Group*. Doug, Alex, and Gordon Berlin have given me some idea of what it's like to grow up surrounded by brothers. Usually the best an in-law can hope for is to be tolerated, perhaps accepted; the Berlins have gone far beyond that in welcoming me into the fold. Exploring the parental pressures under which Henry Adams had to labor makes me all the more appreciative of the nurturing support of my own parents, John and Adeliade Simpson, who gave me the freedom and the opportunity to do what I wanted to do. To see Henry and Charles bicker back and forth in letters, yet display loyalty and concern for each other, brought back memories of my relationship with my sister, Joy—memories refreshed and augmented by many a phone call or visit.

Rebecca was too young to help me write this book, despite her rapt interest in my computer keyboard. Nevertheless, her arrival has enriched my life in countless ways, and I will be hard-pressed to repay the debt, regardless of how many Elmos I buy for her. The newest addition to the family, Emily, has played even less of a role in the process, although now Rebecca has a sibling of her own to hug and harass. My wife, Jean, has been busy with far more important things than this volume, but she has had everything to do with just about anything else that makes me happy. They all remind me of how truly fortunate I am.

THE POLITICAL EDUCATION
OF HENRY ADAMS

CHAPTER ONE

THE EDUCATION
OF AN ADAMS

> Had he been born in Jerusalem under the shadow of the
> Temple . . . he would scarcely have been more distinctly
> branded.
>
> *The Education of Henry Adams*

From his birth on February 16, 1838, Henry Brooks Adams was a marked man. In the game of chance known as life, he recalled nearly seventy years later, "probably no child, born in the year, held better cards than he."[1] To be born into a prominent Boston family with money, prestige, and social connections would be enough for most young men attempting to establish themselves in nineteenth-century America. But Henry Adams held one more ace that made for an excellent hand. He was an Adams, a child born to opportunity.

The Adams family was the nearest thing to a political dynasty in the young United States. Henry's great-grandfather, John Adams, capped a long and distinguished career as revolutionary leader, diplomat, and political thinker by succeeding George Washington as president in 1797. Twenty-four years after John Adams left the White House, his son, John Quincy Adams, entered it after eight years as secretary of state; he was serving in the House of Representatives when Henry was born. Henry's own father, Charles Francis Adams, was about to embark on the same course, winning election to Congress while Henry was still a baby. The tradition of public service and responsibility was ever-present. While Henry later insisted that "the family was rather an atmosphere than an influence," he could not escape its impact. Public service, political independence, a faith in human progress tempered by skepticism about human beings, intellectual excellence, and an education partial to things political and literary—all circulated freely through the rooms of the Adams household and the minds of its occupants.[2]

The family's political creed was simple if strict and exacting, grounded in the ideals of ethics and education. In exercising enlightened statesmanship, an Adams based his decisions upon what was right, not what was expe-

1

dient. To temporize or compromise on matters of principle was wrong. Through extensive reading in history, literature, and philosophy, he learned to distinguish between right and wrong. Because he prized independence both of mind and from party, the only ambition worthy of an Adams was to serve the public good, regardless of personal consequences. He saw political leadership in terms of educating the public about morality and good policy. Character and integrity, not popularity, were the marks of a true statesman; if anything, unpopularity confirmed an Adams's belief that he had done the right thing.

The lessons were embedded in Henry's conscience at an early stage. Grandfather John Quincy Adams allowed the child to roam at will through his library and make his way through a maze of historic documents. At ten, the boy corrected proofs of his father's edition of John Adams's works, exposing him firsthand to the family gospel. Charles Francis Adams lectured his sons to ensure that they absorbed the proper values. To Henry he wrote that "the study of ethics is of the highest value to a man in active life." He reminded Henry's brother, Charles Jr., that the ideal statesman must master "the whole theory of morals which makes the foundation of all human society." Having accomplished this, he then must apply "the knowledge thus gained to the events of his time in a continuous and systematic way." Finally, the elder Adams asserted that "no person can ever be a thorough partisan for a long period without sacrifice of his moral identity." Charles Francis Adams pointed to his own father as the embodiment of his precepts. The conclusion was self-evident to Henry Adams: "His education was chiefly inheritance."[3]

Events reinforced this trend. Childhood was a bookish existence for Charles Francis Adams's children. Although they played outdoors, it was not encouraged, for their father thought physical exercise detrimental to the brain. Henry's early bout with scarlet fever and his frail frame doubtless contributed to his propensity for reading. "Henry is Henry," his mother wrote his father in 1851, "when in the house mostly curled up in your big chair with a book and good natured, of course." The Adams boys competed for family favor through trials of intellectual strength. Even at the dinner table, Henry fought for crumbs of approval with his older brothers, John Quincy II and Charles, as the conversation inevitably turned to literature and politics. Grandmother Adams showed him letters written by officers at the front in the war with Mexico, a topic sure to stir the blood of the Adamses and their fellow Conscience Whigs, who questioned the morality of the conflict and suspected that its main purpose was to secure more land for slaveholders. And could Henry help it if his attention wandered from his Latin grammar to the conversation in the next room, where his father sat discussing political strategy with fellow Free Soilers? A visit to Washington in 1850 during the critical debates over slavery's expansion and sectional compromise made the boy "more political than ever." It seemed likely that he would follow in the direction to which family pointed. "There are two things that seem to be at the bottom of our constitutions," he remarked to Charles in 1858; "One is a continual tendency towards politics; the other is family pride; and it is strange how these two feelings run through all of us."[4]

But being an Adams had its drawbacks. It threatened to rob family members of their individuality as it pressured them to succeed in accordance with the family standards. After all, an Adams had a heritage to uphold. The best schooling, independent wealth, and social standing removed the ordinary obstacles to success. There were no excuses for failure. An Adams could not indulge in selfish pursuits because he was bound by a heritage of duty to serve the republic. Politics *was* in the blood.[5]

To an Adams, a career in public service was not only expected but also inescapable. The family would make sure that the young boy would be educated in such traditions, heedless of individual preferences. One summer morning, Henry decided that he was not going to school that day, and he made his position all too clear. Suddenly the door to the upstairs study opened, and down the stairway came John Quincy Adams. Without a word, the old man put on his hat, took Henry's hand, and walked the little rebel to school. There simply was no way to evade destiny.[6]

It was a demanding burden. Not all Adamses were able to bear it, as Henry doubtless knew. The price of failure was high. John Adams's male heirs had either achieved renown or died in disgrace. Henry's great uncles Charles and Thomas became alcoholics. One uncle, George Washington Adams, committed suicide in 1829, having cracked under his father's stern gaze. Another uncle, John Adams II, died five years later, collapsing after he failed to make the family mill on Rock Creek in Maryland a financial success. Henry's father did not look kindly upon his brothers' fates, coldly confiding to his diary, "I cannot regret the loss of either of my brothers as a calamity either to their families or to themselves."[7]

Even success could be troubling. Each Adams inherited the need to equal if not surpass the achievements of his ancestors. Henry's brother Charles noted that their father had to endure suggestions of a "noticeable family deterioration" by political opponents. Writing a biography of the old man years later, Charles spoke for himself and his brothers as well as his father in celebrating the exhilaration of being "recognized as something more than the bearer of a distinguished cognomen.... To have one's ancestors unceasingly flung in one's face is unpleasant." In an age when many Americans were obsessed with preserving the achievements of the Revolutionary generation, references to "our fathers" had more than an ordinary significance to an Adams.[8]

The family heritage would forever bedevil Henry Adams. "My name is a trifle too heavy for me," he once sighed in exasperation. His father's accomplishments in themselves presented a career difficult to equal; to follow two presidents as well seemed almost too much to bear. As if to remind future generations of their obligations, John and John Quincy Adams had each left behind an enormous sheaf of personal papers, including their voluminous diaries; Charles Francis Adams planned to add to these works his own diary, which was already becoming sizable. There was no way to escape the past. Even success might leave Henry with the reputation of being "just another Adams." Wherever he went, whatever he did, he would never be allowed to forget that he was indeed "distinctly branded."[9]

Henry Adams embraced the family preferences for literary and political pursuits at an early age. He took an active interest in political events and found English novels and histories absorbing. His choice of a childhood idol exemplified these inclinations. Charles Sumner seemed to embody everything Henry aspired to be. As Adams recalled in the *Education*, Sumner was his "ideal of greatness; the highest product of nature and art." Sumner was worthy of a boy's emulation. He had gained early prominence in Boston's social circles through news of his travels in Europe; when he visited the Adams house, he "was rarely without a pocket-full of letters from duchesses or noblemen in England." Henry's brother Charles recalled that Sumner was "very kind and considerate to us children, taking a deep interest in us, and being very companionable." Bostonians looked to Sumner to become the model of the scholar-statesman, someone who could fuse literary interests, social prominence, and an unyielding adherence to principle in public life. Of course, not all Boston was comfortable with Sumner's dogmatic, uncompromising opposition to slavery, and soon State Street merchants, mindful of their profitable relationship with Southern cotton-growers, sought to silence him. This could only enhance his heroism in Henry's eyes. One of the highlights of Henry's childhood was his dash home from the General Court to tell Sumner of his election to the United States Senate in 1851. Henry basked in his idol's glory, hoping that one day it would be his as well.[10]

But education came first. Henry found himself dragged through public and private schools toward Harvard College, a rite of passage demanded of all Adamses. At Harvard he mingled with members of his own social class, scions of long lines of Harvard graduates planning to assume their rightful place among Boston's elite. He tended to look down upon most of his fellow freshmen, found many of his professors boring, and gradually came to detest the mindless disciplinary regulations.[11] Literary and social activities were much more rewarding. He wrote several articles for the *Harvard Maga-*

zine, ranging from recommending a reading list for the benefit of his duller classmates to attacking the fraternity system. He took so much pride in these early productions that he had them bound in a volume entitled "Essays de Henry Adams." Membership in various literary clubs brought him into contact with like-minded young men, who, as one reported, delighted in discussing politics and "all the subjects of the day, which, by the by, Adams is well qualified to do." The debates around the Adams family dinner table had evidently paid off. His classmates recognized his talent for abuse and ridicule when they elected him Hasty Pudding Alligator, although only after he had first secured their promise not to engage in reprisals against his missives.[12]

Harvard reinforced Adams's preferences for things political and literary. His clever talk and broad knowledge soon made him a celebrity among his fellow students, who chose him to deliver the Class Day oration as a senior in 1858. From the pulpit of the First Parish Church, Adams launched a thunderbolt at State Street, deploring the single-minded desire of many of his classmates to make money. In contrast, "some of us still persist in believing that there are prizes to be sought for in life which will not disgust us in the event of success." The United States "furnishes the grandest theatre in the world for the exercise of that refinement of mind and those high principles which it is a disgrace to us if we have not acquired." Henry Adams intended to act out his life on that stage.[13]

With Harvard diploma in hand, Henry faced the task of choosing a career for himself consistent with the obligations of the family heritage. The prospect terrified him. During his senior year he had grown restless, uneasy about what course to take. Law school seemed inevitable. Brothers John and Charles were already lawyers, and the law provided the standard point of departure for a political career. Yet Henry had little taste for a legal career. He needed time to consider his options. A visit to Europe seemed attractive, both on its own merits and as a way to escape the immediate pressures of home. Furthermore, an excursion abroad had sparked Charles Sumner's career. Henry soon persuaded his father to finance the undertaking on the pretence that he wanted to study law in Germany. In reality, of course, he was seeking to postpone making that very choice.[14]

Charles Francis Adams frowned at his son's idea. Although he believed that Henry was in earnest, he held a low opinion of the effect of Europe upon the minds and morals of young Americans: "Some become physically ruined, others morally perverted." To Sumner, in France recovering from wounds sustained when he was assaulted by South Carolina Congressman Preston Brooks in 1856, the worried father confided his belief that "industry will degenerate when out of reach of observation into selfish indolence."

These impressions, according to his namesake son, were formed at an early age, when one of his Harvard classmates "chanced to go to Europe and came home an ass, and remained an ass." The image proved a durable one. But the elder Adams reluctantly assented to his son's wishes out of a determination not to interfere in Henry's future, a resolution that faded as soon as Henry departed Quincy one September day.[15]

Hardly had Henry arrived in Germany when the first signs of meddling appeared. Already his father questioned "whether you had matured in your own mind anything like a systematic purpose, for the promotion of which was designed to employ your time." Two months later, after Henry had settled in Berlin, his father urged him to describe the "religious, social, and intellectual character" of the city "to see if you are really getting any good out of your expedition." After all, "all a man's happiness as well as usefulness in life, depends upon the steady pursuit of some definite purpose." He grimly reminded his son of his belief that Europe "tends to confuse and distract" young Americans, and that Henry was "not likely to make an exception."[16]

If Henry found his father's letters bothersome, he must have boiled when he read his brother Charles's lengthy lectures. For Charles relished the role of the older brother, overseeing the younger sibling's progress ever since he took Henry in as a roommate at Harvard during Henry's freshman year. His letters were pointed barbs pricking at his brother's fragile ego. "What are you going to do? What are you there for?" Like his father, Charles delighted in constantly reminding his brother that "it is necessary to have some end, object, or plan in life fixed in your own mind." He called on Henry to "show what you're made of, or else make way for somebody else." And, lest Henry forget, Charles reminded him of the importance of being an Adams, declaring that his "object in life now is to sustain my family name and position." Candidly admitting that he lacked "the originality to strike out a new path for myself," Charles feared that if Henry were in the same rut, "mediocrity has fallen on the name of Adams."[17]

The correspondence which ensued between the two brothers, lasting a decade, reveals rivalry and jealousy between brothers, yet also makes evident their common problems of wrestling with destiny. For Charles had his own problems with being an Adams. Chaffing at home, struggling with his own legal career, he resented Henry's freedom. By prodding his brother about choosing a career, Charles could avoid the painful job of doing so for himself. Sibling rivalry also played its part. Charles despised having to stand behind eldest brother John, and the competition with Henry irritated him so much that at one point he had considered breaking with family tradition to attend Yale. Such considerations give his letters to Henry their especially sharp edge.[18]

The double-barreled assault from father and brother unnerved Henry. Struggling with both himself and the German language, he did not need to be reminded that much was expected of him. The pretense of legal study did not survive his first law lecture, which was also his last. Confounded by both German and Latin, he cursed Harvard for failing to prepare him for life. As a last resort for justifying his stay, he turned to learning German in the humiliating surroundings of a Berlin *gymnasium*, where he sat next to boys half his age. As expenses mounted beyond his budget, he skimped on meals and moved into cheaper quarters. He spent more time at the beer halls than in front of his law books. Frustrated by the collapse of his original plan, he complained that two years abroad was too short a time to accomplish his designs, which had become ever vaguer. He even went so far as to offer to accompany Sumner on a trip to Siberia on the pretense of assisting in the senator's recovery—a move that would also remove Sumner from the political scene for several months, thus helping the ambitions of Charles Francis Adams, Sr., based as they were on a more conservative approach to the sectional crisis than that taken by Sumner. Nothing came of this idea, and Adams remained in his rooms, devoting his idle hours to feeling sorry for himself.[19]

Henry pondered his future as an Adams. He believed "that an educated and reasonably able man can make his mark if he chooses, and if I fail to make mine, why, then—I fail and that's all." He searched for a suitable career to support himself and establish his independence. To become a writer was out of the question, for it did not pay well and would thus require Adams to remain dependent on his family. As a lawyer he could support himself and make a start at life. "The law must be my ladder," he told Charles. Still, author Richard Henry Dana "insisted that I was looking toward politics; and perhaps he was right."[20]

One idea excited Henry. His grandfather's papers cried for an editor, and some member of the family had "the duty" of writing a biography. As a boy, Henry had watched his father labor away at producing an edition of John Adams's works; perhaps he could do the same for his grandfather. To tackle John Quincy Adams's literary remains soon became the height of Henry's ambition, and he asserted that the task "alone is enough for a man, and enough to shape his whole course." Perhaps he could evade the necessity to make a name for himself by recalling his ancestor's exploits. As the months passed, however, he began to squirm under the burden of his family's expectations as well as his own aspirations. Before long, the mere thought of confronting the family heritage in the form of the grandfather who had once dragged him off to school overwhelmed him, and he dropped the idea, confessing that "it is not *in* me to do them justice."[21] It was apparently difficult enough to endure the criticism of the living Adamses.

7

Failure was unthinkable, but Henry Adams could think of little else. German was "terribly slow and tedious"; visits to the opera or theater provided only temporary relief. Never one for bad weather, he huddled in his dank room while it rained, and he did not find himself good company. Subject to "fits of crossness and disagreeable feelings," accentuated by the weekly lectures in the mail from Boston, he vented his anguish at brother Charles. "I'm doing my best to do well here, God knows, and it's excessively unpleasant to be told without any why or wherefore that I'm becoming a damned fool," he snapped. At other moments he retreated into a corner and whimpered, "I am actually becoming afraid to look at the future, and feel only utterly weak about it."[22]

The letters from home only made matters worse. From his father, Henry received repeated remonstrations rather than reassurances. "There is no such thing in life as holding up people who have not learned to hold themselves" was standard fare from Charles Francis Adams, who solemnly reminded his son that "life is not given for mere pleasure, and that you of all others have responsibilities in proportion to the extent of your advantages." After all, "Life is intended for work and not for play. And you will have had your full share of the latter." Throughout his letters, the elder Adams, recalling the fate which befell his brothers, sounded the theme of impending doom should his son fail to take responsibility for himself and behave like an Adams. But his inability to translate his heartfelt concern for his son into prose resulted in letters resembling Puritan sermons drained of their emotional flair: "Naturally, you were made a gentleman in mind and body. Take care and [do] not degenerate." Henry justly complained that his father's letters "are a little apt to sour the best of cream."[23]

Acutely sensitive to criticism, Henry became all the more defensive because he was aware that his father's charges had much truth to them. Even as he protested that he was working hard, he revealed that he was putting most of his energy into relaxing. "In point of fact . . . I'm doing nothing," he candidly told Charles at the end of his first year overseas. Comments like "This life is regal," "I lounged lots," and "I . . . pretend to read a page of law a day" did little to persuade his family that he was in earnest pursuit of a legal education. Aware of the impression of frivolity conveyed in his letters, he enjoined Charles not to reveal to their father the contents of their correspondence.[24]

Charles had little patience with his brother's pretenses. Frustrated by his own slow start as a lawyer (and perhaps a little envious of Henry's ability to avoid the same fate while enjoying Europe), he knew that his brother's eclectic mind and irresolution would never submit to the discipline essential to the law. Blasting away at his brother's continual pouting, posturing, and procrastination, Charles demanded that Henry begin to make good on his intellectual pretensions. "If you have ability, take the opportunity that is before you to show it," he challenged his brother, ". . . or else make way for somebody else." Henry's repeated false starts and excuses for failure had worn thin. Charles pointed out that Henry's behavior was "justifying the Gov.'s prognostications and giving the lie to your own aspirations," and harshly concluded, "I begin to suspect that you are a humbug."[25]

Charles recommended that his younger brother drop all thoughts of law and turn to journalism. By becoming "a trained Sophist," Henry could be "a teacher of the people—one who leads and instructs them." Through putting into print his insights on public affairs, Henry could make a name for himself, establishing a solid foundation for a career in public service and politics. Henry rejected this suggestion, forecasting that such a career would reduce him to a "dabbler in metaphysics, poetry, and art." He lacked the writing skills necessary to become a successful commentator. "Amusing, witty, and clever I'm not," he claimed, "and to affect the style would disgust me and bore you." No one would have the patience or inclination to listen to his opinions, and even his father looked askance at the idea on the grounds that magazine writing was "ephemeral." The law remained Henry's ideal springboard for his leap into public life. Besides, he sharply reminded his brother, "You have never published a word so far as I know."[26]

Stung by his brother's blunt retort ("Physician, heal thyself"), Charles soon startled Henry by practicing what he had been preaching. Their father, elected to Congress in 1858, had taken the opportunity of the appointment of the House printer to proclaim his independence of party. As his Massachusetts colleagues looked on in exasperation, Representative Adams refused to vote for the choice of the Republican caucus, who had let it be known that he would funnel half his profits into the party coffers. To test public response to the congressman's stand, Charles, under the pen name "Pemberton," published a letter attacking his father's position in the *Boston Advertiser*. As he had hoped, other Boston papers rose to his father's defense. So did an unwitting Henry, who pitched into "Pemberton" in a letter to his mother. Upon discovering "Pemberton's" identity, he reluctantly conceded that his brother had achieved "a great success."[27]

Still perplexed about his future, Henry now found himself challenged by his brother's achievement. "Your Washington letters have stirred me up," he admitted to Charles. His brother had gained the upper hand in their rivalry, and it was his turn to respond. Suddenly his travel plans for Italy took on a new-found importance. He proposed to write travel letters to Charles, coyly leaving it to his brother's discretion whether to forward the letters to a Boston paper. On no condition was Charles to publish any letters which would humiliate Henry, "showing me up to the public amusement." The letters began appearing in the *Boston Daily Courier* in the spring of 1860. Most of them appeared intact, although at times Charles did a little editing.[28]

Henry's notions of a travelogue were pushed aside by a bearded man in a red shirt. Giuseppe Garibaldi's march through Italy electrified most Americans, and Adams was there to report it all. The mobs crowding city streets alarmed him, moving him to ask, "Where is the Sicilian nobility and the gentlemen who ought to take the lead in a movement like this?" Uneasy amid the disorder of social turmoil, he reflected in his letter a marked sympathy for the leaders of the conservative forces, including the Grand Duke of Tuscany and the Pope. Nor could he refrain from keeping one eye on events at home. Reacting adversely to the nomination of an unknown politician named Abraham Lincoln over William Henry Seward, an antislavery disciple of John Quincy Adams, Henry snapped, "In '56 we had the satisfaction of rejecting our Garibaldi [John C. Frémont], and now in '60 we have done still better; we have deserted our Cavour."[29]

Henry's travels in Italy served to round out his overseas tour. His father firmly hinted that it was time to come home: Henry, who had cast aside the pretense of study for the joys of tourism and travel, reluctantly agreed. Events in America interested him, especially the continuing controversy over slavery and its expansion. Some people were speaking of disunion, and an increasing number of Southern whites were advocating it. John Brown's raid on the federal armory at Harpers Ferry the previous October was only the most prominent evidence that the conflict might become violent. On the floor of the House of Representatives, Charles Francis Adams followed the family line, defending the republic in the spirit of his father decades before. Some of those listening thought in more personal terms of self-defense. Sumner's caning was still fresh in the minds of many. Waistcoat pockets bulged with ill-concealed knives and pistols, and when a weapon would slip out and drop to the floor, the noise would bring various members of Congress to their feet, hands reaching into their jackets for firearms.[30]

While most people worried whether the Union would survive the stress of the slavery issue, an eager Henry Adams argued that the crisis provided an opportunity for the Adamses to recapture center stage in American politics. Casting aside once-dear notions of abolition, he hoped that "comparatively conservative men" would seize control of the Republican party. Among this set he classed his father, whose early commitment to the antislavery cause—especially as the vice presidential candidate of the Free Soil coalition of 1848—had clearly faded in favor of a desire to compromise outstanding issues. "If the Governor weathers this storm," he opined, "he has a good chance of living in the White House some day." Like father, like son, he mused. "If all goes right," he told Charles, "the house of Adams may get it's lease on life renewed—if, as I've various times remarked, it has the requisite ability still."[31]

Although Adams feared that William Henry Seward's prediction of an "irrepressible conflict" was correct, he still hoped for peace so that the Adams family could get on with its mission of purifying the American republic of the pollution of political partisanship. Just thinking of the operations of party leaders gave him "a sort of sickness at heart." When foreigners inquired about American politics, Adams found it "humiliating to have to acknowledge the condition of our statesmanship." To elevate "the contemptible tone politics takes with us," the Adams family had to educate the American people on the proper conduct of a democratic republic. "Our task so far as we attempt a public work," he told Charles, "is to blow up sophistry and jam hard down on morality," whether the Union "stands or falls."[32]

Charles Francis Adams's stand on the appointment of the House printer, his son declared, was "the first declaration of the colors we sail under," for it exhibited "the spectacle of an honest man in Congress" for all Americans to see. Other Republicans might grumble that Congressman Adams had made a spectacle of himself and that there were more important issues than patronage to discuss in a time of sectional crisis, but Henry celebrated his father's act as a statement in favor of honest government. Education was "what gives New England its moral power," he proclaimed—his father's example would instruct the rest of the nation as to what was really important. "As for me," he told his mother, "I'm ready and willing, in perfect and common sense, to lay all my hope and ambition for the future, on the same stake." Antislavery was merely a side issue compared to ridding the nation of the political corruption of patronage and party loyalty.[33]

The revived family fortunes gave Henry Adams new life. "It's pleasant to feel that we're going up the ladder still, and that nearly a hundred years hasn't exhausted the family yet," he confided to his mother. At times he still seemed unsure of his own ability to contribute to the tradition. He contemplated "the quiet and sunny prospect" of becoming a historian, since "my ambition for political life dwindles as I get older." But these moments of self-doubt soon passed. More frequently he rejoiced in the future, asserting that "there's hope for the family A. yet." If he was ambitious, it was "not on my own account, but as a family joint stock affair." Far from rejecting his heritage, he embraced it, concerned only that he might not measure up to the standards set by his ancestors.[34]

With his own search for a career stalled and his tour of Europe drawing to a close, Henry Adams looked around for something to do. Charles suggested that he join their parents in Washington, where he could complete his legal studies while bolstering his mother's morale. Henry agreed. "I never knew before this how I liked Quincy and Boston . . . but this course which certainly is the one I should choose and follow . . . finishes setting me afloat." With his interest in politics growing, Washington was "the place that my education has fitted me best for, and where I could be of most use."[35]

The United States was in the midst of a presidential campaign when Adams returned to native soil. Although Charles Francis Adams had been a leading supporter of family associate William Henry Seward prior to the Republican convention, he spoke in behalf of the party's standard bearer, Abraham Lincoln. The family celebrated Lincoln's victory in November, for it meant the overthrow of the slave power and the corrupt Democratic party. With Congressman Adams safely reelected, it seemed that the republic had been saved once more. He scoffed at word that the South Carolina legislature had called a convention to consider secession: "Let them secede from Congress long enough to enable the Republicans to establish their authority in the federal government and the whole game is played."[36]

Henry Adams, who accompanied his father to Washington as his private secretary (having once more shelved the law), agreed. He dismissed secessionists' threats as a game of "bare bluff." So long as Northern hotheads were smothered and "weak-kneed" Republicans kept in line, reason and moderation would triumph under the guidance of Seward and Adams, "the Arch-bishop of antislavery"—a rather inflated and misleading title, for the elder Adams showed little interest in abolition. Henry looked forward to the chance to gain an inside view of politics. A week in Washington confirmed his enthusiasm: "It's a great life; just what I wanted; and as I always feel that I am of real use here and can take an active part in it all, it never tires."[37]

He was particularly enthralled by Seward, finding himself captivated by the senator's "rolling out his grand, broad ideas that would inspire a cow with statesmanship if she understood the language." But Charles Francis Adams was also making his influence felt. "He's a growing man and will soon have a national fame and power inferior to no one unless it be Seward," Henry noted appreciatively. The strategy of defusing secession through conciliation struck him as statesmanlike: his father's willingness to curtail the North's personal liberty laws, secure slavery in the Southern states through constitutional amendment, and admit New Mexico as a slave state was "what the republicans have got to stand on." These measures would thwart secession by splitting the upper and lower South. Included in Adams's second rank of heroes was Andrew Johnson, Senator from Tennessee, who stood by the Union as his fellow white Southerners fell away.[38]

But the young observer soon concluded that his old idol, Charles Sumner, had forfeited all claims to respectability. "Sumner always acts with his eye on his personal figure before posterity and our father with his eye on the national future; which, as you see, are two different ends," he reported to brother Charles. Sumner viewed Congressman Adams's willingness to conciliate the South as evidence of backsliding. When he charged his colleague with abandoning his antislavery principles, the congressman shot back: "Sumner, you don't know what you're talking about. Yours is the very kind of stiff-necked obstinacy that will break you down." When Sumner stood fast, Henry audaciously opened up a copy of Francis Bacon's *Essay on Seditions and Troubles* and proceeded to read some lines to the startled senator. Truly, the mighty had fallen.[39]

Henry Adams did his best to help his father and Seward by following his brother's advice to practice political journalism. He became the anonymous Washington correspondent for the *Boston Advertiser*, supporting the position of the moderates. In these columns he dared the South to secede, celebrated Seward, and at first mocked compromise efforts before following Seward's lead. Adams's articles attracted some notice. The *New York Times*, Seward's paper, reprinted them "with copious italics," as he noted with some chagrin. "Can they suspect or have they been told whence they come?" Before long, Henry's father cautioned his son "against writing too freely." Nor was Henry happy with the impact of the editorial pen on his columns, complaining that the editor "always cuts out the spicy parts of my letters." He concluded that Charles Hale, owner of the *Advertiser*, "does not encourage brilliancy," for "he promptly expunges all that I write of an unfavorable personal character." Still, he had reasoned to be pleased with this initial foray into political journalism, remarking that his columns "have had some good influence in shaping the course of opinion" in Boston and elsewhere, for the *New York Times* reprinted several of them. In short, he had achieved success.[40]

Henry's morale soared and plunged with each new rumor and speculation about secession. At first he made fun of the recurring panics which seized Washingtonians, dismissing the crisis as "the last convulsion of the slave-power." Southerners, especially South Carolinians, were "mad, mere maniacs." Secession would collapse in the face of a patient waiting game, for Southerners would reject separation when they confronted the inevitable "starvation and ruin" which would result from their folly. At times, however, he abandoned his own counsels of calmness, solemnly reporting rumors that the notorious Massachusetts conservative Caleb Cushing and others were fomenting "a cursed dangerous plot." "You've no idea how deep the treason is," he told Charles. Before long, his letters were vacillating from one extreme to the other, displaying either a cocky self-assuredness or despair and disgust.[41]

To Henry, his father was one of the stars of the crisis. "He is making himself a great reputation here and on the whole he is sustained at home,"

Henry reported, claiming that the unity of Republicans "is due in a very great measure to him." Obviously such service required reward from the incoming president, preferably in the form of a cabinet position. Henry thought that the Treasury Department would do just fine. In four more years, perhaps the State Department would follow. He became immersed in speculations about the composition of Lincoln's cabinet slate, only to be disappointed when he discovered that the new president had decided to exclude his father. Lincoln, Adams moaned, "has shown his utter ignorance of the right way to act." The rail-splitter was not "a strong man."[42]

By February 1861, Adams was able to send word to Boston that "the storm is weathered." The border states were still in the Union, and Seward had confidently predicted that secession would collapse by summer. There were casualties. The bond of friendship between Charles Sumner and Charles Francis Adams was severed. "Let Sumner get the idea that his dignity is hurt, and he *is* a damned fool," Henry concluded. But there were also benefits, especially for young Adams. The experience of the past winter, complete with chats with Seward over champagne and the heady experience of seeing one's letters in print, left him "in a continual intoxication." Perhaps holding office was not the only way to exercise political power. Shaping opinion and dispensing advice might produce the same result without one's having to suffer the humiliations of electoral politics. The secession winter had indeed offered the willing student several enlightening lessons in political education and infused in him the aspiration to educate others.[43]

On March 4, 1861, Abraham Lincoln took the oath of office as the sixteenth President of the United States—the first one elected by the Republican party and perhaps the last one elected by the nation. Henry Adams had his first—and only—look at the new president that night at an inaugural ball. He was not impressed. The "awkward" Lincoln, with his "plain, ploughed face," was certainly no Seward, no Adams. Henry found revolting the scavenging of office-seekers, who hungered for scraps of patronage as they circled the streets and offices. With Congress adjourned, he welcomed the chance to return to the purifying atmosphere of Boston, where he might at last get down to reading law.[44]

Hardly had Adams cracked open his Blackstone when he closed it once more. A telegram from Washington disrupted breakfast at the Adams home one March morning. It announced that Lincoln had decided to name Charles Francis Adams as minister to England. Mrs. Adams wailed at the news; the congressman was dismayed; Henry and Charles were astonished. The elder Adams, responding to the call of duty, hurried back to the capital to accept the post in person. After all, it was his by inheritance; both his father and grandfather had held it during critical periods. Maybe the new president recognized talent after all.[45]

Charles Francis Adams returned to Quincy in a foul mood, grumbling about the stupidity of politicians. The lanky Lincoln had made it clear to him that the appointment was merely a political favor to Seward. Humbled, Adams tried to discuss what policies to pursue. But the president was not in the mood. Stretching out, he put his feet on top of the desk and began talking to Seward about the Chicago postmastership. This was too much for Adams. Presidents simply did not sit that way, as he knew from personal experience. He left the White House convinced that the great days of the republic were over.[46]

Henry had even more cause for dissatisfaction. Early reports had suggested that he would become the secretary of the legation. The appointment of offspring had been customary as a means to supplement the inadequate salary accorded the minister. Whatever expectations he had were soon dashed, however, by the news that Charles Lush Wilson, a Chicago newspaper editor, had been named to the post, compensation for losing the postmastership of his home city. Once again, Chicago concerns had slighted an Adams's ambitions. "As I suppose this to be one of Mr. Lincoln's selections," Henry snapped, "of course there is no use in commenting on it." He took steps to make sure that no further damage would be done by the appointment of another "incompetent Westerner" by urging upon Sumner the retention of the present assistant secretary of the legation, Benjamin Moran. In making this recommendation, he ended any consideration of himself for the office, cutting short an offer which would be more of a humiliation than an honor. Rather, Henry announced that he would be accompanying his father as a private secretary.[47]

Preparations commenced in the Adams household for the move to London. Henry welcomed the opportunity to assist his father, for it offered an escape from dreary law books. At the time, it looked like little more than a temporary assignment, for most people assumed that the war would be a brief one. Still miffed at Lincoln's indifference, Charles Francis Adams took his time preparing to leave. Even the firing on Fort Sumter failed to hasten his departure. The Adamses did not board the Cunard steamer for Liverpool until May 1, some six weeks after news of the appointment broke up the family breakfast.[48]

No one, least of all Henry Adams, anticipated what lay in store for Americans. Over the next four years, minor crossroads, winding creeks, and tangled thickets furnished the stage upon which the bloody tragedy was played out. Many of Adams's peers, among them Oliver Wendell Holmes, Jr., were marked for life by the conflict. As Holmes put it, "the generation that carried on the war has been set apart by its experience. Through our great good fortune, in our youth our hearts were touched with fire. It was given to us to learn at the outset that life is a profound and passionate thing." For others, like William Dean Howells, who was the American consul to Venice at the time, the war brought shame. "Every loyal American who went abroad during the first two years of our great war," Howells later wrote, "felt bound to make himself some excuse for turning his back on his country in the time of her trouble."[49] For these people, the Civil War would be a troublesome legacy.

No such problems perplexed Henry Adams as he set foot in London in May 1861. Thanks in part to his father's dallying in Boston, the Adamses were met with the news that Great Britain had just declared its neutrality in the American conflict. The minister's son was more concerned about learning the rules of etiquette. He admitted that he was "easily tired and irritable." Part of his condition was due to the after-effects of seasickness; his quarters added to his misery: "The hotel is poor, our quarters confined, our eating to my overeducated mind miserable." Worse still, he found London society impenetrable. "No one has asked me to dinner; nor have I found that my reputation has crossed the Atlantic before me," he grumbled only half in jest. To be introduced to society was "a repulsive piece of work." No one cared to make his acquaintance; the dinners were "dull, heavy, lifeless affairs"; the balls were "solemn stupid crushes." Society, he concluded, "is a frightful and irredeemable bore to me." Only his position as a correspondent on English affairs for the *New York Times*—a position that required anonymity and was kept secret from his father—relieved the monotony.[50]

Occasionally, Adams became so dejected at his position in London that he contemplated joining the Army of the Potomac. After receiving news of the Union defeat at Bull Run in July 1861, he begged Charles to "get a commission for me" and outlined his preference to serve in a regiment commanded by "Boston fellows . . . to make it pleasant." But patriotism had little to do with Adams's threat to "raise Heaven and earth" to join the army. Having tasted London's social life and found it sour, he feared he could not "stand the taunts of every one" over Union setbacks "without being able to say a word in defence." At least in Virginia "he would have only bullets to wound him," as he later recalled, not the slights of London society assailing his sensitive soul.[51]

This moment of panic soon passed. Before long, Adams retreated to his earlier claim that he was "hardly the material for a soldier." Charles vigorously concurred that his brother would be of more use to the cause abroad. He added that Henry's motives to enlist were personal, not patriotic. "Like a coward," he charged, "you want to run home because our reverses make the post abroad . . . very uncomfortable." There was much truth in his assessment. Periodically Henry would admit to Charles that "when things go wrong, I feel a good deal as though I would like to cut and run," but he never donned a blue uniform.[52]

Henry's father encouraged his son to stay in London. The minister saw "small glory in a civil war" and was not eager to waste a son in the conflict. His namesake son, conscious of the family's reputation as well as of his civilian garb, disagreed. "It seems to me almost disgraceful," Charles commented, that not one Adams "stood in arms for that government with which our family history is so closely connected." He, not Henry, should enlist as the most fitting representative of the Adams clan. The family had been "most prominent in the contest of words" with the South. Rather than shrink away in this "hour of greatest danger," Charles decided to fight "to show that in this matter our family means what it says." He secured a lieutenant's commission in the cavalry.[53]

Chagrined, Henry expressed dismay at his brother's "throwing yourself away like this." Charles exploded when he read this. "How am I throwing myself away? Isn't a century's work of my ancestors worth a struggle to preserve?" Henry never answered. Nor did he ever enlist. To the end of his life, he maintained that he "found obstacles constantly rising in his path" towards enlistment. He did not explain what the obstacles were or why he never tried to surmount them. Perhaps it was better to pass over such matters in silence, especially after his previous posturing about joining the fray. He never spoke of joining the army in terms of fighting for his country, but instead considered it as a chance to flee embarrassment abroad. Enlistment was a matter of convenience, not conviction; the humiliations of London society, great as they were, could not drive him away. Others felt differently. Many of his Harvard classmates, including several close friends, rallied to the colors. Several were killed. Henry scanned the casualty lists as if they were class notes, but he never came close to sharing the fate of his more unfortunate friends.[54]

Instead, Henry followed his brother's advice "to make yourself heard" by writing articles on Anglo-American affairs for the American press. Once more he sought to shape public opinion with his pen. His articles were unsigned, but he knew that Secretary of State Seward would read his columns in the *New York Times*, for it was edited by Seward ally Henry J. Raymond. Most interesting were his columns on English reaction to the seizure of two Confederate diplomats aboard a British mail carrier, the *Trent*, by a Union captain. Although he scored some minor victories and was gratified when the Lincoln administration, in line with his dispatches, sought a peaceful resolution of the *Trent* affair, he expressed frustration over his inability to shape opinion in the North, once complaining that important paragraphs concerning English reaction during the *Trent* affair had been cut. Charles's own efforts in the press were "devilish good," but sibling success served to make Henry "blue for a day, thinking of my own weak endeavors."[55]

Henry's endeavors came to a sudden halt early in 1862 when the *Boston Daily Courier* proudly announced his authorship of an article containing remarks critical of London society. The London papers gleefully seized upon the opportunity to lampoon the American minister's son in print. One January morning, to his "immense astonishment and dismay," Adams found himself "sarsed through a whole column" of the *London Times*; a day later the *Examiner* scored some hits. Humiliated ("I . . . am laughed at by all England," he moaned), he found no solace in the *Courier's* statement that "he has by no means degenerated from the hereditary ability of his family." Ironically, having come to prominence as, of all things, a social critic, Adams had to quash his more useful career as a foreign correspondent for the *New York Times*, lest that too be revealed and imperil his father's mission.[56]

The incident capped several months of soul-searching by Henry Adams. He came away from his introspective reevaluation mortified at what he found. "I am tired of this life," he complained to Charles. "Every attempt I have made to be of use has failed more or less completely." He was "ashamed and humiliated" by his civilian status. He felt insignificant serving as his father's secretary. "Coward" echoed in his mind; he would not deny that he could not bring himself to enlist. When dispatches reporting a battle arrived at the legation, he "trembled" so much that he sought the steadying influence of brandy. Defeat confirmed his bitterness; victory reminded him that while his friends were "acting such grand parts at home," he was living a "thoroughly useless life." Anxiously he scanned the casualty lists to see if his friends had fallen victim to the bullets he feared to face.[57]

Slighted at court functions, burdened by news of Union defeats, "unable" to enlist, and humbled by the London press, Henry Adams assessed himself a failure. His efforts to shape public opinion through the press had been halted by the threat of exposure. For the moment, at least, his career in politics had come to an end: "I've disappointed myself, and experienced the curious sensation of discovering myself to be a humbug." The past four years, he confessed to Charles, had "done little towards giving me confidence in myself." He lacked the determination and perseverance to make good his grandiose predictions of importance. Failure stared him in the face. "The future is a blank to me."[58]

CHAPTER TWO

A NATIONAL SET OF MEN

It will depend on the generation to which you and I
belong, whether the country is to be brought back to its
true course and the New England element is to carry the
victory. . . .
Henry Adams to Charles Francis Adams, Jr., 1863

"The year 1862 was a dark spot in Henry Adams's life, and the education it gave was mostly one that he gladly forgot." So Adams recalled it in 1906. But 1863 brought light and enlightenment. As the Union war effort finally turned the corner, Adams's isolation from London society ended, and he felt increasingly useful at his post. Most importantly, he began to develop a political philosophy which reconciled family heritage with contemporary thought—a cornerstone which promised him a role in public life. He found himself, so to speak, in 1863.[1]

As the Union cause went, so went Henry Adams. The narrow Union victory at Antietam failed to reassure him, but the promulgation of the Emancipation Proclamation on January 1, 1863, lifted his spirits. Adams had been urging such a step for nearly a year. "If some real emancipation step could be taken," he wrote to Secretary Seward's son Frederick at the beginning of 1862, "it would be the next best thing to taking Richmond for us here." When news of the proclamation reached London, Adams rejoiced. "It has done more for us here than all our former victories and all our diplomacy," he told Charles, for it had sparked "an almost convulsive reaction in our favor all over this country."[2]

Success on the political front was matched by success on the social front. To Adams's great surprise, he suddenly found the once-closed doors of London society, if not wide open, at least ajar. Richard Monckton Milnes turned the handle. A member of Parliament and one of England's foremost liberals, Milnes was sympathetic to the Union cause; he was also a patron of literature, a credential scarcely less important in the young American's eyes. Milnes invited Adams to his country estate several times when no one else would talk to him. Adams admired his host's intelligence and wit almost as much as his taste in guests; he was even more pleased when Milnes put him up for membership at a social club, even though it was for minor diplomats. He still professed to find "fashionable society . . . intolerably stupid," but by then he had decided that he would never make it in London's conservative social circles.[3]

Instead, Adams found his associates in the ranks of English liberalism. He attended mass meetings in support for the Union cause and delighted in seeing what he called the "'moral influence' of American democracy" at work. "There are all the elements of a great, reforming, liberal party at work here," he chimed to Charles.[4] He began to mix with "the cultivated radicals of England," including John Stuart Mill, John Bright, and Richard Cobden—men "whose acquaintance I make desperate efforts to make," he admitted. Sympathetic to the Union cause, these men admired the American political system but saw room for improvement. Having expressed his own doubts about his native polity for some time, Adams listened as the Englishmen discussed how to rectify the excesses of democratic government and society. Just to witness such minds at work pleased him no end. "I confess that I always feel a little self-satisfied in such society," he told Charles. "I feel my self-respect increased by the fact of standing beside, and feeding with such men." Not only did those men accept the Northern cause as right; they accepted young Adams as well.[5]

Adams particularly idolized John Stuart Mill, whom he pronounced "the ablest man in England." Attending a dinner with the political economist in February 1863, he "took particular pains" to be introduced to his hero. Mill's writings on the tension between democratic society and intelligent governance, mentioned in *On Liberty* (1859) and developed in *Considerations on Representative Government* (1861), had attracted many readers and none more eager than Adams. Not only did they reinforce the young man's assessment of democracy's virtues and vices, but Mill's insistence that a democratic society must be overseen by an intellectual elite willing to restrain its excesses and guide it down proper paths outlined a role for Adams to play in the American experiment, one similar to that of his forefathers. Alarmed at rampant materialism and perturbed by the tendency of democracy to shun its best men in favor of mediocre leaders, Mill called upon the able and intelligent to express opinions and to publicize knowledge. Educated themselves, they must now educate society and its elected leaders along the lines of right reason. Indeed, to Mill the best government was one which allowed "the individual intellect and honesty of its wisest members" to be brought to bear on government, "and investing them with greater influence on it than they would have under any other mode of organization." Only then could a democracy reconcile political equality with the pursuit of excellence by learning to make correct choices. As he reminded his readers, "the most important point of excellence which any form of government can possess is to promote the virtue and intelligence of the people themselves." Thanks to Mill, Adams was now confident that there was a place for men of the mind in American politics.[6]

Adams also immersed himself in the writings of Alexis de Tocqueville, especially after Henry Reeve, the editor of the *Edinburgh Review* and one of England's leading liberal advocates, reissued his translation of *Democracy in America*. The Frenchman endorsed the notion of the necessity for rule by the best in a democratic society, reminding readers like Adams that an aristocratic elite had to curb democratic tendencies toward materialism, mediocrity, and majority tyranny. Doubtless the young diplomat nodded in agreement with Tocqueville's conclusion that the "best government is not that in which all have share, but that which is directed by the class of the highest principle and intellectual ambition." Together, Mill and Tocqueville furnished the foundation for what some called "aristocratic liberalism," a political and social creed of rule by the best, infused with the notion that a virtuous and educated citizenry was essential to good governance. Adams took to these ideas because they comported so well with his own notions; his selective reading of Mill and Tocqueville was designed to reinforce long-evident tendencies in his mind about the way things ought to be.[7]

While Mill and Tocqueville furnished the twin pillars of Adams's reading, he explored other thinkers as well, and was drawn to Auguste Comte's theory of positivism. Comte asserted that man's attitude toward his environment had evolved through three stages. At first, man submitted to his environment; then, he worked to comprehend it through empirical reasoning, experimentation, and investigation; now he sought to control it through manipulating the universal laws previously revealed through investigation. Of course, those best fit to manage the environment were members of an educated intelligentsia equipped to discover and apply these laws for the benefit of society—something Adams embraced as part of his natural order. That much of Comte's thought came to Adams through Mill's 1865 study of the French thinker also whetted the young American's interest. Perhaps surprising by its omission from Adams's London correspondence—especially in light of his later writings—is any mention of Charles Darwin. Although Adams read Darwin's works, he refused to apply his theories to societal development, noting several years later that "Mr. Darwin has, after all, announced only a theory, supported, it is true, by the greatest ingenuity of reasoning and fertility of experiment, but in its nature incapable of proof."[8]

Mill, Tocqueville, and Comte reinforced Adams's axiom that the best and the brightest should rule, a mainstay of his family's political philosophy. As Ernest Samuels later put it, Adams read such authors "with a recurring thrill of recognition." He also read them rather selectively, turning to them

primarily to refurbish notions of aristocratic leadership in a democratic society that had long buttressed the political philosophy of the family Adams.
Tocqueville's prescriptions were even more pertinent because he endorsed
the moral superiority of New England's moral philosophy; moreover, during his excursion to America he had visited with John Quincy Adams.[9]
Henry's ancestors would have vigorously agreed with Mill and Tocqueville
about the ills of democracy and the need for enlightened leadership. But
Mill and Tocqueville gave these notions legitimacy apart from the family
tradition. Henry Adams could conclude that he was responding not merely
to the legacy of the past but to the necessities of the present as well. Together, family tradition and the political philosophy of "aristocratic liberalism" outlined his obligation to serve his society as a member of the elite.[10]
    Adams devoted most of his spare hours in 1863 to reading Mill and
Tocqueville, "the two high priests of our faith." He no longer wanted to
join the army ("I should be like a bewildered rabbit in action, being only
trained to counsel"), and he dismissed thoughts of pursuing a career in law
as a "convenient fiction." Mill and Tocqueville prescribed remedies for the
ills that Adams had diagnosed in the democratic body politic; through their
emphasis on elite rule, they also had presented Adams with a sense of purpose and a role to play in renewing the republican ideal. "I have learned to
think De Tocqueville my model, and I study his life and works as the Gospel of my private religion," he told Charles. "The great principle of democracy is still capable of rewarding a conscientious servant." Mill and
Tocqueville provided "a vague and unsteady light in the direction toward
which I . . . must gravitate."[11]
    Having discovered his political models in Mill and Tocqueville, Adams
soon found a contemporary Englishman who embodied the lifestyle to which
he aspired. In 1863 he met a young aristocrat, Charles Milnes Gaskell, who
was a distant cousin of Adams's benefactor, Richard Monckton Milnes. Although four years Henry's junior, Gaskell became his close companion, and
the two remained friends for life. Gaskell exemplified the young intellectual of refined tastes who became involved in politics on his own terms.
Henry James called him "an excellent fellow, an entertaining companion
and the prince of hosts," although he privately added that Gaskell was somewhat of a snob who took himself too seriously. Perhaps this was all the more
reason for Adams to be charmed. He envied Gaskell in his family home in
West Yorkshire, entertaining guests with witty and knowledgeable conversation, occasionally lapsing into conceit. It was the kind of life Adams wanted
to lead—that of the cultivated gentleman, equally at home in the library,
the social club, and the political meeting. "I have learned that there are
objects of ambition which may be held separate from the opinions of men
or the applause of listening Senates," he told his brother Charles.[12]

Gaskell also served to exacerbate Henry's love-hate affair with England, a syndrome rooted deep in the Adams heritage. Once an admirer of all things English, Henry had to confess by 1862, in the wake of his manifold embarrassments, that "my own Anglicism is somewhat wilted." He freely criticized London society as a "nasty set," finding the "tone of people here . . . insufferable to me." London's social season was "a sort of canonization of mediocrity. No one attempts to have a good time, and if they did, they would be voted vulgar." English politics were even worse. Adams was astounded at the behavior and policies of Lord John Russell, Lord Palmerston, and William E. Gladstone both at home and towards the North, bemoaning their "contemptible equivocations and evasions and dishonest subterfuges" in foreign policy. He found a warm home among English liberals in part because they, too, were restless under the status quo and hoped for the triumph of the Union.[13]

Underneath his harsh strictures about London society, however, Adams retained a deep admiration for English ways and manners. As he broke out of his social isolation, he began to look more favorably on his surroundings. "Society in London certainly has its pleasures," he sighed early in 1863. By the end of the year, he spoke of "young England, young Europe, of which I am by tastes and education a part." The Democratic politician and newspaper editor Henry Watterson, who met Adams during the 1870s, noted: "In manner and manners, tone and cast of thought he was English." Adams cherished his memories of his England: thirty years later, he told a young diplomat, "It was a golden time for me."[14]

Adams exemplified a classic dilemma of American culture and society during the nineteenth century. He asserted that American politics and society were superior to their English counterparts, yet inwardly he always feared that the reverse was closer to the truth. For all of his talk about the need to judge the American experiment on its own merits, he often measured its successes and failures according to English standards. When London society gave him the cold shoulder, he dismissed it as a product of its "laziness, stupidity and self-distrust," but his letters to Charles revealed his fear that the real shortcomings were to be found in himself. So concluded legation secretary Benjamin Moran, who noted that at one society gathering Adams walked about, "pretending that he disliked it and yet asking to be presented to everybody of note." Charles Gaskell had teased Adams by showing him how delightful society could be, while the rest of London suggested that he was not fit to take part in it. Adams's sneaking sense of inferiority, reinforced by his personal experiences in England, redoubled his ambition to improve American society and politics until his country was second to none.[15]

Fusing his family legacy with the principles of aristocratic liberalism, Adams developed a conception of the good society based upon the rule of an educated elite who would provide the direction and set the standards for democratic society and politics. "We want a national set of young men like ourselves or better, to start new influences not only in politics, but in literature, in law, and society, and throughout the whole social organism of the country," he told Charles at the end of 1862. This "national school of our own generation" would guide the course of American development, using its superior intellect to solve society's problems and applying its refined sensibilities to provide America with brilliant triumphs in art and literature. These gentlemen were equipped to rule, and Henry Adams was to be one of them.[16]

The Civil War threatened Adams's ideal. He feared the war's "demoralizing effects more than anything else." It was "hard enough work to keep our people educated and honest," he complained, but the "general repulsiveness" of army camp life (which he had never experienced in actuality) threatened to put America on "a permanent course towards every kind of idleness, vice and ignorance." America's "worst passions and tastes have been developed by a forced and bloated growth." He worried whether the destiny of his country was to go "from war to war and debt to debt . . . till we lose all our landmarks and go ahead like France with a mere blind necessity to get on, without a reason or a principle."[17]

But Adams also noted that the war presented Americans with an opportunity to correct the excesses of democracy. As John Stuart Mill himself pointed out in a letter to the historian and diplomat John Lothrop Motley, a friend of the Adams family, "If you have among you men of calibre to use the high spirit which this struggle has raised . . . as means of moving public opinion in favor of correcting what is bad and strengthening what is good in your institutions and modes of feeling and thought, the war will prove to have been a permanent blessing to your country." Henry Adams saw that he and his fellow gentlemen had the chance to "put the country on the right track." He was ready to seize the opportunity. "It will depend on the generation to which you and I belong," he told Charles, "whether the country is to be brought back to its true course and the New England element is to carry the victory." The rising generation "must bring back or create a respect for law and order and the Constitution and the civil and judicial authorities." Adams eagerly accepted this great responsibility as a task equal to that undertaken by his ancestors. "Our generation has been stirred from its lowest layers and there is that in its history which will stamp every member of it until we are all in our graves," he lectured his elder brother. "We cannot be commonplace. The great burden that has fallen on us must inevitably stamp its character on us."[18]

This vision inspired Henry Adams. He stayed awake until the early morning hours, reading and writing. When visitors from America arrived,

Adams sat down with them to discuss "affairs at home and philosophical statesmanship, the Government and the possibility of effectual reform." The news of Union victories found him "internally singing Hosannahs and running riot in exultation." His post as private secretary now interested him: "I am better satisfied with my position now than ever before, and think I am of use." He concluded in July 1863, in the wake of Union victories at Gettysburg and Vicksburg, "I believe I never was so well off physically, morally and intellectually as this last year."[19]

Henry Adams was in Italy with his mother when he heard about Appomattox and Lincoln's assassination. He viewed these events as both a climax and a transition. "To me this great change looks like a step downward to our generation," he mused. "New men have come. Will the old set hold their ground, or . . . make way for a young America which we do not know[?]" It was time for the reunited nation to confront the challenge of democratic governance, to establish a national meritocracy to direct the development of the nation. He had yet to consider in detail how this goal would be attained or how it would be manifested in government policy. Nor did he feel in any hurry to address these concerns. Instead of returning to America immediately at war's end, he chose to enjoy England three years more while his father remained at his post.[20]

Events in postwar America confirmed Adams's belief that his country needed direction from the able. He characterized the politics of Reconstruction as chaotic and deplorable, for mere political advantage, not principled statesmanship, appeared to motivate political leaders. Adams quickly abandoned earlier notions of revenge, military rule, and treason trials in favor of reconciling the wayward white brothers of the defeated Confederacy. Horrified at the passage of the Civil Rights Act and the Fourteenth Amendment in 1866, he charged that the Republican-controlled Congress was "violating the rights of minorities more persistently than the worst pro-slavery Congress could ever do" as it "habitually" ignored the Constitution. Besides, Congress was incompetent, "having botched every single measure demanded for the public good. . . . It is time that this is stopped." He predicted that the Military Reconstruction Act—which Congress passed in March 1867 in an effort to create loyal governments in the Southern states through the enfranchisement of the freedmen—would result in the South's becoming "a society dissolved, and brigandage universal." Some of the Radical proposals were simply "monstrous." Infuriated, he told Charles that "my blood boils" just thinking about Reconstruction. Perhaps with unintended irony, he concluded: "Things look awfully black to me at home."[21]

Adams's dark view of events did not include a sympathetic look at the millions of recently freed blacks in the South. After all, he reasoned, slavery was dead. "Free opinion, education, and law have now entrance into the South. Why assume that they are powerless and precipitate hopeless confusion?" Never did he betray the slightest awareness, let alone concern, about the plight of American blacks. When he spoke of minority rights, he meant the right of white Southerners to home rule, and he sounded far more like his grandfather's old adversary John C. Calhoun than the abolitionist he had once professed to be. It was ironic—to put it mildly—that to someone who vividly recalled sixty years later his anger at witnessing the return of fugitive slaves in Boston, the deepest evil of Reconstruction was not the violence against blacks in the South, but the alleged violence done the Constitution by Republicans seeking to protect those blacks.[22]

Adams also deplored the inflationary tendencies of government fiscal policy. It had been a tenet of the family philosophy that irredeemable paper money was evil, a notion endorsed by most English liberals, including Mill. Henry focused his attention on the repeal of the Legal Tender Act of 1862, which made irredeemable paper money—the supposedly infamous "greenback"—a circulating medium of currency in the United States. Using historical parallels to make his point, Adams published two anonymous essays in the *North American Review* which, though ostensibly studies of British financial policy in the early nineteenth century, held implied lessons for contemporary problems. The first, "British Finance in 1816," criticized protective tariffs and paper money for hindering the growth of the economy in the aftermath of the Napoleonic wars. Adams suggested that history furnished "instruction to other nations which are placed in circumstances more or less similar." His second effort, a study of the suspension of specie payments in England between 1797 and 1821, further cautioned against any policy that neglected immediate resumption of specie payments. Justifying his efforts on what appeared to be an obscure topic, he told Charles Eliot Norton, editor of the *Review*, "The American people may instruct themselves in the interim, but this seems highly improbable." Of more interest is Adams's unexplained decision to maintain anonymity. Perhaps he sensed that readers would not credit such work if they knew it came from a young man; perhaps he once more sought to evade the burden of being an Adams inherent in identifying himself—or sought to prove the strength of his intellect independent of his heritage; perhaps he knew that those most eager to discover his identity could do so anyway.[23]

To Henry Adams, the changed character of Massachusetts Republicanism exemplified the decline of American politics. Once he had been proud of his Republican affiliation. The party contained its share of misfits, malcontents, and extremists, but men of virtue, ability, and intelligence also flocked to its standard. Yet the war had transformed it for the worse. Once the gallant defenders of the Constitution against the Southern "slave power,"

Bay State Republicans were now "little better than a mob of political gamblers and timid time-servers." Party leaders, including Charles Sumner and George S. Boutwell, were "permanently insane." Perfectly content to let white Southerners determine the destiny of their region, Adams could not comprehend Sumner's fervid desire to protect the freedmen. Once an idol to be worshipped, Sumner was now in Adams's eyes an irrational, stubborn, half-crazed egotist. His mind, Adams commented in later years, "had reached the calm of water which receives and reflects images without absorbing them; it contained nothing but itself." If Sumner was what Massachusetts Republicanism had to offer, then Henry Adams wanted no part of it.[24]

Adams's understanding of Massachusetts Republicanism was uninformed, as might be expected given his location (although ignorance rarely restrained him from expressing his opinion in definitive fashion). Moderate as well as radical forces were present in the ranks of Massachusetts Republicans. It had been the obstructionist behavior of President Andrew Johnson that had driven the two together, as was evident in former governor John A. Andrew's decision to abandon his challenge to Sumner's claim to party leadership in the wake of the president's attacks on the senator. Nor was Sumner the controlling force in establishing the outlines of congressional alternatives to the president's Reconstruction policy. Moreover, Adams surely felt that any program to protect the freedpeople in the postwar South was "insane": his opposition to slavery, tepid as it was, included no case for egalitarianism. Of course, in expressing these sentiments Adams was not alone: he would have found a white supremacist soul mate in Secretary of the Navy Gideon Welles, who confided similar notions to the pages of his diary.[25]

Henry's brother, John Quincy Adams II, soon discovered that the dislike of the Adamses for Massachusetts Republicans was reciprocated and then some. As a Republican member of the state legislature, he had supported Governor Andrew's reconciliationist posture and had battled Sumner's supporters. In August 1866, he attended the National Union convention in Philadelphia, signifying his support for Johnson's conservative Reconstruction policy. Immediately the *Boston Advertiser* labeled him an apostate and drummed him out of the Republican ranks. The next year, Sumner meted out the punishment, blocking John's appointment to head the Customs House. There was nothing left for John to do but to be true to his name and declare his independence of party discipline—although, in truth, he had already done so when he had sided with Johnson in 1866. He bolted to the Democratic party, heading the state ticket as its candidate for governor in 1867 and 1868.[26]

Henry interpreted John's fate as a sign of the times, concluding that the Adams brothers should follow the family tradition of deserting party in the name of principle. Like their father, they were "again in a miserable minority in Massachusetts, without a friend to work with," looking toward "another period of political banishment" in the Bay State. Echoing Tocqueville, he declared that the "tyranny of majorities in our country must be tempered by resistance." It was time to break with the Republican regime. He blasted his brother Charles's desire to "fight it out within the party" as "a piece of self-delusion which you use to cover your own intellect from seeing and confessing what is really fear of public opinion." Look at what had happened to Richard Henry Dana when he had tried to juggle self-respect with party regularity: he "had been whipped and kicked like a mangy spaniel by Sumner and his party." Only brother John was man enough to say "that his soul was his own."[27]

The grotesque presence of Benjamin F. Butler in Republican ranks symbolized to Adams the degradation of a once-proud party. A former Democrat who had gained infamy for his behavior as a commander of occupation troops during the war, Butler seemed a vulgar joke to most Massachusetts gentlemen. His mere existence in politics made a sham of the idea of rule by the best. That he was elected to the House of Representatives in 1866 was both a disgrace and a sign of the dangerous ignorance of the populace. Espousing greenbacks and tariffs, both of which were anathema to Henry Adams, Butler had exacerbated class divisions to gain votes. "You must crush him now," Adams warned fellow gentleman and free trader Edward Atkinson, "or he will grind your faces in the dirt." But it was Butler who would do the crushing in 1868, steamrolling to victory over Dana in the Fifth Congressional District, which included Lowell, home of many gentlemen but of far more workingmen.[28]

Adams watched apprehensively as the old Republican party disintegrated during Reconstruction. He had once believed that the destruction of the "slave power" would free the United States from stifling partisanship and allow it to grow and flourish with the revival of republican values. Instead, the party which had saved the Union now seemed intent on destroying the republic. "If the country doesn't stop, it's going to Hell," he warned Charles in 1867. The emergence of men like Butler complicated Adams's desire to revamp the republic. It confirmed his distaste for professional political electioneering. "I never will make a speech, never run for an office, never belong to a party," he concluded. Besides, the political environment in Massachusetts, as Adams perceived it, plus his own unprepossessing presence, made it unlikely if not impossible that he could ever win the popular favor he delighted to scorn. Instead, he planned to embark upon a career as a political journalist, thus indulging his taste for criticism while seeking to exercise influence on those in power. "There are still heads to hit in this world," he announced to Charles. Moreover, he would abandon Boston for the intoxicating atmosphere of Washington, D.C., where he might make more headway and where he seemed to feel more at home.[29] Although Adams had announced that his decision would "make it impossible to follow the family go-cart," the fact was that he was simply choosing a different path.[30] The choices were in line with his education. Mill and Tocqueville had emphasized the importance of a well-directed press in governing and disciplining a democracy. Suited for electoral politics neither by appearance nor by personality, Adams would instead educate and guide the thinking of the people who actually governed, thus circumventing the need to curry approval from the people at the polls. The issues of reform—tariff policy, finance, and the appointment of qualified individuals to office—needed articulate spokesmen. He would settle in Washington, revive old connections, make new friends, and push himself into the inner circle of government. While the politicos might reap the rewards of public applause, Adams would take pride in the knowledge that they had acted upon his advice, allowing him to control the engine of government by telling the nation's leaders which levers to pull.

Henry Adams never paused to consider that significant obstacles stood in the way of his plan. He had no previous political experience. In fact, he had precious little contact with American politics, aside from his stint as a political reporter during the secession winter of 1860–1861. He had been out of the country since the opening of hostilities. Could he reasonably expect to play such a critical role in politics upon his return? He had developed his notions of governance and reform by candlelight in his London bedroom. Did they bear any relation to American reality? For political news he had relied on diplomatic dispatches, newspaper reports, private correspondence, and the observations of an occasional visitor. Did these give him an accurate perception of American politics? In the past, Adams's lack of firsthand knowledge had not prevented him from passing judgments, as his opinion of the South prior to Fort Sumter had suggested. A more cautious person might have admitted that he had much to learn before he presumed to teach.

Serious as these shortcomings were, Adams's biggest obstacle was his own personality. Subject to emotional extremes, he could be exhilarated and boastful one day, only to sink into deep depression and despair the next. He tended to magnify both his triumphs and his failures out of all proportion. Benjamin Moran, assistant secretary at the American legation in London, was particularly irritated by Adams's arrogance, no doubt in part out of resentment and personal pettiness at the upstart's intrusion into diplomatic circles. Moran found Adams "pompous and assuming" and lashed out that the pretentious young man "is very conceited, and talks like a goose. . . . He will ere long get a hard slap in the face from fortune and that will sober him and give scope to the good sense he really possesses." Brother Charles was more pithy: "My brother has grown to be a damned, solemn, pompous little ass."[31]

Adams's bouts with depression, evident in his wartime correspondence, were so frequent that one wonders why he never tried to commit suicide—although it appears that he may have contemplated it at least once. Labeling himself "a full-blown fatalist," he admitted to Charles that "I despise the world and myself so honestly and reflectively that whatever fate comes, will probably find me ready to bow to it with a good grace." Charles termed him "morbid"; another brother, John Quincy Adams, reported that he "cusses everything." Even Henry admitted that at times he became "horribly solemn," a trait that earned him the nickname "Mausoleum." Such a psyche reflected Henry's awareness that his personality, coupled with the changes in American politics over the past century, would make it very difficult to duplicate his ancestors' accomplishments. Nor did his appearance help matters. Slight in frame, light in weight (120 pounds), his five-foot-four-inch body topped by a balding head—Henry "feels pitiably," brother Charles commented, "the want of physical presence." Henry complained bitterly about his physical shortcomings. "You have a physique, brass, and a disposition for society," he told Charles; "I suffer from a want of all these qualities, and perpetual and incessant mortification on that account." Perhaps his pugnaciousness and arrogance toward others reflected his pessimism and compensated for his physical disadvantages. Adams himself suggested such an explanation in later life when he confided to a niece that he overcame his shortcomings by bad manners—a habit he admittedly developed during his years in London. He added that he often strutted when walking "to increase his sense of importance." No wonder Charles once called his younger brother a "damned little cuss."[32]

In submitting his first article to the *North American Review* in 1866, Adams exhibited both self-deprecation and conceit within the space of a few sentences in a letter to John Gorham Palfrey. "I am by no means proud of my literary powers," he confessed. "Had I possessed any real confidence in myself I should not have almost reached thirty without an effort to win my spurs." But he could not resist adding arrogantly, "There is more study and laborious application in the enclosed portfolio than in any number of the *North American Review* that I usually see." Holding that "the public is a pretty contemptible thing," Adams cared little for an audience outside of the elite that he hoped would bring the country into a new era. Adams's belief that he could best persuade people by offending them at least let him rest safe in the assurance that he was not currying popular favor, but it was an ominous sign for someone who needed to make friends in order to shape policy.[33]

For someone desiring to influence others, Henry Adams seemed bliss-fully unaware that his personality could influence people adversely. Perhaps he recognized that his arrogance often drove people away, but he rational-ized this fact by deeming such people as not worth knowing. Shy and re-served, fumbling when performing social niceties, Henry displayed an aloof and curt demeanor that may have been a sign of defensiveness, or an awk-ward way of expressing himself. Certainly his warm and deep friendships with Gaskell, John Hay, and others demonstrate that he could be a likeable fellow when someone penetrated his veil of diffidence and conceit. Such traits are easier to describe than to analyze, but it is safe to say that Adams's personality proved detrimental to his chosen career. Perhaps he had some knowledge of this, for he once admitted, "My enemy is only myself."[34]

On December 1, 1867, Charles Francis Adams, Sr., resigned his post as minister to the Court of St. James's. After seven trying years, the Adamses would returning to the United States—although the retiring minister made sure to schedule his return to New York so that he would arrive after the Democrats were to meet to nominate a candidate for president in July 1868, an opportunity he preferred to pass up. No one was more anxious to leave London than Henry Adams. "As to the future, I know that the prospect is misty, but I have made my plans and am ready to begin the march," he told Charles. But he doubted that he would return to Boston, because it "is not big enough for four Adamses." He was headed elsewhere. "I claim my right to remain what I have been for ten years, an independent cuss": his target was Washington, D.C., and his aim was to save the republic.[35]

CHAPTER THREE

THE ROAD TO WASHINGTON

Since no other path seemed to offer itself, he stuck to his
plan of joining the press. . . . One announced one's self
as an adventurer and an office-seeker, a person of
deplorably bad judgment, and the charges were true.
                            The Education of Henry Adams[1]

Henry Adams debarked from a Cunard steamer in New York City one
muggy July night in 1868, prepared to take the country by storm. Paying
scant attention to the swarms of Democrats who had descended on Man-
hattan for their party's presidential nomination (the convention proved to
be longer than anticipated), he scurried to Quincy with his parents. The
summer social season revived him. "Everyone was cordial," he told Charles
Milnes Gaskell, "and the young women mostly smiled upon me more
beamingly than I had been accustomed to, during my residence among the
frigid damsels of London." Amid excursions to the coast and the clatter of
teacups, he confirmed his plans to try politics on his terms. In October, he
departed by train for the nation's capital, determined, in his father's words,
"to try his future as a writer on public questions of a higher class."[1]

Adams's first stop was New York. He quickly arranged to be the Washington correspondent for the *New York Evening Post* and for Edwin L.
Godkin's reform weekly, the *Nation*, to supplement his connection with the
North American Review. Both his name and his previous writings served as
admirable qualifications for such positions; more important, however, was
his clear commitment to reform. With credentials in order, he now needed
only a chance to peek down the corridors of power. He found it when he
stumbled into his old London acquaintance, William M. Evarts, on a New
York sidewalk. Evarts had made a name for himself since the war, climbing
to the cabinet as attorney general after offering a brilliant defence of Andrew Johnson during the president's impeachment trial, completely defeating prosecutor Benjamin F. Butler as Charles Sumner looked on in dismay.
Such enemies made Evarts all the more endearing to Adams. The young

journalist enjoyed Evarts's easy wit and convivial disposition; Evarts also served as a pleasant and highly placed guide to the political labyrinth. Having laid the groundwork for a successful career in the political press, Adams clung doggedly to Evarts as the pair traveled to Washington.[2]

Adams settled into a boarding house on G Street—lodgings which, if modest, had "more civilisation in it that the rest of Washington all together," according to the new occupant. "The great step is taken, and here I am," he informed Gaskell, "settled for years, and perhaps for life." Before long, he ventured forth into the chaotic world of Washington politics: "the people and the mode of life," he remarked with a touch of prescience, "are enough to take your hair off." The city was not totally foreign to him, for his idol from the secession winter, William Henry Seward, was still secretary of state. Adams's relationship with Evarts also opened some doors. The attorney general ushered him into the White House to meet Andrew Johnson, who treated Adams to a discussion of constitutional law, a subject dear to both men. Evarts also introduced Adams to various cabinet members who welcomed the young man so warmly that he could not resist confiding his successes to Gaskell. "In about five years I expect to have conquered a reputation," he declared, as he settled down to work. Yet such a snug position was doomed to be short-lived. "Unfortunately this whole Cabinet goes out on the 4th of March," he noted, "and in the next one I shall probably be without a friend. Politics makes a bad trade."[3]

Indeed, much of Adams's early work might well go for naught. On November 4, 1868, voters chose Ulysses S. Grant, the hero of Appomattox, as the eighteenth president of the United States. Many hoped that as chief executive he would rescue the republic a second time. The Adams family's impressions of the president-elect were shaped in large part by Henry's brother Charles, who had observed Grant at close range during the Wilderness campaign of 1864 while his company was attached to headquarters. "Grant is certainly a very extraordinary man," he concluded after a month of hard fighting: "He handles those around him so quietly and well, he so evidently has the faculty of disposing of work and managing men, he is cool and quiet. . . . In a crisis he is one against whom all around . . . instinctively lean." Grant, Charles observed, exercised great tact in overseeing the Army of the Potomac's operations, preserving harmony while building confidence. Such political skill augured well for a potential president; Charles was an early advocate of Grant's candidacy, attending a meeting at Faneuil Hall to endorse the general. Even more surprising was John Quincy Adams II's ringing endorsement of Grant during the 1868 campaign. Although he headed the state Democratic ticket that year as candidate for governor, he had only good things to say about the opposition's presidential standard-bearer: "He finished the war, and that is enough to entitle him to my respect and admiration." He shocked his fellow Democrats by concluding, "I do believe he is an upright, honorable man, who will try, if elected, to do his best, not for a party only, but for the whole people of the country." Grant was well aware of these remarks, for his private secretary, Adam Badeau, had read the speech to him.[4]

But Grant would not take office until March 1869. In the meantime, Henry got to work educating people about politics even as he was finding out about it firsthand. Given his interest in finance, it was understandable that he chose the Treasury Department for his initial foray into public policy. He quickly made the acquaintance of the department's head, Secretary Hugh McCulloch, who impressed Adams as a man sincerely interested in administering his office without regard for political considerations—a very laudable trait in the eyes of an Adams. The young journalist was also reassured by McCulloch's availability and friendliness. He proudly wrote Gaskell that the secretary "pats me on the back, not figuratively but in the flesh." Given free run of the department's records, Adams dug in and went to work on an article on American financial policy.[5]

Adams's frequent visits to the Treasury Department allowed him to observe the type of young men who were bent upon a career in public service, and he liked what he saw. He noted approvingly that McCulloch was "surrounded by all the active and intelligent young men in the country." Adams's fear that his absence from the war would forever scar him in the eyes of his peers soon faded. These ambitious fellows shared his eagerness for reforming the machinery of government, and displayed wit, intelligence, and learning to boot. As he later recalled, he "was greatly pleased to be admitted as one of them." Adams's superiors also flattered him. Evarts, aware of Adams's interest in financial policy, sounded out arguments about currency questions with the young man in preparation for his defense of the constitutionality of the Legal Tender Act before the Supreme Court. Adams, who maintained that the legislation had been both unconstitutional and unnecessary, enjoyed jousting with the attorney general. Soon his curiosity led him into the home of Chief Justice Salmon P. Chase, who was secretary of the treasury when the Legal Tender Act became law in 1862. Chase confided to Adams his doubts about the law's constitutionality; Adams made clear his own reservations when he reported on the oral arguments before the Supreme Court for the *Nation*. Doubtless it helped to be an Adams to secure such immediate entry into the corridors of power, but Henry proved impressive on his own. Surely a newcomer to Washington could not have asked for a warmer reception than this.[6]

One of Adams's new Washington acquaintances had an especially sympathetic ear for his doctrines. David A. Wells had met Adams in England while collecting information about the British economy as Special Commissioner of the Revenue. There—from the sparkling conversations at that haven of English liberalism, the Cobden Club—Wells, like Adams, had gleaned much about free trade and hard currency that had disabused him of his protectionist beliefs. He was also a staunch advocate of civil service reform. Wells provided the close companionship Adams thirsted for, as well as a possible job, for he was rumored to be on the president-elect's cabinet list, and Henry's brother Charles had already offered to serve under him. As snow fell on Washington, Adams listened in rapt attention as Wells, who both looked and acted the part of the professor, outlined the proposals for revenue reform and tariff reduction contained in his annual report, sure to stir the anger of many Republicans. When Wells's report was published, Adams praised it as the "first statesmanlike expression of policy I have seen, and though I know and care too little about popular opinion to say whether you will meet a warm popular response, I am at least sure that if the people do not respond, it will be so much worse for the people." As he told Charles, "Things are beginning to move."[7]

Adams also encountered two more fellow spirits in Congressman James A. Garfield of Ohio and fellow Massachusetts native Francis A. Walker. The Ohioan embraced specie resumption, favored free trade (although he often voted to protect the productions of this constituents), and revealed a deep interest in political economy—all of which attracted Adams to him. Garfield also fancied himself an intellectual. While this may have been stretching the term a bit, he was both well-educated and widely read, so much so that his colleagues in the House, growing tired of his extended remarks garnished with classical allusions, referred to him as "the learned gentleman from Ohio." Walker also found political economy compelling, and specialized in statistical analysis; he worked for Wells. That these two former army officers welcomed the non-combattant Adams into their ranks was heartening for the newcomer.[8]

His sense of self-importance confirmed, Adams soon became convinced that the major test of the incoming administration's desire to reconstitute the constitutional order would be how closely its financial policy adhered to his beliefs. In his articles on British finance for the *North American Review,* he had used the past to educate the public about present policy; now he intended to lecture the incoming administration through the press on the proper course to follow. "American Finance, 1865–1869" appeared unsigned in the *Edinburgh Review* for April 1869. The author claimed that whatever progress the government had made in resolving its financial difficulties was due not to skillful management but to abundant resources. He deplored the lack of expert advice employed in formulating policy and ridiculed the "wildest financial theories" set forth by politicians. Whether the sheer growth of the American economy could compensate for such ineptitude remained a matter for speculation. It was up to the incoming administration to inject reform principles into government operations. But the *Edinburgh Review* was less than an ideal forum for the propagation of his views. Very few Americans, let alone Ulysses S. Grant, read it; even the *Nation* dismissed it as a journal of no consequence. Adams, however, distributed offprints to those whom he most wanted to impress and influence— Wells, Garfield, and Walker.[9]

On a more mundane level, Adams waxed ecstatic over the prospect that Wells or Evarts would enter the new cabinet, opening up more opportunities for himself. Along with Wells, Walker, and Garfield, he plotted strategy against common enemies such as Ben Butler, who was holding forth on the merits of paper money. He made plans for another article on speculation, noting that such fields "are gloriously rich and stink like hell." Meanwhile, he anxiously awaited the call to public service which must inevitably come after March 4—although he craved the invitation, not the office. "I have bluffed people so damnably on the idea of my wanting office that they are now humbled at my feet and if someone would only offer me something handsome so that I could refuse, I should be secure from such suspicions for ever," he bragged to Charles. "If Evarts gets the State or the Treasury, I shall be supposed to have my choice of positions, which will answer the purpose just as well."[10]

Adams was shrewd enough to clear away one possible obstacle on the path to power. Charles Sumner still loomed over his future; having seen the senator stand in his brother John's way, Henry could not be sure that he would not suffer a similar fate. Charles Francis Adams did what he could for his son, dining with the senator in 1868. The engagement passed without incident: "This will smooth your path," he reported to his son. Not long after, Henry encountered Sumner on the street one day, greeted the senator, then anxiously awaited a response. Caught off guard, Sumner, perhaps placated by Henry's father, decided that Henry should not be held accountable for his family's moral turpitude. Not only did he generously return Henry's handshake, but he also invited him to dinner at the senator's house on Lafayette Square, just across from the White House. Adams soon became a frequent visitor, mixing with diplomats, politicians, and fellow New Englanders. As he recalled in the *Education*, "All this favored a young man who had come to make a name."[11]

One person who had occasion to observe Adams in action during these months was Sumner's private secretary, Moorfield Storey. One evening Storey encountered Adams in vintage form, "monopolizing the conversation, as it seemed to me; and laying down the law with a certain assumption." Resenting this newcomer's arrogance, Storey was prepared to dismiss him as an obnoxious upstart when the two met on the street the next day.

Adams, perhaps aware that he could not afford to offend someone in Storey's position, turned on his charm with intended effect. Storey warmed to Adams's personality, and the two young men made the rounds of Washington's social circles, competing for the reputation as the best waltzer in Washington.[12]

Storey enjoyed Adams's company but cared little for his pessimistic view of politics. The two spent long hours one night at Sumner's after dinner debating the quality of American politics, with the senator's secretary vehemently opposing Adams's contention that politics and society had declined since the beginning of the republic. Doubtless Sumner sat to one side, amused to hear two earnest young men pass judgment on the politicians of past and present, including himself. As Storey commented when he reported this conversation to his fiancée, "Men talk much of corruption and jobbing in private matters, but it could probably be found that almost every charge if examined was groundless. It is very easy to make sweeping assertions, and to none more easy than the gentlemanly democrats of Boston, who, having always gloried in their ignorance of politics, have evolved from their own conscience theories about it, which can only be excused by that very ignorance." According to Storey, Adams sorely needed to be educated rather than to educate others about politics in America.[13]

Yet Adams was only one of several people who looked to the new administration to provide the opportunity for those of intelligence and taste to shape American governance. It would be hard to compose a coherent list of this cadre, although among those who claimed membership were journalists Adams, Samuel Bowles of the *Springfield Republican*, Godkin, Horace White of the *Chicago Tribune*, and, to a lesser extent, George William Curtis of *Harper's Weekly*; politicians Carl Schurz and Jacob D. Cox; and social scientists Atkinson, Wells, and Walker, as well as Henry's brother Charles, who dabbled in all sorts of pursuits. They hailed from Republican ranks; they were far more absorbed by issues of finance and civil service reform than by Reconstruction, which they saw as a distraction from the real issues at hand; they spoke of the need to educate politicians and the public. Some historians, like Geoffrey Blodgett, have identified "an interlocking directorate of liberal intelligence," a network of the like-minded. But it is unclear exactly what served as the foundation of their common identity other than a desire to shape the future by providing for rule by the intelligencia. "Reform" was a rather broad concept: although it was usually grounded in shared sentiments about free trade, civil service reform, and a lack of interest in Reconstruction, it nevertheless is better understood as a shared set of assumptions about the need for an American version of aristocratic liberalism than by agreement about specific proposals. Defining such a cadre is problematic at best, for many reformers were far more united by what they opposed than what they proposed. Whether they would exercise influence and power, and to what extent would they implement their agenda, remained an unanswered question.[14]

Much would be determined by the man who would become president on March 4, 1869. Given the assurances of his elder brothers, Adams, despite his lack of first-hand knowledge about Grant, had reason to welcome the advent of his presidency. Many of his fellow reformers did. Massachusetts Congressman George F. Hoar later remembered that many reformers "looked to Grant with an almost superstitious hope. They were prepared to expect almost any miracle from the great genius who had subdued the rebellion." Godkin hoped "that we have in Grant a man who will break up the present system, and in breaking it up will reveal to the country the possibility of being both great and prosperous without the aid of party charlatans." Here was the man, freed from the bonds of political obligation, capable of restoring the republic.[15]

As Henry Adams recalled nearly a half-century later, "Grant represented order." The president-elect was no friend of many Radicals. Charles Sumner had opposed his candidacy, and many remembered Grant's distaste for Ben Butler from the war. Some political observers suspected that Grant had secretly encouraged Dana's candidacy against Butler the previous fall. To Adams, Grant represented reform; to a young man on the way up, he also represented opportunity. The president-elect's open dislike of politicians fueled Adams's hopes that he would cast aside partisan considerations and restore merit as the sole qualification for public office. Under Grant, the existing political order, so hostile to the Adamses, might give way to the rule of the best. Henry Adams smiled at the idea. But, as he later recalled of Grant, "One seemed to know him so well, and really knew so little."[16]

The incoming president's sphinx-like attitude concerning his cabinet choices, founded upon his sensible desire to forestall efforts to alter his selections, touched off rampant speculation. Among names frequently mentioned was that of Charles Francis Adams, Sr., for secretary of state. The old man sat in his Quincy home, snipping out newspaper columns praising his virtues and qualifications for the honor, yet all the while reassuring his diary that he wished to enjoy retirement from public life. However, he also reiterated the traditional Adams theme of his reluctant willingness to respond to a call to duty. When Grant traveled to Boston, the elder Adams met him at a dinner. Determined not to look eager for position, the former minister was reserved, yet he interpreted Grant's own reserve as a sign of dislike.[17]

If his father seemed ambivalent over the prospect of a cabinet post, Henry Adams was dead set against the idea. He spent the early weeks of winter determined to stifle any "call to duty" for his father. But his concerns did not touch upon the restfulness of a retirement so well deserved. "I don't want him there," he told Charles. "He would be in my way." Besides, he added, sounding an ominous note, "this first Cabinet will be a failure." Better, he thought, to sit around and await events. Grant, enjoying the confusion and speculation, remained silent about his preferences. "Everyone is in the dark," Adams observed in January 1869. The following month, he reported that bewilderment had engendered anger: "The politicians, I am told, are furious at not being consulted by Grant. . . . I know as much as any fellow, and that is, they say, the highest wisdom." He watched as Wells, Evarts, and Sumner fretted over their chances for office. Even Adams found Grant's silence unnerving. Puzzled and exasperated by the president-elect, he grew somewhat cynical, as if to brace himself for the worse. "I pity the man that goes into that Cabinet," he told Charles as inauguration day approached. "We here look for a reign of western mediocrity, but perhaps one appreciates least the success of the steamer, when one lives in the engineroom." Uncertainty gnawed at him. So much depended on a man who during the last decade had risen from obscurity to the presidency. Yet Adams also knew that there were limits to what the new president could do. "Grant's position is *very* difficult, between the Senate and the people, but he alone can do little," Adams told John Bright. "The reform we need must come from the people and the people show no signs of it." It was time to stir things up.[18]

Adams realized that his search for reputation and influence had to take him beyond the drawing rooms of Washington society, so he made plans for his first salvoes in the reform press. He planned to commence firing with an article, tentatively titled "Rings," that attacked the corrupt workings of the political system. As he contemplated his initial sally into the field of political journalism, he could hardly restrain his joy at the odium he felt sure the piece would bring upon him. "I want to be advertised," he confessed to Charles, "and the easiest way is to do something obnoxious and do it well. . . . I am not afraid of unpopularity and I will do it." In his efforts to achieve instant infamy, he considered offering "Rings" to an English journal, a move he thought would add insult to injury to the American ego: "No home publication will act on America like foreign opinion."[19]

Soon Adams became enamored with the idea of unpopularity. By writing a "monumental" article, "a piece of history and a blow at democracy," he hoped that public reaction would "make me a 'degenerate son,' and a 'traitor,' a 'cynical skeptic,' and a 'person whose career is closed before it has begun.'" This desire for infamy not only bore the imprint of an Adams; it was also a curious transposition of cause and effect. All three of Adams's paternal predecessors, in predicating their actions on personal principle rather than on political expediency, had accepted public calumny, although not always in stride. Unpopularity was to be expected, since it confirmed their skeptical view of "the people" and reassured them that they had done the right thing. They pointed to personal attacks as proof that they acted irrespective of personal ambitions. Henry Adams seemed far more interested in the sensation he would cause than in the cause of the sensation. "One's value is fairly measured by his abuse," he reasoned. Infamy would give him the reputation he needed to exercise influence on public officials. He failed to consider that it might produce the opposite result.[20]

As his first step toward notoriety, Adams set down his impressions of Washington in the winter of 1868–1869. "The Session," modeled upon Sir Robert Cecil's annual review of British politics in the *London Quarterly*, appeared in the April issue of the *North American Review*. It revealed the young journalist's profound disillusionment with the workings of American government during the third session of the Fortieth Congress. Congress, Adams argued, was collapsing under the immense pressure of resolving increasingly complex issues and withstanding the incessant clash of special interests against the public good. The machinery of legislation "groans and labors under the burden, . . . spasmodic and inefficient." Congress was unable to devote more than "superficial attention" to the major issues of the day. Adams generously listed them: "Reconstruction, establishment of the Executive in its Privileges and Proper Functions, Revenue Reform, Monetary Reform, Administrative Reform, Internal Improvements, Foreign Policy."[21]

In a lifeless and cursory discussion of Reconstruction, Adams dismissed the passage of the Fifteenth Amendment as "of small practical value" and declared Reconstruction at an end—evidence of his own impatience with this distraction from what he judged to be the real issues of the moment. Much more important was the issue of presidential power, "where a battle is unavoidable and imminent." He focused on the Tenure of Office Act, legislation passed to hamstring Johnson by preventing the president from removing anyone appointed with the approval of the Senate from office without the Senate's concurrence. It was time to repeal this travesty upon the separation of powers—although Adams was embarrassed to note that on this issue he found as his ally none other than Ben Butler. Nevertheless, Adams called upon Grant to "wrest from Congress the initiative which Congress is now accustomed to exercise." This revealed the true purpose of Adams's essay—to attack the present state of Congress and political parties as subversive to good government. Throughout the remainder of "The Session," he used issues merely as pegs upon which to hang his indictment of the political system and its "debauching effect . . . upon parties, public men, and the morals of the state."[22]

According to Adams, political parties were at the beck and call of "rings"—now known as special interest groups—which prostituted government to serve their own needs. They "formed a hedge which marks the limit within which argument and reason may prevail." Parties, which had "no decency and no shame," bargained away their support to the rings in return for money. As a result, the "condition of parties precludes the chance of reform." Thus, Wells's reports concerning the tariff were doomed to oblivion because they were not the product of a party or a ring. Through the patronage system the rings wormed their way to the heart of the administrative process. Thus infected, the body politic was crippled in its attempt to serve the public good. Adams hinted that the whole system would soon collapse if left unreformed.[23]

Adams also pointed his sharp pen and wit at Congress. Corruption was not his major concern, he said with a straight face; after all, "not more than one member in ten" ever accepted bribes. Instead, he lashed out at the inferior quality of men in public life. Uneducated in the fields of political economy or constitutional law, congressmen fumbled with intricate issues. The chaos of Reconstruction had contributed to this degeneration because "it has brought into Congress a class of men whose influence has not been favorable, and who have increased the power of the lobby rather than the dignity of either House." With such men in office, reform was smothered. Claiming that he "saw no reason why a democracy should be necessarily corrupt," Adams called upon Grant to undertake a thorough reform of the system. He willingly admitted that this was a "superhuman task" and might merely "postpone the day when corruption will become intolerable." Nevertheless, it seemed the only real alternative. Incremental changes in policy were not enough: it was time for "a wise and careful correction of the system itself." Only then could programs like revenue reform receive due attention, and government return to its purpose of serving the people.[24]

"The Session" represented a shift in Henry Adams's attitudes toward American politics. Once he had thought the mere introduction of men of merit and intelligence into politics would solve any problem; now, as he told Edward Atkinson, his observation of corruption and jobbery convinced him that "we have got to take the matter up with a high hand and drag it into politics if we are to hope for success." Political reform crowded out all other concerns. Free trade was "a false scent"; Reconstruction was no longer important. "The whole root of the evil is in *political* corruption," he concluded. The next battle would be fought along the lines of reform. "Our coming struggle is going to be harder than the anti-slavery fight, and though we may carry free trade, I fear we shall be beaten on the wider field." Without hesitation Adams enlisted in the ranks of the reformers, fighting to preserve the republic, as had his ancestors. He held few illusions about the difficulty of the task before him. To the aged John Gorham Palfrey, a veteran of past political struggles against slavery, he expressed skepticism: "How a mere change of administration is to help us, I cannot see, and am rather inclined to think that it will only improve our affairs so far as to make the system endurable, and so blind our people to the necessity of true reform." He concluded that the "idea of democracy in itself, by the mere fact of giving power to the masses, will elevate and purify human nature" was humbug.[25]

Such dark comments contrast starkly with Adams's earlier bright optimism that the levers of power were within his grasp. Ecstatic about his rapid acceptance into some political circles, he dramatized and exaggerated the problems facing the nation in order to bolster his confidence, assuring himself that his struggle against democratic excesses was worthy of his family name. At the same time, his correspondence sounded a tone of flippancy tinged with sarcasm, spiced with arrogance and more than a touch of conceit. Expecting access to the corridors of power as a matter of course, Adams, "laying down the law," promised to offend many practical politicians who had earned their keep in the sweatshop of Washington politics. By claiming piously that he courted unpopularity, Adams reassured himself that others disliked him because of his political ideals rather than his irritating personality, which only increased his contempt for most politicians.

From Quincy, Charles Francis Adams, Sr., encouraged his son to rein in his runaway ambition. "I warn you not to be too sanguine of early success from any efforts you may be able to make," he wrote Henry early in January. Knowing his son all too well, he continued: "Especially beware of overconfidence which is apt to breed conceit, and to weaken your influence in the long run." Puzzled by Grant's peculiar behavior, uncertain as to the president-elect's qualifications for office, and no doubt a little chagrined that he would probably be omitted from the cabinet slate, the elder Adams concluded that the announcement of the cabinet "will be the signal for new combinations." In any case, he advised Henry, "The game will be well worth watching as a study for young men like you."[26]

On March 5, 1869, Henry Adams walked up Pennsylvania Avenue to the Capitol. Ulysses S. Grant had been inaugurated the previous day, and the new president had assured the nation that he was determined "to do to the best of my ability all that is required of me. The responsibilities of the position I feel, but accept them without fear." But Adams cared little for what Grant had to say. Like everyone else, he wanted to find out who would be in his cabinet.

Once at the Capitol, Adams was forced to wait outside the Senate chamber, for the Senate had gone into executive session to consider Grant's list of nominees. If he was close to the door, he might have heard a few muffled cries of anguish and astonishment, punctuated by several choruses of "yeas."

In a few minutes, the large doors opened. Senators streamed out, some with looks of shock. Sumner seemed especially grim. Over the buzzing crowd, Adams heard the names called out. Several were familiar. Ebenezer Rockwood Hoar as attorney general was a family friend; Jacob D. Cox as secretary of the interior was well-known for his conservatism on race; and Elihu B. Washburne, who headed the cabinet slate as secretary of state, was an eminent congressman credited with being Grant's political patron—although secretary of state hardly seemed the position for him. Adams has even placed on his personal slate John M. Schofield as secretary of war— the lone holdover from Johnson's cabinet, and a temporary one at that. But other selections stunned and mystified him. John Creswell, a somewhat obscure Maryland Republican, for postmaster general? Alexander T. Stewart, the department store magnate, as secretary of the Treasury? Exactly who was Adolph Borie, the new secretary of the navy? What had happened to Wells? To Evarts? What, indeed, had happened to Henry Adams's vision of the future?[27]

The following week only added to the confusion. Stewart was barred from the Treasury post by a 1789 statute excluding from that office men with commercial investments. Stewart volunteered to place his business affairs in trust; Grant asked the Senate to repeal the law. Several senators, embarrassed that the Senate had approved Stewart unanimously before discovering the law, supported the idea, but Charles Sumner, furious with the new president for failing to consult him over Cabinet selections, thwarted the plan. Then Washburne, against Grant's wishes, gave up the State Department after several days, pleading ill health—although it seemed that all along he wanted the mission to France instead (which he received). In the first week of his presidency, Grant had lost his nominees for the two most important cabinet positions. Adams eagerly awaited to hear whom Grant would nominate to replace Washburne and Stewart. Perhaps Evarts and Wells—and Adams—would come into power after all.

But when the announcement came, the young reporter received several more jolts. For the State Department, Grant turned, not to Evarts, but to New Yorker Hamilton Fish, who reluctantly agreed to serve. Fish was an old-line Whig with conservative views, and eventually Adams would warm to him. The same could not be said for Grant's choice to head the Treasury Department. Anxious to quiet Radical opposition to his appointments, Grant turned to George S. Boutwell of Massachusetts. There was much to recommend Boutwell for the position. Originally a Democrat, he had twice been elected governor of Massachusetts before the war—elevated to office by the same coalition of Free Soilers and Democrats who had first elected Sumner to the Senate. During the war, he had been in charge of the Internal Revenue Office; he left that office to enter Congress, where he played a

43

significant role in framing Reconstruction legislation. Although in later years, people would declare that Republicans in Congress forced Boutwell on Grant, the fact was that Boutwell had already turned down Grant's offer of another cabinet post—ironically, from Adams's point of view, as secretary of the interior (now held by Cox). But for Adams the appointment was a great setback. Not only did it deprive Wells of office, but it also elevated in his stead a man Adams loathed. In Adams's mind, Boutwell was a hack politician who had no respect for learning: he had once recommended that Harvard be recast as a vocational school for farmers, mechanics, and merchants.[28]

By the end of Grant's first week in office, Adams had recovered his composure. He had reserved some space in "The Session" for a discussion of the new president's initial actions and spent several days pondering what to say. His comments were restrained but to the point. Grant's decision to keep his own counsel had proven a disaster. "The idea now so popular that politicians are bad counsellors, is one of the most unfortunate mistakes of our day," Adams gravely informed his readers. "To exclude politicians would imply also the exclusion of statesmen, and to conduct the Government without the aid of trained statesmen is as dangerous as to conduct a war without the aid of trained generals." The annoyance expressed by Congress, extreme as it was, was justified. While Adams denied any desire "to express any unfavorable opinion of General Grant's cabinet," he warned that "there must be no more mistakes in administration, and no hazardous experiments, whose failure may shake public confidence." Privately, Adams was much harsher. The president, he reported to Charles, "has made Congress madder than the devil." The cabinet selections "are not what we want. I am afraid there is more favoritism than public good in them." Much to his disgust, he discovered that Boutwell did not share Wells's plans for financial reform. "It's the old game with fresh cards," he moaned. Worst of all, though he did not say it, the Adamses were lost in the political shuffle.[29]

Adams was unnerved by Grant's final slate. Several decades later, he would recall that "Grant's nominations had the singular effect of making the hearer ashamed, not so much of Grant, as of himself." Neither Evarts nor Wells had secured a position. Boutwell's appointment marked a clear setback: Adams remarked that "this particular damned fool is the damnedest of all." But there was also reason for Adams to be pleased. Cox, who shared Adams's interest in finance, was a close friend of Garfield; Hoar appeared to be just the kind of public man Adams dreamed would be in politics; Fish, a New York aristocrat, had been a friend of William Henry Seward. None of these men were professional politicians; rather, they were the high-minded men above politics. Adams's disgruntlement was a sign that he had expected too much.[30]

After one month of the new administration, Adams remained perplexed as to its policy. "That I am politically dissatisfied is unquestionable," he told Gaskell; "but then I have yet to find anyone who is not in the same situation." Everywhere he went, he heard disgruntled politicians muttering: "I go from Wells to Evarts and from Evarts to Sumner and so round the list, and find them all disgusted in their own branches." Newspaper editors made sport of the president's struggles with Congress. As for Adams himself, he confided to his brother that Grant was no improvement over Johnson: "I am astonished by his behavior, but I am even more puzzled than astonished." He waited to see what would happen next. Meanwhile he kept himself busy by looking into the widespread fraud in the New York elections the previous fall, and speculated that he might return to England with the new minister. "I don't care for such a position," he claimed, but his thoughts were already drifting back to London. So much for being "settled for years, and perhaps for life" in Washington.[31]

Foreign affairs were much on Adams's mind. In May, the Senate, following Charles Sumner's lead, overwhelmingly rejected the Johnson-Clarendon Treaty, which had proposed to settle outstanding grievances between the United States and Great Britain from the Civil War, especially the damage done United States shipping by British-built Confederate cruisers—the so-called Alabama Claims. Both Sumner and Grant took a tough stand on renewed negotiations: Sumner was interested in the acquisition of Canada, while Grant looked toward a European conflict to give the British a taste of their own medicine. Adams, who had looked to preserve Anglo-American ties, sought to set himself up as a private intermediary by corresponding with John Bright and William Forster. In so doing he hoped to supplant none other than Sumner himself, who had once used his transatlantic ties to great effect during the war. According to Adams, Sumner's mind was overrated; Sumner was now intent on "seizing the direction of our foreign affairs," although Grant and Secretary Fish were determined that this would not happen. In Sumner's place, Adams would offer to assess public sentiment and the possibilities of settlement. Bright, always a friend of Anglo-American accord, seemed willing to cooperate, although Adams's suggestion that Great Britain abandon her possessions in the Western Hemisphere doubtless struck him as unrealistic.[32]

As spring came to the capital, Adams fretted over the success of his experiment in reform. Anxiously awaiting the appearance of his "blows at democracy" in print, he railed at his inability to exercise influence. "My hopes of the new Administration have all been disappointed; it is far inferior to the last," he frowned. The reason was obvious: "My friends have almost all lost ground instead of gaining it as I hoped. My family is buried politically beyond recovery for years. I am becoming more and more isolated so far as allies go." He worried whether he could find "an independent organ to publish my articles," given the growing indifference to reform. To brother Charles he revealed the more mundane aspects of isolation. "I can't get you an office," he announced. "The only members of this Government that I have met are mere acquaintances, not friends, and I fancy no request of mine would be likely to call out a gush of sympathy." His friends were in trouble. Wells could not protect his own clerks from Boutwell's housecleaning of the Treasury Department, and Attorney General Hoar was preoccupied with defending his freedom from patronage-seekers.[33]

Yet the young reporter took almost a perverse delight in his powerlessness. "I rather like all this," he smiled, "for no one can touch me and I have asked nothing of any living person." As he often did, he preferred to transform his handicaps into virtues. Freed from the responsibilities of place, he prided himself in his ability to "express pretty energetic opinions all around," regardless of the audience. He announced that he would "wait till the cards are played out. I can afford to wait. We have won our rubber on the old game."[34] Of course, he had no other choice.

Courting unpopularity, Adams initially was overjoyed when his articles finally appeared in late April. "I find that I have unexpectedly jumped into notoriety," he announced to Charles. In proclaiming his triumph to Gaskell, he revealingly declared, "For once I have smashed things generally and really exercised a distinct influence on public opinion by acting on the limited number of cultivated minds." Light-headed with success, he seemed determined to make "my annual 'Session' an institution and a power in the land." His enthusiasm paled a bit when he read the reviews of "The Session." Not many newspapers noticed it. The *Nation* approved of it in a short notice, describing it as "a thoughtful, forcible, and highly suggestive article" that reflected the author's "independence of thought and plainness of sensible speech." The *Springfield Republican* gave the article more attention partly because of editor Samuel Bowles's friendship with the Adams family. In an editorial entitled "Another Adams," reviewer Franklin B. Sanborn declared that Adams "has as quite as good a chance of becoming prominent in the future politics of the country as either of his brothers, although he is yet but little known." Sanborn commented that Adams, who "had the reputation of being one of the three best dancers in the capital," had written "a long and brilliant paper" which, however, displayed "some conceit and some pedantry." The most important critic read the article sequestered in his Quincy study. "We . . . generally like it," Charles Francis Adams told his son. But he preferred to emphasize the *Republican*'s criticisms. Enclosing a copy of its remarks, he observed, "I think there is a little modicum of justice in the objection to the tone of parts of the article as savoring conceit more or less. . . . Shy natures age given to it from a necessity to support themselves from within against the first struggles with the opinion of the world." If Henry expected "to mix much with men," he added, "I advise you to remove this obstacle to your influence with them altogether."[35]

Having flailed away at democracy, Henry Adams retreated to his corner to prepare for the next round. The meagerness and nature of public response made him wonder whether he had chosen the correct career. "I'm sick of the whole concern of publishing articles which are neither worth writing to me, nor reading to anyone who counts," he impatiently told Charles before the articles appeared. Later he admitted that his finance article in the *Edinburgh Review* "has attracted no notice so far as I know." Such comments overlooked the response to "The Session," but even they fell short of what he craved. In frustration he lashed out at his own writing. After looking at "The Session" in print, he grumbled, "I don't think much of it and I grind my teeth to think how much better I could do it now." Such self-denigration served as a caustic counterpoise to his conceit. "High appreciation of ourselves was always a strong point in our family," he told Charles, "though I protest by Heaven that my conceit is not due to admiration of myself but to contempt for everyone else." In a lighter vein, he noted that Sanborn's reference to his dancing ability had appeared in several personal columns. "I am in an agony of terror for fear of seeing myself posted bluntly: 'H.B.A. is the best dancer in W[ashington].' This would be fame with a vengeance."[36]

Charles, used to his brother's moodiness, snapped at Henry's conceit over his political productions. In reply, the younger brother confessed, "I do think too much about my own productions and myself generally." He refused to "go down into the rough-and-tumble, nor mix with the crowd" in pursuing his political goals; he preferred "taste and dexterity" to "roughness and strength." If politics meant soiling one's hands in hard work, wrangling over jobs, speaking to the unwashed, or making practical compromises, it was not for him: "My path is a different one; and was never chosen in order to suit other people's taste, but my own. . . . I mean to be unpopular and do it because I must do it, or do as other people do and give up the path I chose for myself years ago."[37]

Adams worked out his rationalizations on paper as he wrote to friends, revealing far more than he realized. "My opinions and dislike for things in general will probably make my career a failure," he told Gaskell. This was all too true, especially "so far as any public distinction goes." Then he began to defend himself: "I am contented to have it so." He attributed his failure to the inability of society to appreciate him: "There are no very clever men here, but some very fair ones, and as things are generally going to the devil, I don't much care who is uppermost and am well-pleased to have no strong personal friends in power." Washington was socially and politically too primitive to understand him. "I am looking forward with great rejoicing to my visit to England next year," he continued, where at least some people welcomed his presence. Those few cultivated men in America who applauded his critiques relentlessly demanded more: "Work pours in on me, and I can't do half what men urge me to do."[38] Within the space of four sentences, he had thus transformed himself from total failure to someone above his peers, appreciated by a select few.

Adams's path was a difficult one, but then he had chosen it freely. By equating unpopularity with influence, he had braced himself for abuse, interpreting it as evidence that he had struck at a sore point. His elitist notion of politics served several purposes: he could justify his literary efforts as aimed at an audience composed of "cultivated minds"; he could rationalize his inability to gain position as due to his distaste for the "rough-and-tumble"; and, by endorsing rule by the best and the brightest, he could claim membership in the ranks of the elite. Unable by personality as well as preference to "mix with the crowd" in the political scuffle, he argued that his weaknesses were actually strengths. Unfettered by patronage, he could speak freely; he could attribute his powerlessness to the truth of his charge that there was no place in politics or government for men of intelligence, breeding, and merit. "These party organizations have little honesty in them and are ruled by ignorant and ambitious men," he told John Bright. It was time for a change. "Sooner or latter the old parties must break up. . . . Without large internal reforms our Government and Union will go to pieces."[39]

Adams returned to Quincy early in July to escape the stifling heat of Washington. But he took his politics with him. Garfield, Wells, and other free traders came up to discuss future plans for reform. "If you could see the gravity with which I attend the private meetings . . . which are to settle our coming policy, you would roar with delight," he chuckled to Gaskell. "What a humbug one is!" Garfield seemed more interested in viewing the Adams house, but it was clear to him that Henry Adams was "rapidly rising as a clear and powerful thinker and writer."[40]

CHAPTER FOUR

A POWER IN THE LAND

> Grant's administration outraged every rule of ordinary
> decency, but scores of promising men, whom the
> country could not well spare, were ruined in saying so.
> *The Education of Henry Adams*

At Quincy for the summer, Henry Adams labored away at "another ponderous article" for several months. His experiences at Washington had convinced him that civil service reform was the key political issue for reformers. Without subverting the patronage system, the basis of party power, reformers could not hope to dethrone the party bosses from policy-making positions; until reformers ascended to those positions, they could do nothing about the tariff or the currency. It was the control of administration, not the framing of legislation, that was essential to reform; civil service reform, in Adams's eyes, would secure to reformers control of the bureaucracy. John Stuart Mill had characterized the quadrennial patronage sweepstakes as "the one great blot and disgrace on American institutions" in a public letter that spring. Adams could only agree with his mentor that politicians were "the greatest perverters of free institutions."[1]

Adams made plans to ensure that this time he would be heard. He would not wait for congressmen, senators, or other government officials to turn to the *North American Review*; he planned to circulate his latest "blow at democracy" as a pamphlet. To guarantee that people would read and talk about it, he made it "very bitter and abusive of the Administration." As a result, he might get into trouble, but, as he told Charles Milnes Gaskell, he had "nothing to lose."[2] The product of a vitriolic pen wielded by an ambitious author, "Civil Service Reform" appeared in the October number of the *North American Review*.

Casting aside for the moment the usual arguments made in support of civil service reform, which concerned administrative ability, Adams maintained "that among the precautions absolutely necessary for the maintenance of a free government is a frequent recurrence to the fundamental principles of the Constitution." In his opening paragraph he placed himself firmly in the family tradition of supporting the principle of separation of powers, quoting with approval the clause of the 1780 Massachusetts Constitution explicitly declaring that constitutions were intended to make sure that "*it may be a government of laws and not of men.*" The purpose of civil service reform, Adams continued, was to reestablish the independence of the executive branch by restoring to it the complete power of appointment, shredding the power of political machines, special interest groups, and Congress.[3]

"The whole executive system has become the avowed plaything of the legislature," Adams wrote. "Whatever happens, Congress has established the right to seize and overthrow the whole administration once in every four years forever." He located the origins of the decay of presidential power in Andrew Jackson's theory of "rotation in office," taking a swipe at an old family enemy. Although Jackson's vigorous leadership obscured the serious damage that a policy of political patronage portended for the republic, his successors had buckled under the pressure of party leaders, seated in the Senate, demanding a price for their support. Members of Congress assumed the right to nominate candidates for office; Abraham Lincoln finally acknowledged the legitimacy of the system, crippling (in Adams's eyes) the president's power.[4]

Adams recalled how reformers had waited with high hopes for the advent of Grant's presidency. The new president despised politicians; his qualities of honesty and perseverance seemed ideal for the task at hand. Grant's cabinet selections reflected his ideals, possessing a "common freedom from political entanglement"; even after the Republican Senate secured Boutwell's appointment, "the Cabinet contained only one member who was distinctly a representative rather of the Republican party than of the Republican sentiment of the country."[5] This seemed a positive beginning; the new president appeared to be free of party dictation.

Whatever hopes reformers held that the new administration would make "no sweeping and partisan changes" were dashed within the first month, however, as hordes of office-seekers descended upon the nation's capital. Adams claimed that Grant and his advisers were not at fault: "No distant observer can judge fairly of the difficulties to which a President is subjected when he attempts to maintain such a position in the face of the party organization which supports them." Adams reminded his readers that "in the struggle that followed, the President stood alone" and "did not surrender with a good grace." Rather, it was the political system which was at fault. Patronage destroyed the constitutional order by giving too much power to Congress. Grant had to listen to the demands of party leaders: "A senator may be tedious, ill-mannered, and a notorious rogue, but the double maj-

esty of State and Senate speaks from his lips and commands a hearing."
Adams concluded that "members of Congress cannot be honest with such a
power in their hands."[6]

The rush for office was so serious that "even a President so determined
in character and so strong in popular support as General Grant shrank from
the attempt to reform the civil service as one which was beyond his powers." He was not alone; Adams condemned "a long line of Presidents who
have failed to respect their trust." Nevertheless, it was Grant's duty "to
originate any reform in the civil service which may seem to him useful or
necessary; and if he understands the meaning of an oath, he is bound to
carry out such a reform in spite of all resistance." This assessment is somewhat puzzling. Adams claimed that Grant, who had "stood alone" for reform, realized that even as the president, to reform the system "was beyond
his powers"—a judgment which implied that reform was futile. In the next
paragraph, however, Adams accused Grant of betraying his oath of office
for not attempting what he had just said was "beyond his powers." Such
claims revealed more about Adams's priorities than they did about Grant's
performance. Reform was all-important: all other issues would have to wait
their turn, for reform was the prerequisite to good governance.[7]

Adams used Attorney General Hoar and Treasury Secretary Boutwell,
both from the same congressional district in Massachusetts, to compare the
ideal to sordid reality, in the process revealing his prejudices. Ebenezer
Rockwood Hoar was by "birth and training a representative of the best
New England school." He was a member of the "class of men who had been
gradually driven from politics, but whom it is the hope of reformers to
restore." In stark contrast stood George Sewell Boutwell, a man of "narrow
political morality," a "product of caucuses and party promotion." Given
such crass credentials, it was only to be expected that Boutwell would distribute the patronage at his disposal to secure political support. With men
like Boutwell in power, Adams concluded, "the administration of President
Grant as a whole will be considered as having carried the principle of rotation in office and submission to external interference in executive powers to
a point beyond anything that had been reached before."[8]

Adams offered a simple solution. He asked for no new legislation, merely
that Congress "keep its hands off executive powers." He challenged Grant
to be "equal to his post," to stand forth as "a bold and honest leader." Reformers would do their part by appealing to the public to support the president in his struggle against Congress and party organizations, and to hold
the president accountable for his actions. They had to convince the people
"that reform is a vital question, that the evils and dangers are real, and not
mere inventions of lively fancy." This done, reform would become a reality.[9]

Adams's article revealed much about his notions of presidential power, the politics of reform, and the selective memory of reformers. His proposal for a new tactical approach by reformers illustrated some of the problems inherent in reform politics. He urged reformers "to act outside of all party organizations, and to appeal, with all earnestness that the emergency requires . . . to the people," by displaying examples of corruption for all to see. Yet this appeal for popular support, appearing in the elitist *North American Review*, came from a man who once proclaimed that "whoever is right, the majority is wrong." Rather, Adams thought that he could best exercise "a distinct influence on public opinion by acting on the limited number of cultivated minds"—an attitude that, if shared by all reformers, would result in an elite-oriented movement where the leaders talked to each other and to no one else. More startling was his intention to "send copies to all members of the Government and of the legislature." Since he had characterized the article as "rather bitter, rather slashing, very personal," one is left to wonder whether he believed that the best way to influence someone favorably was to alienate him.[10]

Adams's blindness to reality seemed all the more incredible because he appeared to understand the position of presidents once in office. Grant had to listen to the leading men of his party and had to gain their support to be a successful president. Adams acknowledged that if Grant continued to battle Congress, he "would provoke a personal rupture with so many members of the legislature, and secret hostility in so many more, as to endanger the success of the administration." One might conclude that Grant displayed political pragmatism (to say nothing of common sense) in deciding to work within the system. Given the problems of Reconstruction, financial affairs, and foreign policy, for Grant to have followed Adams's policy of setting as his top priority a battle with the Senate over control of the patronage would have been insane. The president needed only to recall the fate of his predecessor to remember what awaited a proponent of an "independent presidency" ready to defy Congress at the drop of a hat. But Adams called for precisely that.[11]

Adams had noted that Grant had "stood alone" in resisting the initial onslaught of office-seekers. Where were the reformers? Most, including Adams, had failed to give the president any support. Adams reported that it was "one of the unfortunate but inevitable results of the situation that the better class of politicians on whom a President ought to rely, men of dignity and self-respect, will not lower themselves to this struggle for patronage." However, he failed to recall that he had assured his brother that the first cabinet would be a failure, and had discouraged his father from seeking or expecting position, advice that Charles Francis Adams eagerly followed. Fish, Cox, and Hoar, his favorite secretaries, had to be coaxed into accepting their cabinet posts. How could one blame the president for not select-ing members from the "better class" if such men drew back from public service?[12]

Selectivity was also evident in Adams's discussion of Boutwell. He at-tacked the treasury secretary for opening up his department to patronage-seekers; but within a year, Boutwell instituted an examination system designed to filter out unqualified candidates. The secretary was seeking the best of both worlds: administrators qualified both by ability and political affiliation. Nor had Boutwell been eager to accept his post, contrary to Adams's image of a spoilsman hungrily anticipating an office. Adams like-wise failed to mention that Representative George F. Hoar, the brother of the virtuous attorney general, found enough time to search out postmasterships and census recorder positions for his supporters.[13]

Never were Adams's ancestral traditions more evident than in "Civil Service Reform." His conception of the presidency was a direct outgrowth of the principles to which his grandfather and great-grandfather adhered during their administrations. Both John and John Quincy Adams had in-sisted that the president should be independent of Congress, watching that body to make sure that it did not exceed its bounds. While Henry Adams probably did not realize that the section of the Massachusetts Constitution that he quoted at the start of the essay concerning the separation of powers was one of the few paragraphs John Adams did not draft, the doctrine had been the core of the family's belief in the Constitution. In fact, near the end of his essay he justified reform in terms which doubtless held great meaning for the author. To build public support for the movement, he had written, was "a work not inferior to that of the Republic's founders, . . . an aim high enough to satisfy the ambition of one generation."[14]

The press greeted Adams's latest offering coolly. Horace Greeley's *New York Tribune* remarked that it "ought to attract a good deal of thought." The *Nation* applauded his comparison of Hoar and Boutwell. Adams, the re-viewer continued, had "made for himself an enviable reputation as a coura-geous politician," although he tended in his writing "to be at times a little too forcible" and "a little too fond of hard hitting." The *Springfield Republi-can* called "Civil Service Reform" the "best reading in the number" but contended that Adams had made "some wild statements of fact." In a sepa-rate column, entitled "An Adams on the Administration," the *Republican* took issue with Adams's gloomy picture of the spoils system, declaring it a practice which "grew up with the system of parties, and will last, in some shape or another, as long as politics exist. It is the fuel which runs the politi-cal engine." The *Republican* dismissed Adams's description of the "self-deg-radation" of the administration as a sign of inexperience. "The fact is notoriously otherwise," it insisted. Had Adams forgotten the disgraces under Presidents Pierce and Buchanan? It speculated that Adams was "possessed by a wild unreason, and a total inability to see persons and things as they are." He had exhibited the "sort of impartiality which consists in finding fault with everybody who is still unburied."[15]

To the *Republican*, the "crowning piece of absurdity" in Adams's essay was his comparison of Hoar to Boutwell. It charged that the portraits were drawn with a prejudiced pen and "embodied the fancies of his own brain, or those of persons equally incapable of seeing men as they are." Indeed, Adams was vulnerable to this criticism; for by establishing Hoar and Boutwell as opposite types, he had oversimplified the characters of both men. Still, the *Republican* gave credit where it was due: "No man has stated better the herculean nature of the task" facing civil service reformers, and Adams had done it "with ancestral vigor and eloquence, and with an acuteness of analysis peculiar to himself."[16]

Most importantly, someone in the Grant administration took notice. Garfield told Adams that Secretary Cox had read the article. Encouraged, Adams made several visits to Cox's quarters, only to find the secretary out. Finally he sat down and wrote Cox a note. The letter casts a confusing light on the intent of the article. Adams claimed that he wished to bring the civil service bill of Representative Thomas A. Jenckes to the attention of the administration, although the article castigated Jenckes's bill as "calculated to aggravate rather than to check the evil." Ironically enough, Grant had met Jenckes and had endorsed the bill, which featured competitive examinations administered by a board of commissioners. Adams must have been chagrined, for his objections to the Jenckes bill were "numerous and to my mind fatal."[17]

Adams presented an alternate course of action to Cox, after buttering up the secretary by assuring him that "you are the reserved force, the silent agency by which I hope this contest is to be decided." Adams wanted Grant's cabinet, as part of its deliberations prior to Grant's first annual message, to prepare "a distinct measure of reform to be offered as a Government proposition to Congress." He hoped it would reject the notion of competitive examinations in favor of tossing aside congressional influence and restoring the full power of appointment to the president. If other means of urging reform measures on Grant failed, Adams expected Cox to "take the responsibility of bringing it up. Give the country a lead! We are wallowing in the mire for want of a leader."[18]

Adams declared that he would "be disappointed if no one retaliates on me." Aside from a few critical notices he could not find much to go on. "I would like to show you some of the attacks I have met in the press here," he told Gaskell. "They are usually based on my great-grandfather, but occasionally on my extreme youth, and I expect to catch it hotter than ever in the course of the winter when the subject comes up in Congress." But the pamphlet did not have any visible effect on most people in Washington. People were more amused at his portrayal of Boutwell and Hoar than interested in what he had to say.[19]

One reason for this lukewarm response was that few people could agree on what civil service reform was. Reformers agreed that the present system was deplorable. They hoped to remove administrative positions as political bargaining chips between the president and Congress. However, they did not want these offices for themselves. Rather, once these positions were placed beyond the pale, professional politicians, bereft of patronage, would give way to the intelligentsia. Policy-making positions would be filled by men interested in formulating policy, not in dispensing patronage. These positions, not the purely administrative jobs, were what many reformers sought for themselves. Some reformers stressed the need for administrative expertise in appointments: others, like Adams, were more concerned with the policy positions. Reformers also differed as to the means by which to implement reform. Many civil service reformers, including Jenckes, favored competitive examinations in an effort to establish a nonpartisan government bureaucracy. Others, like Adams, looked to it as a means of stripping political parties of their power. Adams went a step further: he wanted to strengthen the president's hand by restoring his complete autonomy in matters of appointment.[20]

Henry Adams, Carl Schurz, and James A. Garfield formed a strange trio in favor of civil service reform. All three men claimed to support it, yet in practice Schurz and Garfield behaved in ways that make one question the sincerity of their commitment to reform. Schurz, a freshman senator from Missouri, had little sympathy for notions of an independent executive or a vigorous president. "Nothing could be better for Grant, just now, than to learn that the legislative power is as such independent and somewhat animated by an independent spirit," he wrote a friend in early 1869. He proclaimed that the "growing tendency of flinging down legislative powers at the feet of 'personal government,' when that personal government is carried on by one who starts out with a certain capital of popularity is rather too much for my republican blood." Schurz was not reluctant to demand his rights, either, telling Secretary Fish that the secretary had better not refuse his patronage requests: "If you do, mark the inevitable consequences. ... Mark my words." He assured a friend, "I have worked very hard for my friends." This was exactly the behavior Adams had attacked, yet he expressed to Schurz his strong, sympathetic interest in the senator's career, and Schurz himself believed that he would "become the leader of reform in the Senate."[21]

James A. Garfield was little better. Like Schurz, the Congressman from

Ohio had served in the Union army. Also like Schurz, he upheld political principles that should have kept him from gaining Adams's warm friendship. He opposed the repeal of the Tenure of Office Act, as did Schurz, and demanded that the administration respect his patronage demands, flying into a rage when Grant appointed a postmaster in Garfield's district without consulting the Congressman. Garfield dunned his appointees for campaign expenses, including distribution of a pamphlet supporting civil service reform. He also willingly accepted stock in Credit Mobilier—a device to mobilize capital for the Union Pacific Railroad—without paying for it, although he later returned it. But no matter. Garfield's support of the concept of civil service reform endeared him to Adams, who at best remained blithely ignorant of Garfield's less-commendable practices.[22]

Adams returned to Washington in late October and waited for Grant's first annual message. When it came, he, along with Schurz and Garfield, was disappointed. Cox had failed to persuade Grant to follow Adams's advice. Worse, the president's message said nothing on the subject of civil service reform. Schurz quickly introduced his own bill, which followed the competitive exam approach. Congress refused to consider the proposal. It also ignored Illinois senator Lyman Trumbull's plan, which resembled Adams's scheme. Regardless of which road civil service reformers took, they ran into a dead end.[23]

Adams feared that his article had ended his chance for political influence under Grant. Instead, as Congress met in December, he found himself caught "up in a coil of political intrigue and getting the reputation of a regular conspirator." Several cabinet members, far from being upset over the article, were "in perfect sympathy with me in abusing themselves." Adams thought that, in a divided cabinet, he was "on the side which has the strongest men, and Reform is always a sure card." Relating to a friend his close relationships with cabinet members, he had to remind himself that he was "only a very small fly on the wheel."[24]

Adams was busy with other things as well. He was on the track of a scandal sure to singe the administration. In September 1869, New York had witnessed a "speculative mania" over gold, culminating in "Black Friday," when the Gold Exchange nearly collapsed in panic as prices soared, then plunged. Adams shook his head in dismay when he heard that Jay Gould and Jim Fisk were at the center of the confusion; his brother Charles had already revealed their shady railroad dealings in several articles. What drew him towards the incident were rumors that members of the Grant administration were involved: Boutwell, perhaps Grant's family, maybe even the president himself were suspect. Some stories said that Gould and Fisk acted on inside information obtained by Abel Corbin, Grant's brother-in-law; a few suggested that Mrs. Grant and some of Grant's staff also enriched themselves. Luckily for him, Garfield headed the congressional committee that was to investigate the "gold conspiracy," and he willingly let Adams examine all the evidence before the committee. Within a few months Adams had the whole story.[25]

The situation was not as horrible as it had been rumored to be, but it was bad enough. Gould and Fisk had been looking for a good way to make money, and they thought they had found it when Gould happened upon Corbin, a lobbyist with a shady past who had just married the president's sister. The three men concocted a plan whereby they would use insider information on government gold sales to corner the gold market—a prime area of interest in an era when the worth of legal tender was measured in terms of how much it would take in greenbacks to purchase an equivalent amount of dollars in gold. Corbin secured access to Grant for Gould and Fisk, but the reticent president offered little more than vague generalities—although he displayed rather poor judgment in allowing himself to meet with Gould and Fisk in the first place. It would be neither the first time nor the last that the general's family relations would entangle him in trouble. Unable to deliver his brother-in-law, Corbin decided instead to tell Gould and Fisk that he had brought Mrs. Grant in on the scheme (just as Gould had tried to entice Grant's private secretary, Horace Porter, to invest in gold). In fact, neither Julia Dent Grant nor Porter would have anything to do with such investments. However, Corbin continued to engage his brother-in-law in discussions about gold sales, arguing that if the government did not sell gold, its price would go up (in terms of greenbacks), thus helping farmers who received gold dollars for their harvests on the international market (which, by the way, would mean that more agricultural goods, especially grain, would be shipped east on railroads such as Gould's Erie line).

For a while, Grant accepted this reasoning and advised against an increase in government gold sales in September. But before long, he grew suspicious, and at last, upon discovering that a missive from Corbin reiterating his advice had been delivered by a private messenger employed by Gould, he responded, warning Corbin (through a letter from Julia to Mrs. Corbin) to stop his speculations with Gould and Fisk. Several days later, the president met with Secretary of Treasury George S. Boutwell. Soon afterward, the government announced a new sale of gold. The news struck hard in New York, where speculation had driven up the price of a hundred dollars in gold to a hundred and sixty greenback dollars; within moments, the price fell nearly thirty dollars. Gould, tipped off by Corbin that something was awry, had gotten out; Fisk found it a little more difficult to shake his obligations.[26]

In the recriminations that followed—including accusations that Julia Grant, Porter, and perhaps even the president himself were in on the deal—

the real story was often overlooked. The president, the First Lady, and Porter were not guilty of anything; had they been so, Grant would have let the speculation continue. Corbin's statements to the contrary to Gould and Fisk were simply a way of promoting the scheme. Nor were Grant's remarks on government gold-sales policies any different from the usual speculation about future policy. Where the president erred—and seriously so—was in having any dealings whatsoever with Gould and Fisk, especially after he began to grow suspicious of them. It is unclear exactly what Grant knew of Corbin's relationship to Gould and Fisk prior to the climax of the affair; once convinced that Corbin was engaged in speculation, Grant grew distant and refused to share his opinions on future policy. Nevertheless, the letter he had Julia write, although it contained no explicit description of policy, set off enough alarms in the minds of Corbin and Gould that they correctly deduced what course Grant would pursue. In all of this, there was more than enough to do Grant damage, and Democratic papers made what they could of the president's embarrassment. It was difficult to agree with the *Nation*'s assessment that "nothing could have been more sensible or upright than the President's course throughout the whole affair."[27]

Instead, Adams's "The New York Gold Conspiracy" aimed at describing how Gould and Fisk attempted to corner the Gold Exchange, although it loosed some random shots at the Grant administration. Adams merely grazed the president, finding him unfortunate in attracting a corrupt brother-in-law. He reserved his blasts for his favorite target, the treasury secretary, asserting that "the success of a speculation would depend on the action of Mr. Boutwell." Implicit was the suggestion that the secretary was caught unawares by the trickery of the conspiracy—which was not entirely accurate, although it was not without a shadow of truth, either. Nevertheless, Adams's three primary targets remained Gould, Fisk, and Corbin, with the first two gathering the majority of his attention.[28]

Even as he observed how politicians' fumbling enhanced the chances for financial fraud, Adams addressed the potentially more disastrous consequences entailed in the rise of corporate power. Gould and Fisk had created a corporation which "has proved itself able to override and trample on law, custom, decency, and every restraint known to society, without scruple, and as yet without check." Adams forecast the growth of corporations so vigorous that they "will ultimately succeed in directing government itself." The current American policy was unable to stop this threat. The federal government would have to move beyond the bounds of the Constitution in the direction of "an absolute central government" to tame the monster. Unless Americans developed an appropriate response to the rise of the corporation, "popular institutions may yet find their very existence endangered."[29]

Although the monstrous corporation was an old theme, Adams sounded it with new urgency. He had once compared the Southern slave power to a corporation, expressing the fear that both would "pervert the whole body politic." While in England, he noted "how sudden, direct, and unduly powerful a pressure the overgrown commercial interests . . . can put upon their Government."[30] Certainly corporate power was of growing concern to many Americans, and had Adams stuck to the theme, he might have gained a wider audience. But he preferred to subordinate it to his desire to reform the process of government. Having defined a serious problem, he failed to devote his intellect to solving it.

For Adams, his most serious problem was finding a publisher for his article. Knowing that it contained "a good deal of libellous language," he looked to place it with an English journal. The *Edinburgh Review* wanted no part of it. The *London Quarterly* turned it away. Finally, the *Westminster Review* picked it up and published it in its October 1870 issue. But the long delay was costly. Readers had forgotten the scandal and were so caught up with Adams's lively account and his colorful description of Gould and Fisk that they missed the moral of the story.[31]

But Adams could not spend all his time worrying about the fate of one article. In occasional pieces in for the *Nation*, he sharpened his satirical prose on some of his favorite subjects, including Boutwell and Butler. One column went beyond such concerns to broach an idea designed to encourage the formation of a governing elite. In "Men and Things in Washington," he adopted the persona of a foreign diplomat observing Washington's intellectual society: "Society itself exists only in disjointed fragments, and that there is no established centre of intelligence and social authority." Adams called upon his fellow intellectuals to "combine and establish . . . a cosmopolitan club, if only to assert a social influence which might assist their private purposes." Such a club would provide a place for politicians, intellectuals, and other notables to mix and to exchange ideas, thereby raising the tone of government.[32] This suggestion reflected Adams's London experiences, where at dinner he mingled with Mill, Bright, and other English liberals.

"I have no power whatever and am held up solely by social position and a sharp tongue, yet I float," Adams reported to Gaskell as 1869 ended. After all, things could be worse: "I am tolerably intimate with some members of the Cabinet, and have no enemies that I know of." True, there were few "cultivated people" in Washington ("Your friend—que voici—alone, and a few others, have any brain," he bragged to Gaskell), but at least he was part of its society. Still, political office was out of the question—for the moment, anyway: "I don't expect that anything except perhaps literary reputation will ever come of it. The pressure for office from every part of the country is so tremendous that unless one is backed by strong party support and personally worries the Government, there is no chance of obtaining anything."[33]

Adams's frequent socializing once led him to one of the most interesting encounters of his Washington experience. In the spring of 1869, he met General Adam Badeau, who had served on Grant's staff during the war. To his surprise, the two men hit it off at once, and when Badeau returned from a tour of diplomatic duty in London, he took the set of rooms below Adams's quarters. "We dine every day in state, and full dress, and white cravats," Adams reported to Gaskell. He also saw in Badeau a source of information about the president, and began to pump him about his boss. Flushed by drink, which accentuated his ruddy face, Badeau boasted that only he and John A. Rawlins, Grant's chief of staff and secretary of war until his death in 1869, understood Grant. The general possessed "an intermittent energy, immensely powerful when awake, but passive and plastic in repose. . . . For stretches of time, his mind seemed torpid." Even Badeau could not describe how Grant thought; indeed, he was "not sure that Grant did think." This left Adams puzzled, so Badeau offered to do more. He took Henry Adams to the White House.[34]

Badeau and Adams walked into a room to see the president and his friends seated, engaged in light discussion. Grant quietly smoked as he listened to the conversation, which Adams judged "rather dull." Mrs. Grant joined the group. "She squints like an isosceles triangle, but is not much more vulgar than some Duchesses," Adams allowed generously. Bored by the discussion, Adams began to talk. "I chattered," he recalled in a statement that combined self-deprecation and condescension, "with that blandness for which I am so justly distinguished, and I flatter myself it was I who showed them how they ought to behave." Adams did not report Grant's reaction. Suspicious of strangers, especially strangers from Boston, Grant probably just watched and smoked. Perhaps he just ignored the young chatterbox. It never occurred to Adams that his condescending behavior might well alienate the person whom he most needed to influence.[35]

Adams left the White House as puzzled about the president as when he came. Grant reminded him of Garibaldi. Both were men of action, not of thought. Of the several presidents Adams ever met, he later recalled, "Grant was the most curious object of study among them all." To Gaskell he was more blunt: "Our President is as narrow, as ignorant, and as prejudiced as ever a George (I, II, III) among you."[36]

"Confusion beyond idea! a universal free fight, with everyone abusing everyone else, and tripping each other up whenever they can!" So Adams described Washington politics during the winter of 1869–1870. The three branches of government warred with each other over financial policy, appointments, and foreign policy, with Adams looking on. Certainly there would be opportunities for reform in such chaos.[37]

Adams had long waited for the Supreme Court to rule on the constitutionality of the Legal Tender Act of 1862. A case before the Court, *Hepburn v. Griswold*, appeared to present the perfect opportunity. It concerned whether greenbacks could be used to pay off debts incurred before the passage of the act. Adams followed the case carefully, reporting on the arguments of both sides for the *Nation*. He was peculiarly qualified for the task, for he had argued that the act was unconstitutional in discussions with William M. Evarts, who as attorney general had defended the acts before the Supreme Court. On February 7, 1870, the Court by a vote of four to three declared unconstitutional the section of the Legal Tender Acts allowing greenbacks to be used in payment of debts contracted prior to the passage of the act. Adams was pleased by the decision. However, victory came at some personal inconvenience. For Attorney General Hoar, one of Adams's friends in power, opposed the ruling, while Chief Justice Salmon P. Chase, another of Adams's friends, had delivered the decision. Adams found himself caught in the middle, with Hoar and his son Sam, another member of the Washington waltzing corps, on the one side, and the chief justice and his captivating daughter Kate—whom he had offended by telling her that she was full of "twaddle and cant"—on the other.[38]

More infuriating was the Senate's refusal to confirm Hoar as an associate justice on the Supreme Court. Hoar's refusal to bend to partisan considerations while making appointments as attorney general infuriated many Republicans, and the nomination gave them a chance to retaliate. "What could you expect for a man who had snubbed seventy senators?" commented Senator Simon Cameron, one of Hoar's friends. In the *Nation* Adams blasted the Senate's willingness to lay aside the public good in order to gratify private grievances. Grant's "anxiety to keep the peace was notorious, and has weighed heavily in his course of administration. He has already yielded much—too much—to the legislature." Now the Senate had made a "scandalous and utterly unpardonable attack" on Hoar. The attorney general had "done his utmost to raise the Administration above the dirt of local politics." If Grant retained Hoar in the cabinet, "he practically slaps the Senate in the face, and accepts the war it has declared." If he allowed Hoar to resign, the separation of powers doctrine would be at an end. Unfortunately for Adams, the war he anticipated never broke out. To be sure, Grant sensed that retaining Hoar might well hamper his efforts to cultivate members of Congress, but for the moment he was willing to retain the attorney general—until he could gain something more concrete in exchange for his departure.[39]

Foreign policy differences threatened to drive a wedge between another pair of Adams's allies, Secretary of State Fish and Senator Sumner. The two men divided over how to resolve differences with Great Britain— notably the question of English responsibility for the damage caused Northern shipping by Confederate vessels constructed in English ports. Sumner spoke of making the English liable for all of the North's war expenditures after Gettysburg. Fish eventually pushed on along more moderate lines but, afraid to offend Sumner, initially conceded too much in the realm of diplomacy to placate the senator. Similarly, Grant had acceded to Sumner's wish to have the historian John Lothrop Motley head the English mission, despite Grant's uneasiness over Motley because, among other things, the historian parted his hair in the middle—as Fish later confided to Adams. While others laughed, Adams observed, "Very shrewd men have formed very sound judgments on less material than hair."[40] Grant's suspicions were soon confirmed when Motley conducted his first negotiations with the English foreign minister along Sumner's lines, disregarding Grant's and Fish's wishes.

As important as Anglo-American affairs were, they were not the most divisive foreign policy issue. Rather, what transformed the long-smoldering friction between Grant and Sumner into blazing hatred was the annexation of San Domingo. Grant deeply believed in the project. He thought that San Domingo was rich in natural resources, possessed strategic advantages as a naval base, promised to bolster American trade, and could provide Southern blacks with an alternative to remaining in the South. Adams was ready to give Grant's policy "ardent support"; but when he went to visit Sumner, he realized that conflict was imminent between the occupants of the two houses which faced Lafayette Square. Sumner was dead set against annexation—he was rightly suspicious of some of the financial dealings involved—but Adams could not believe Sumner's own expansionist schemes based on his desire for the acquisition of Canada by the United States as payment for American claims against England.

Adams later recalled that he came away from the senator's house with "the gravest doubts of Sumner's sanity." That the United States could conquer Canada, Adams had no doubt; that Great Britain would simply give it up, he found ludicrous. He also wondered about the wisdom of Sumner's opposition to the San Domingo scheme. Even Adams knew that "a quarrel with General Grant was lunacy." Sumner was "a very light weight in the Republican Party"; he lacked the skills of party management, and many Republicans would gladly see him destroyed. Even worse from Adams's point of view, annexation might split Fish and Sumner, and Grant's first battles would be over annexation, not reform.[41]

Adams's description of Sumner and his assessment of the senator's position hit false as well as true notes. Sumner was far from alone in his opposition to the annexation of San Domingo, although historians who mock

Grant's plan overlook the degree to which it attracted support from able people. Moreover, although the Massachusetts senator engaged in wild and fanciful allegations of corruption about the project, there was enough to question in the behavior of Grant's envoy, Orville Babcock. It was not the mere fact of Sumner's opposition but the way in which he went about it—including casting aspersions about Grant's intelligence and integrity—that angered the president beyond reconciliation. Nor was Sumner quite the lightweight recalled by Adams: among his most loyal supporters was Carl Schurz. Indeed, Sumner knew that he could block annexation if Senate Democrats joined dissident Republicans in opposition. It was not Sumner's initial opposition to annexation, but his persistence in leveling fantastic charges against Grant and the threat of his opposition to other administration initiatives in foreign policy which doomed him to being ostracized by his colleagues—although it must be added that a good number of them had been waiting for just such an opportunity for years. And as for Canada, Sumner was not alone in desiring it—Grant and Fish had also expressed an interest in its acquisition—nor did he desire it unless Canadians did as well.[42]

Adams was understandably troubled by the course that events were taking. Reform was not among the issues being discussed. The issues confronting the government threatened to set his political allies at odds with each other, and would force him to choose sides. "The President and his Cabinet and the Senators and the Congressmen are all squabbling together," he reported to Gaskell, "and if the ill-temper goes on increasing as rapidly as it has done for three months past, we shall have an earth-quake again as we did four years ago." But he remained optimistic about his position in Washington. "My side is undermost, but precious wicked and pretty strong," he concluded. "There is soon to be a very lively fight, and I dodge about with my pen in my hand, lampooning the other side." This style of journalism "suits my black-guard tastes." His side was "strong in the press, but weak in power. We despise all the people in control, and all we can do is only to make a little more noise." Still, he had high hopes that his side would eventually triumph: "Personally I am still at a loss to know what the devil I want, or can possibly get, that would be an object, in case my friends came into power. So far as I know, however, my hands are still clean. I want nothing and fight only for the amusement of fighting."[43] Gaskell was probably not taken in by Adams's pose of carefree flippancy; he had heard too much about his friend's strong feelings about reform.

"People here are beginning to acknowledge me as some one to be considered," Adams rejoiced. Cabinet members invited him to dinner; reformers sought him out. Early in 1870, Wells and Adams collaborated on a plan of attack against the protective tariff system. "I had a dozen of the leaders at a meeting in my rooms the other night, and we effected a close alliance," he told Gaskell. Among those in attendance were Horace White of the *Chicago Tribune*, Francis A. Walker, Hugh McCulloch, and Charles Nordhoff of the *New York Evening Post* as well as Henry, his brother Charles, and Wells. Henry liked the idea of rubbing shoulders at "a secret but weighty political caucus" with "the small number of high panjandrums"—a remarkably inflated description of the participants (perhaps he was simply joking). He imagined that this new coalition "over revenue reform, free trade and what not" would tear the Republican party asunder if it did not adopt the reformers' agenda. Such a party would bury Reconstruction as an issue and realign politics on issues of political economy and governance. Within a week, the conspirators would see "whether we can control Congress"—a wish that was not father to the fact. It was all part of the "eternal whirl of politics," and Adams enjoyed the idea of being "up to the roots of my hair" in such dealings.[44]

The balding reformer also prepared to launch another dart at financial policy, although he was aware that Hoar would be stung. The day that the Supreme Court announced its ruling in *Hepburn v. Griswold*, Grant sent to the Senate the names of his two newest nominees to the Supreme Court in place of Hoar and Edwin M. Stanton, who had died within a day of his confirmation. Grant and Hoar were well aware of Joseph P. Bradley's and William Strong's positions in favor of the Legal Tender Act—although charges that they had "packed" the Court go too far. The Senate confirmed both nominations, and Hoar immediately pressed the new Court to consider two cases involving the constitutionality of the Legal Tender Act concerning debts contracted *after* the passage of the legislation. Adams knew what was afoot, and he went to work on "a piece of intolerably impudent political abuse" to demonstrate not only that the act was unconstitutional, but that it had been unnecessary and had violated the laws of political economy as well. "Never since the days of Cleon and Aristophanes was a great nation managed by such incompetent men as our leaders in Congress during the rebellion," he assured Gaskell. Francis A. Walker had originally offered to write the article, but when Cox appointed him to head the 1870 Census he turned his notes over to Adams.[45]

Adams said little that was new to anyone in "The Legal Tender Act," which appeared in the *North American Review* in April 1870. He called the passage of the act "one great disaster," a "catastrophe," and a "calamity." He deplored "the want of education" displayed by congressmen discussing the issue. The late Thaddeus Stevens, who held only "contempt for financial knowledge," was labeled as "grossly ignorant upon all economical subjects and principles." Such sentiments reflected Adams's opinions, not agreed-upon fact. Having carefully crafted a portrait of congressional incompetency, Adams urged policy makers to apply the principles of political economy and not those of partisan advantage to future decisions. But it was his abusive rhetoric, not his argument against the Legal Tender Act, that became the object of controversy. The *Nation* claimed that Adams had his grandfather's "instinct for the jugular," displaying "deliberate contemptuousness" at all times. But a reviewer complained that Adams tended to "indulge too much his aptitude for general ridicule and satire," distracting readers from his argument. The *New York Tribune* concurred, characterizing the piece as "a real old-fashioned 'slashing article'" and remarking, "It is a great pity he could not say all this without losing his temper." Adams appeared to prefer it that way. "I have brought all the respectable old fools of the country down on me by a mighty impudent article," he told Gaskell. "Well! it certainly was savage!"[46]

Adams's desire to be "impudent" irritated many people who met the journalist in person. William S. Robinson, Boston correspondent for the *Springfield Republican* under the name "Warrington," thought little of Adams's "wreaking on the subject" of civil service reform. In writing on the Adams brothers, Robinson concluded that John Quincy Adams II was "the best inheritor of the Adams qualities." Not so with Henry and Charles, who, "instead of being . . . bold and downright, are politically timid." Henry "has altogether too much of the English and diplomatic and supercilious character . . . to allow him to become a useful public man." Adams offended others as well, James Shepherd Pike, a Maine Republican, noted in March 1870, that Adams "has grown old . . . crotchety and conceited."[47] Adams did little to change this impression in his last effort, completed just before he left for England in 1870. The July number of the *North American Review* contained his most biting attack yet on the Grant administration.

In "The Session, 1869–1870," Adams argued that the American political system, as outlined in the Constitution, had collapsed. The Founders, striking out against European political theory, chose through the Constitution to make "an issue with antiquity." Europeans had insisted that the government was sovereign; the creators of the American republic, fearing centralized power, invented the theory of federalism and applied the concept of separation of powers to preserve public liberty. Their purposes "were perhaps chimerical," their hopes "almost certainly delusive." However interesting the experiment, its history "demonstrates the impossibility of success through its means."[48] For an Adams to articulate such ideas was heresy; previous generations had celebrated and defended that document.

Adams asserted that the American Civil War temporarily "obliterated the Constitution." By 1869, the time had come to see whether its principles could again prevail. For if the Constitution "restored itself," the American experiment would be vindicated: "A brilliant opportunity occurred for the new administration, not perhaps to change the ultimate results, but to delay some decades yet the demonstration of failure." How the system could both "restore itself" and be restored by the new president remained unclear, especially if in any case the achievement would do little more than postpone the inevitable demise of the document. But Grant seemed ideal for the job. He possessed "unbounded popular confidence" and was "tied to no party . . . under no pledges." His military experience, far from being a hindrance, was "an inestimable advantage" because it helped him to distinguish between right and wrong, something impossible for a politician. This was obviously a picture drawn for effect: Adams had never expressed such opinions after March 5, 1869. As a portrayal of public attitudes, however, it hit the mark. Certainly people believed that Grant "would grasp with a firm hand the helm of the government, and give the vessel of state a steady and determined course."[49]

Grant failed to live up to such expectations. The general was aggressive, confident, and competent; the president appeared hesitant, uncertain, and fumbling. His "personal notions of civil government were crude"; he was "not imaginative or highly cultivated"; in truth, he was little better than "a feudal monarch." Since Adams had once said similar things of Lincoln, Grant enjoyed good company. But Adams's claim did have its sting of truth. In summarizing Grant's inaugural address, with the president's promise that he would not enforce any policy against the will of the people, he justifiably concluded that Grant "assumed at the outset that it was not his duty to steer; that his were only the duties of discipline." That Grant had made such a statement to draw a contrast between himself and Andrew Johnson did not occur to Adams (or to subsequent critics of the general-president). To Adams, the ship of state drifted along, without direction, attracting only barnacles.[50]

How could Grant fall so short of expectations? In two paragraphs that mixed insight with arrogance, Adams offered an explanation. He argued that the "conservative class of citizens"—who, Adams disingenuously claimed, "had no partisan prejudices"—had "not perhaps overrated so much as misconceived the character of Grant." Employing what Badeau had confided to him, Adams said that Grant's "character is still in some respects a riddle" even to his closest friends. He was an enigma, a man who assimilated ideas almost unconsciously and who was dependent on the suggestions of his associates. Adams next examined these "surrounding influences," hoping to discover a ray of hope, a spark of intelligence. He found George S. Boutwell. The treasury secretary was second only to the president in terms of political power and importance, since nearly every issue involved financial questions that required his opinion. Because these issues had "assumed overruling importance" now that "old issues were passing away," according to Adams, it was imperative that Grant "should have in the Treasury a man who could command and compel respect." Unfortunately, Boutwell "was not a person to make good the needs of the President." Believing that "knowledge was a deception," the secretary sat in his office, deaf to any advice, unenlightened by economic theory. For Adams, Boutwell was the negation of all he believed in; intelligence and creativity (to say nothing of Henry Adams) were no longer welcome at the Treasury. Any success Boutwell might have would be due to the nation's economic growth, not to his policy.[51]

Boutwell's course rendered a dismal picture all the more grim. The confusion and lack of purpose in the executive branch presaged "the certain abandonment of the original theory of the American system." Adams had expected Grant to check the overweening power of the Senate; but "without a purpose, without followers, and without a head," such a prospect remained in the realm of fantasy. As Adams saw it, nowhere was this more evident than in Grant's first annual message, in which "the want of plan and unity of idea was so obvious" that it drove men to despair. Grant and Boutwell, he reported, proposed differing economic policies, though he did not say how they differed. Likewise he claimed that the press ridiculed the administration's economic policy, though only his own articles stood out in lonely proof of his assertion.[52]

The rest of "The Session" was calm by comparison. Congress had "uniformly ignored" the administration's recommendations on policy. Sumner had stifled annexation; Hoar had been humiliated; the administration was only a minor irritant to Congress. Reconstruction, according to Adams, had been brought to an end. Reformers were scoring minor successes in revising the tariff. Grant, Boutwell, and Hoar packed the Supreme Court to gain a favorable decision on the Legal Tender cases. "The success of any Executive measure must now be bought by the use of public patronage in influencing the action of legislators," Adams concluded. As a result of the Grant administration, "the internal fabric of the government" was "wrenched from its original balance." The machinery of government was no longer equal to the task of governing the country. Whatever had been the value of the Constitution in the past, it could no longer cope with the demands of an industrializing nation.[53]

Like "The New York Gold Conspiracy," "The Session" showed that Adams was coming to grips with a serious problem: the inability of existing political institutions to respond to the economic transformations of the nineteenth century. Perhaps the structure of the state and the political ideology of republicanism that furnished its blueprint were out of date. Once committed to the preservation of the constitutional order at all costs, he now wondered whether the Constitution could cope with an increasingly complex society. "The amount of business has become so enormous as to choke the channels provided for it," he pointed out. "The government does not govern." Instead, the "efficiency of the machine grows steadily less. New powers, new duties, new responsibilities, new burdens of every sort are incessantly crowding upon the government at the moment when it has become unequal to managing the limited powers it is accustomed to yield." Without the administration's open, active, and united support, reformers were doomed to patching up the system instead of overhauling it. In light of Adams's bleak portrayal of the future, one might well wonder what was the use of trying.[54]

Yet the fact was that many people were interested in the problems of governance, and not all of them were reformers. Debates over the scope and purpose of the American state, sparked during the Civil War, continued during Reconstruction. What should be the role of the federal government in the lives of daily Americans? How widely should it cast its net? What of familiar notions of federalism and laissez-faire? What about the impact of economic change upon hallowed principles of the American polity? During the remainder of the nineteenth century, in fact, the question of governance would be one of the major themes of American political discussion. Here were issues worthy of consideration by an able intellect who wanted to serve his nation. But Adams never followed up on his promising initial insights to take part in the dialogue. In reciting his litany of complaints about the failure of the American republic to meet the standards set by his forebears, Adams failed to engage in his own generation's debate over governance. Sometimes emulating one's ancestors means more than reciting them; sometimes it means participating in the same process of founding a new order.

This time Adams's efforts attracted a great deal of public attention, and he found himself a minor political celebrity. In the *Springfield Republican* Samuel Bowles exclaimed, "Nobody can deny the brilliant ability displayed in it, or fail to recognize those perennial traits of the Adams intellect." "The Session" was pirated, then printed by several Democratic papers, and drew return fire from Republican organs. Democrats seized upon it as a partisan attack on the Grant administration and reissued it as a campaign pamphlet. Godkin's *Nation* announced that the article "impartially, scalps everybody all around." But it was Adams's biting satire, rather than the deeper implications of the article, that gave "The Session" its notoriety. The *Nation*'s reviewer took note of this in commenting on the "just" complaints voiced by many readers over Adams's "clever and fierce attacks on official personages." Even this journal, a vocal advocate of reform, found Adams's essay "too unmitigatedly and severely fault-finding and critical." The *New York Tribune* dismissed it, complaining that Adams "seems to pass his life in a condition of chronic political anger."[55]

One of Grant's supporters, Senator Timothy Otis Howe of Wisconsin, was so provoked by "The Session" that he responded to Adams's charges in an extensive letter, published in the Madison *Wisconsin State Journal*. Howe's sarcastic rebuttal revealed Adams's inconsistent logic, his preference to assail rather than to evaluate policy, and his faulty knowledge of history and politics. Adams's account of the writing of the Constitution had only one saving merit, according to Howe: it was original. "He neither seems to comprehend the current history of the times nor the text of the Constitution," the senator claimed, "and he utterly mistakes the motives of those who framed the Constitution." Responding to Adams's assertion that Congress, in passing its Reconstruction legislation, had "obliterated" the Constitution, Howe reminded Adams that while an act of Congress might "contravene" the Constitution, it could not "obliterate" it: "On the contrary, the Constitution obliterates the act." Much of the article sniped at Adams's logic. After contending that the Constitution would "restore itself" to its prewar condition, Adams had gone on to state that it was up to Grant to restore it. If the Constitution could restore itself, Howe commented, then why did it need Grant's assistance? Adams chided Grant for failing to lead, claiming that the Constitution called upon the president to lead; Howe triumphantly retorted that no such clause appeared in the document.

The senator's rebuttals were petty, and at times pedantic. But they exposed Adams's tendency to allow his prose to obscure his arguments. Much more telling were Howe's counterpunches directed at Adams himself. What made "The Session" notable, Howe suggested, was "the distinguished paternity claimed for it. The author is proclaimed to be not only a statesman himself, but to belong to a family in which statesmanship seems to be preserved by propagation—something as color is in the leaf of the Begonia, perpetuating resemblance through perpetual change." He recounted the frequency with which members of the Adams family changed parties. To the senator, party loyalty was a sign of principle and character; men who changed parties were consistent only in their opportunism. What Adams saw as a virtue, Howe attacked as a weakness. Having thus abused Adams, Howe went on to make some perceptive comments about "The Session." He chastised Adams's desire to criticize everything indiscriminately. Adams shifted ground continually, smugly poking away at any and all errors, without stopping either to analyze the substance of political issues or to offer alternatives. Such nonsense struck Howe as the "emptiest of all possible cavil." He closed his review with some left-handed compliments. Adams possessed "talent for depicting character," even if he had "none at all for expounding the Constitution." He concluded with a statement which would come to be ironic: "He might succeed as a novelist. He must fail as a historian."[56]

Howe's response was that of an enraged partisan who, unable to come to grips with Adams's argument, responded in kind to his sarcasm. Like Adams, Howe excelled at vindictiveness; however, he lacked the ability to analyze. He also ignored Adams's somber closing remarks about the end of republican government—possibly the most interesting aspect of the essay. Perhaps it was evidence of the degree of Adams's influence that he could stir only someone like Howe to respond to his bitterest assault on the Grant administration.

Amused by Howe's reply, Adams rejoiced that he had at last drawn blood. "To be abused by a Senator is my highest ambition, and I am now quite happy," he wrote Gaskell. He was especially delighted to see Howe compare him to a begonia, cherishing the term for the rest of his life. In the *Education* he saw deeper irony in the simile: the begonia was "curious and showy . . . conspicuous . . . seemed to have no useful purpose, and it insisted on standing always in the most prominent position." As Adams concluded, "My only regret is that I cannot afford to hire a Senator to abuse me permanently." But beneath Adams's pleasure at seeing his article gain attention lurked some chagrin. To be noticed by Senator Howe was only a shade better than not being noticed at all. Critics were ignoring his message— that the system was falling apart—in their rush to pore over his caricatures of Washington celebrities. Instead of being regarded as a penetrating analysis of Grant's first year in office, "The Session" was soon relegated to the ranks of partisan rhetoric. Furthermore, critics could not let go of the inevitable comparison between Henry Adams and other members of the family. He was, as the *Springfield Republican* had once put it, just "another Adams."[57]

Perhaps Adams would have been happier had he known that both his effort and Howe's reply had reached the ears he wished to singe. Ulysses S. Grant had read "The Session" and had heartily congratulated Howe on his retort, saying that he "didn't know when he had read anything with so much pleasure." The president told Adam Badeau, Adams's old neighbor, that the Adams family "did not possess one noble trait of character that I ever heard of, from old John Adams down to the last of all of them, H.B." "The Session" meant an end to whatever hopes Adams entertained of exercising influence in high places during the Grant administration.[58]

Washington politics was the furthest thing from Henry Adams's mind in the summer of 1870. He enjoyed the season with Gaskell in his country home. After several months, he would be ready for Washington once more. Even when he was called to Italy to visit his sister, who had just been injured in a nasty carriage accident, he seemed determined to renew his political career in the fall. When Charles W. Eliot, the new president of Harvard, offered him a position on the faculty, Adams turned it down. "Having now chosen a career," he replied, "I am determined to go on in it as far as it will lead me." Events soon shook Adams's determination and optimism. His sister contracted tetanus, fell victim to lockjaw, and died. It was the first time that Henry Adams had to deal with death as an adult, and he was thrown into a morbid state of mind. The quiet of mourning was soon shattered by the outbreak of the Franco-Prussian War. He spent the rest of the summer tracing the movement of the armies on campaign maps. He also began to pick up news of another contest which promised to upset his America as the war threatened to destroy his Europe. For, at long last, Ulysses S. Grant was preparing to wage war on his political opponents.[59]

Henry Adams had been right about one thing. When Grant became president, he had very little idea of how the job was done. Except for a few successes in Reconstruction policy, his first year in office had been disappointing and at times dismal. He had been embarrassed by the early cabinet shuffle, and Black Friday cast a further shadow on his competence. His minister to England took his orders from Charles Sumner, not from the State Department. Now Sumner stood in the way of his cherished plans for the annexation of San Domingo. It had not been a promising beginning: as Adams had noted, "the machinery of government works clumsily when no responsibility, or subordination, or harmonious action can be enforced between executive and legislature." James Russell Lowell, visiting the White House in March 1870, characterized Grant's expression as that "of a man with a problem before him of which he does not understand the terms."[60]

But the president proved a quick learner. He soon abandoned his initial conception of the presidency as a purely administrative office, replacing it with a conception of presidential leadership based upon the bargaining power of patronage—just what Adams feared would destroy the system. Grant thought otherwise. "An executive must consider Congress," he later said; "The members have their rights as well as himself. If he wants to get along with Congress, have the Government go smoothly, and secure wholesome legislation, he must be in sympathy with Congress." Patronage was the key, creating a link between president and Congress, giving incentive for both to cooperate, and striking down the inhibitions to concerted action imposed by the doctrine of separation of powers. This model was in direct contrast to Adams's model of presidential leadership, which looked to the balances between branches of government established by the separation of powers doctrine. Grant rejected that model because he had witnessed the fate of its last advocate, Andrew Johnson. Much better, he thought, to follow the example of Abraham Lincoln, a master practitioner of the bargaining model.[61]

It had been a long and costly education, but Grant immediately put it to use. Aware that Attorney General Hoar's behavior had created friction between the Executive and Congress, he looked around for a replacement for the gentleman from Massachusetts. After all, Hoar was not supporting annexation, and Grant was tiring of cabinet members who persisted in opposing settled policy decisions. To gain the support of several Southern senators for annexation, as well as to bolster the Justice Department's efforts in support of the freedmen, Grant replaced Hoar with Amos Akerman of Georgia. The president next trained his sights on Charles Sumner, announcing to his cabinet on June 14 (a day before he requested Hoar's resignation) that he would "not consider those who oppose his policy as entitled to influence in obtaining positions under him; that he would not let those who oppose him 'name Ministers to London,' etc." On June 30, the Senate failed to ratify the San Domingo treaty by a vote of twenty-eight to twenty-eight. On July 1, Grant demanded that Hamilton Fish request the resignation of John Lothrop Motley as minister to England. When Fish protested that "it is not Mr. Sumner but Mr. Motley at whom you are striking," Grant snapped, "It is the same thing."[62]

Adams learned of Grant's counterattack when he returned to England in July. He dined at the Motleys', noting that they were "enjoying a state of mind anything but cheerful." He knew that Grant's new approach spelled doom for his political ambitions. Still, he sailed home, ready to take part in the new battle. There seemed nothing else to do. But when he arrived at Boston, he was once more offered the teaching post at Harvard, along with the editorship of the *North American Review*. This time, Adams accepted both posts. As with his failure to enlist in the army, he later asserted that his flight from Washington was due to family pressures. He blamed his family, especially his father and his brother Charles, for conspiring to "drag him away" from his chosen career. There was some truth to the charge. Charles Francis Adams had used his position on Harvard's Board of Overseers to advantage, prodding Eliot to offer his son the position. Writing to his brother, Charles urged him to seize the opportunity to edit the *Review* and add to his reputation in the reform movement—hardly dragging him away from his chosen career.[63]

But no one forced Henry Adams to accept Eliot's offer. If at twenty he had convinced his father to let him go abroad, there was no reason for him to bow meekly to the dictates of family at thirty-two. Having battled his brother over his future for some twelve years, why would he now give up the career he had always wanted, just to please him? Adams's egotism and pride did not render him amenable to submitting abjectly to the wishes of others. Contrary to the image he created in the *Education*, Henry Adams decided his own fate. He had reason enough to leave Washington. "There are few of my political friends left in power now, and these few will soon go out," he told Gaskell. Hoar was gone. Sumner raged at Grant from his house across Lafayette Square. Wells was not reappointed to his position when his term expired, a casualty of the war over revenue reform. Garfield was scurrying for cover. Schurz, who was advocating a fusion between moderate Republicans and Democrats in Missouri, was no longer welcome at the White House. Only Cox was left.[64]

And not for long. Even as Adams packed his possessions, Cox contemplated severing his ties with the administration. Grant had lost patience with Cox's insubordination and arrogance. He repeatedly reminded Cox that it was he, not Cox, who was president, but the secretary ignored the warning. When Grant revoked Cox's order prohibiting his clerks from taking a second paid vacation in order to go home and vote, Cox, claiming that Grant was subverting civil service reform, tendered his resignation. It was quickly accepted.[65]

Watching the exodus of his friends from power, Adams realized that his influence at Washington was at an end. Once a warm home, it was fast becoming the enemy camp: "Things have taken a political turn there which is by no means favorable to me," he reported to Gaskell. His last article had placed him clearly in the opposition. Given these circumstances, a post at Harvard and the editorship of the *North American Review* were godsends. Far from being a step down, it would increase Adams's standing in reform circles.[66]

"All we poor privates ask is a leader, but all our leaders run away," Henry Adams told Cox after he had resigned. "Look at men like Evarts, my father and the rest, and tell me what we can do."[67] But some of the privates were fleeing as well. Unwilling and unable to battle Grant on the front lines, Adams withdrew to his scholarly sanctuary at Cambridge with plans to continue the struggle—and as a general, not as a private.

CHAPTER FIVE

FROM FIGHT TO FLIGHT

Not one young man of promise remained in the Government service. All drifted into opposition . . . Adams's
case was perhaps the strongest because he thought he
had done well.

The Education of Henry Adams

Arriving at Cambridge in the fall of 1870, Henry Adams prepared to
teach medieval history—"of which, as you are aware," he reminded Gaskell,
"I am utterly and grossly ignorant." The prospect both charmed and challenged him. But Adams planned to educate more than just his college students. He could not wait to take over the editorship of the *North American
Review*. He proposed to become one of the powers of the land through the
Review, passing critical judgment upon American society, manners, culture,
and literature as well as instructing his readers on the correct course to
pursue in politics. The *Review* would become "a regular organ of our opinions," Adams informed Wells. The editorship would prevent him from breaking "entirely from old connections." At last Adams had control of a vehicle
which influenced "the limited number of cultivated minds" he wished to
address. His move from Washington to Cambridge was hardly a retreat; it
was a change of base for conducting operations; and, as he told Gaskell, it
"has by no means thrown me out of politics."[1]

Editing the *North American Review* renewed Adams's spirits about his
political fortunes. He became optimistic enough to announce that he anticipated "the day when we shall be in power again as not far distant." Having rid himself of the delusion that he could influence policy through gaining
a reputation at Washington, he basked in the freedom that open opposition
gave him. No longer need he pretend to be concerned about offending
Grant, Fish, or other members of the administration. He could now hurl
abuse to his heart's content. Moreover, his position allowed him to claim a
place among the leaders of the insurgent Republican movement against the
president.[2]

Adams prodded his old friends "to stand by me on my first appearance as editor" by contributing articles on political reform. He urged Cox to write about civil service reform and asked Wells to submit a piece on revenue reform. With such writers, he told Cox, "I believe I can secure my success and assist the reform movement." Lest Cox back out of his commitment, Adams impressed him with the importance of acting: "What we want from you now is a lead. . . . You must lay down for us the great principles of our movement." To Carl Schurz, Adams composed a flattering appeal, requesting the Missouri senator to describe the "true nature of the Liberal Republican movement."[3]

Adams's editorship enabled him to play a larger role in promoting the insurgent Republican movement against Grant. In November, the movement's leaders assembled at New York to plan for the upcoming congressional session. The new professor, making clear where his priorities lay, hurried down from Harvard to join them, explaining that "my flock must wait for their historical fodder till I return." At New York, he huddled with brother Charles, Godkin, Bowles, Horace White of the *Chicago Tribune*, and several other editors and members of the Free Trade League. Noticeable by their absence were Schurz—still undecided over whether to break with Grant—and Cox. The course of the meeting soon exposed the diverse aims of the participants. House Speaker James G. Blaine had offered to let the insurgents organize the all-important Committee of Ways and Means "and any other positions that might be required of him, even beyond our expectations," Adams reported to Cox. Garfield would chair the committee as a nod toward tariff reduction. The Free Traders wanted to refuse the bait, bolt the party, and join the Democrats on the issue of free trade. Adams and his fellow editors dissented, preferring to hold the threat of a new party in abeyance, accept Blaine's offer, "and to throw on the Republicans the responsibility of a rupture if they dared to try it."[4]

Further discussion revealed that those present could agree on little more than their "indifference or contempt for the administration." Adams and White battled to place the issue of civil service reform on the agenda, much to the dismay of the Free Traders; divisions appeared again over whether to establish a permanent organization. Adams soon saw "that there was great danger of our committing a serious blunder by acting without sufficient preparation" and "resisted the movement to the utmost," eventually carrying his point. Wishing to maintain his freedom of action, he refused to tie his hopes for reform to the single-minded Free Traders. Since those present could not agree on a plan for action, the meeting soon broke up. The participants would have to wait and see what happened. Adams reported to Cox that "the advance since last spring was very marked" and that he was "amused" to see how confident the insurgents were about their power. He could barely contain his satisfaction with his own position. He was power-ful and influential among his peers, exercising leadership in political mat-ters. Charles noted that "Henry and I had clearer ideas of what was wanted than any one else and finally shaped the course of events." The *New York Evening Mail* soon reported that the *North American Review*, "which used to have a strictly private circulation among a few hundred cultivated and re-spectable 'old fogies,' is waking up." Under Adams's editorship, the quar-terly "may yet become a power in the arena of the discussion of contemporaneous questions." It was just like the old days, when Henry over-heard his father and his compatriots plan Free Soil tactics in the living room of their Boston house. Back at Cambridge, he settled down for the winter, prepared to observe events at Washington while keeping an eye on his stu-dents.[5]

Events soon shattered Adams's confidence. The reform machine sput-tered to a halt as the administration geared into action. Blaine remained silent over whether Garfield was to chair Ways and Means. He had outwit-ted the political amateurs, holding out the promise of Garfield's appoint-ment to stifle any notions of open revolt. The post remained empty until the next Congress, when Blaine named Henry Dawes to the position. Then Grant, in his annual message, launched a few rockets into the camp of the insurgents. The president, seeking to confine the damage caused by Cox's resignation, spoke in general terms about the need for civil service reform: "The present system does not secure the best men, and often not even fit men for public place." He urged Congress to examine the matter. He side-stepped the issue of revenue reform, claiming that it "has not been defined by any of its advocates to my knowledge, but seems to be accepted as some-thing which is to supply every man's wants without any cost or effort on his part." Having dealt in summary fashion with the two major concerns of the reformers, Grant turned to the San Domingo issue once more, calling for Congressional approval of a committee to investigate the feasibility of an-nexing the Caribbean republic—even to the point of negotiating a new treaty of annexation.[6]

The message threw reformers into disarray. They had prepared to fight the administration over civil service reform and revenue reform; Grant en-sured that the lines of battle would be drawn over the San Domingo issue. As Charles Sumner realized, the president did not need Congressional au-thorization for the investigating committee. In fact, whatever hope Grant still had for annexation—and these hopes were slim—he soon let fall, as he settled for a committee charged only to investigate the island republic, with-out any power to negotiate a new agreement. Instead, Grant used the com-mission proposal as a way to count heads, enforce party loyalty, and contest Sumner's insinuations about his integrity. Adams called the message "a queer document," but it served its purpose well. During the winter, the Senate was racked by acrimonious debate over San Domingo. Senators hurried to defend the president from Sumner's bitter attacks. Garfield noted near the end of the session that "the Senate has done almost nothing in the way of legislation. Their time has been almost wholly devoted to politics . . . making and unmaking presidents."[7]

Adams missed the entire point of Grant's message and the politics of the session. Failing to understand its political purpose, he preferred to evaluate it as a statement of policy, and characterized it in condescending terms of petty ridicule. "As to Revenue Reform it is particularly droll, but rather in the style of a very ignorant collegian," he confided to Cox. "We shall teach him as much as he will be able to learn, before long." He enlisted Wells to perform the task of educating the president through writing an article on the subject. Adams was more surprised to see Grant's paragraph on civil service reform, concluding that Cox's removal was responsible for it. "But I still see a long fight before us," he warned the former cabinet secretary.[8]

Visiting Washington in January 1871, Adams "found anarchy ruling our nation. I don't know who has power or is responsible, but whoever it is, I cannot find him." Sumner, after launching a characteristic philippic against Grant over annexation, found himself thrown on the defensive by a fierce counterattack which ultimately seized his cherished chairmanship of the Foreign Relations committee as spoils of war. Carl Schurz protested loudly about Grant's use of executive power and his interference with the Senate, portraying the general-president as a tyrant. Oblivious to these results, Adams observed that Grant "has succeeded in breaking down everybody of any value, including himself." But he also admitted that "the prospect of getting rid of him is distant"—inadvertently testifying to Grant's political success. Far from "breaking down" his presidency, Grant was "breaking down" his opponents within the party and reforging a Republican party whose members were loyal to the organization and sometimes to the president, while blunting the thrust of the reformers' attack. Returning to Cambridge, the dejected editor begged Wells to hurry up with his article: "We need it badly now, for San Domingo is demoralizing all our issues."[9]

Meanwhile, Grant's political offensive moved forward relentlessly. Having caught the reformers flat-footed, he now delivered a blow that sent them reeling. When Congress reacted sluggishly to his call for civil service reform, the president gave up on pushing any specific bill. Instead, he approved a resolution drafted by Pennsylvania Representative William H. Armstrong which directed Grant to appoint a commission to draft a set of civil service guidelines. In the dying moments of the session, the resolution, attached as a rider to the civil appropriations bill, passed Congress. The president's quick response to a potentially grave situation showed that he had learned how to lead on the political battlefield, marshalling his troops in the Senate and choosing his own terrain for the struggle. Annexation confused reformers; the president's support for civil service divided them. Some reformers still urged resistance to the Grant machine, but others were satisfied by the president's efforts and stayed in the party. Editor Samuel Bowles exclaimed, "How completely our good President comes over to the advanced platform in his message. . . . If he would only practice as well as he preaches, he would not leave a single inch for us to stand on." The removal of Sumner from his committee chairmanship was a grim reminder of the possible fate the insurgents faced if they broke ranks.[10]

Adams was stunned. By April, he had become desperate. Godkin's *Nation* had little positive to say about the first number of the *North American Review* put out by Adams. In light of recent events, Cox's article on civil service reform had a hollow ring to it. Schurz continued to resist Adams's efforts to put his thoughts on paper, despite the editor's eager pursuit. Adams offered to polish any notes or a rough draft into an article. When Schurz refused, Adams, growing frantic, tried to impress the senator with the notion that while stump speeches were "ephemeral," a good piece of "political diagnosis . . . will last." He pointed out that Schurz's "other efforts have little or no effect upon the class of readers who can only be reached by more permanent influences than the daily press." But Schurz preferred speaking to writing. Only Wells responded to his friend's pleas, but with little effect. Appearing in the July issue of the *North American Review*, his discussion of revenue reform was cluttered by tables and dry language that served to bore rather than educate the reader. Even Adams pronounced the issue dull.[11]

Adams's attitude stood in stark contrast to that of his colleagues in the reform movement. Many of his fellow reformers took new strength from the events of the winter and spring of 1871. A majority of them began to abandon the notion that Grant could be denied renomination: they increasingly accepted instead the need to form a new party founded on the reform agenda. In the rush to form a new organization, its founders had little time for writing articles or for Adams. They already knew what they wanted: to decapitate Grant, transform American politics, and enact the reform agenda of civil service reform, hard money, free trade, and reconciliation with the white South. Stump speeches might be "ephemeral" to Adams, but they were the stuff of political rallies and the mobilization of voters—a part of politics for which Adams had no taste and less ability. Intellectual though he might be, Schurz knew from his previous experiences in politics that voters would judge articles in the *North American Review* to be "ephemeral." Better, he thought, to look for voters where they could be found, through newspapers and political rallies. Better to cultivate Horace White of the *Chicago Tribune,* Horace Greeley and Whitelaw Reid of the *New York Tribune,* Samuel Bowles of the *Springfield Republican,* and Murat Halstead of the *Cincinnati Commercial* than Adams and his handful of readers. It was no accident, then, that Schurz chose to make his break with the administration and the party through a speech at Nashville, Tennessee, in September 1871—for he knew full well that the press would carry his remarks.[12]

Adams's hopes for political influence were trampled by reformers in their rush to form a third party. Struggling to find contributors, he no longer cared much for the *North American Review* as an organ for reformers—nor did they turn to his journal to express their ideas. Historical and scientific articles filled its pages. Political aspects were no more encouraging. "What between the Force Bill, the Legal Tender Case, San Domingo, and Tammany," he told Schurz, "I see no constitutional government any longer possible." Even his teaching suffered, and the professor "nearly had a rebellion" and was "the object of unlimited cursing." He gratefully escaped to the West, relieved from teaching students and politicians alike—a task made doubly hard when it was apparent that he was losing both of his cherished audiences.[13]

Surely, Adams exaggerated when he spoke of the collapse of constitutional government. In light of his initial demand that Grant exercise the powers of the presidency, his protests against the president's behavior reflected Grant's failure to follow Adams's agenda: to Adams, that crime was alone sufficient to indict him as weak and ignorant. But his protests against the president's policies were overblown. Grant had long ago dropped any idea of annexation; the Force Bill was a circumscribed measures, due to expire in a year, and necessary to subvert lawlessness and white supremacist terrorism in the South (something Adams, for all his love of law and order, never protested). Nor was Adams on the mark in other areas. The Supreme Court's decision in the Legal Tender cases, delivered in May 1871, while it overturned *Hepburn v. Griswold* (which had denied the use of legal tender to pay off debts contracted prior to the act's passage in 1862), left unchanged the status of debts contracted after the act's passage (as had *Hepburn v. Griswold*) while helping to bring some stability to the nation's financial markets. Adams overestimated the impact of the Court's recent decision while overlooking the rather limited scope of *Hepburn v. Griswold.* As for Boss William Marcy Tweed and the reign of Tammany in New York City, Adams would have done well to exercise a little forbearance, for before long, the Tweed Ring would be assailed and broken—and among the leaders in the assault would be cartoonist Thomas Nast of *Harper's Weekly,* who alternated between attacks on Tweed and on Adams's cherished colleagues, most notably Schurz, while defending the president of the United States. Rather than the collapse of constitutional government, what grieved Henry Adams was the disintegration of his political future. At a time when others were responding to the call for battle, he preferred to nurse his pretended wounds, many of which were self-inflicted.

Yet his frustration was understandable. In the April issue of the *Review*, he had launched another attack on James Fisk and his lawyer, David Dudley Field, when he published two articles, one by Charles, critical of both men; this followed the revelation that he was the author of "The New York Gold Conspiracy." Having already gone into opposition with the publication of his second "Session," it made no difference now to Adams if Grant and his supporters knew he was the author of a piece critical of the administration. Although Adams anticipated and even eagerly welcomed a confrontation with Fisk or Field, the promised combat fizzled after a few exchanges with Field. In the fall, Henry and brother Charles assembled a selection of their writings under the title *Chapters of Erie and Other Essays*. Among Henry's pieces were "Captaine John Smith" (which did not seem to fit at all alongside the other essays), "The Bank of England Restriction," "British Finance in 1816," "The Legal Tender Act," and "The New York Gold Conspiracy." The mask of anonymity was thus lifted from several of his essays; at last, American readers would be able to read his discussion of the causes and consequences of Black Friday. Perhaps Adams thought that the collection would serve as a bible for reformers. A less generous observer might comment that Adams was simply gratifying his ego much as he did when he bound his undergraduate essays—a motive which would at least explain the inclusion of "Captaine John Smith," for it was his initial foray into the pages of the *North American Review*. Oddly enough, Adams omitted his two best essays, his reviews of politics in 1869 and 1870. Reviewers politely complimented the effort as an examination of financial questions, railroads, and scandals, although Henry's desire for English notices was fulfilled only when Gaskell took it on himself to place one and write another. Such solicited praise did little to reverse Adams's sinking influence among reformers or his declining interest in politics: rather, the volume served as a tombstone to both.[14]

Grant jolted the Adams household once more in November 1871, when he appointed Charles Francis Adams, Sr., as the American representative to the Geneva Tribunal that would arbitrate American claims against Britain resulting from English support of the Confederate navy during the war. Given Henry Adams's attitude towards the president, some might have thought that Grant had gone mad. In fact, Grant was reluctant to make the appointment at first, and only the entreaties of Hamilton Fish changed his mind. But the decision to name Adams was a political masterstroke. It drew applause, satisfied many people that Grant was willing to appoint "the best men" to office, and sent a possible political opponent abroad.[15]

Despite his father's good fortune, Henry Adams steadily continued to lose interest in politics. In December, he reported to Gaskell that he had "dodged a meeting of politicians at Washington" and was "sinking into provincial professordom with anguish." Nor did his friends seem particularly eager to rescue him from that purgatory. A desperate call to Cox for "a pronunciamento" which "would attract interest and rouse action" failed. Samuel J. Tilden, whose efforts against the infamous Tweed Ring in New York City gained him national attention, also turned down a request to contribute a commentary. Adams complained that reform was "rapidly subsiding into political indifferentism," but the words really described his own apathy, for many of his fellow insurgents had decided that the time was ripe to make an open break with the Republican party and set up an independent movement. Schurz's Missouri supporters had called a national convention to meet at Cincinnati on May 1, 1872. Among the names mentioned as possibilities for heading the independents' ticket was Charles Francis Adams, Sr. Henry appeared unmoved by such prospects, and he "groaned with pleasure" when he saw his father off to Geneva. As for himself, he was "comparatively little disturbed by the infernal row which is going on."[16]

The sources of Adams's political apathy were personal. He had lost his feeling of importance in the movement. Unable to solicit articles for the *North American Review* and burdened by the operations of the quarterly, he quickly lost his enthusiasm for reform. Nor did his old friends miss him. One sign of his growing insignificance in the reform movement as it prepared to contest Grant's reelection was the fact that Thomas Nast, whose cartoons for *Harper's Weekly* savaged Grant's opponents, apparently never included Adams in his cast of characters. Adams sulked. If he was not to play an influential role in the movement, he preferred to play none at all. His letters to Gaskell, once sparkling with political news, now spoke only of getting people to review recent literature and of Cambridge society. Yet there was reason to smile: he was getting married. Henry had met Marian Hooper in May 1871, and was soon in full pursuit of a woman who by most accounts was something special. Henry "found her so far superior to any women I had ever met" that he determined to win her, finding the chase more entertaining and fulfilling than politics. On February 27, 1872, Marian (or "Clover," as she was known) accepted his offer of marriage. And, "what with teaching, editing and marrying, I am a pretty well-occupied man," he remarked. The engaged couple planned a European honeymoon after a June wedding, removing the groom from politics at election time.[17]

As his wedding approached, Adams busied himself with plans for the honeymoon. But he could not avoid commenting on the impending meeting of reformers at Cincinnati. "The gathering will be tremendous and my old political friends are deep in it," he reported to Gaskell. He knew that his father did not want to be nominated president, although somewhere deep inside the elder Adams craved the unsolicited call to duty—a fact he made clear in setting his terms for accepting a proposition from Roscoe Conkling to serve as Grant's running mate (he would consider the idea only if nominated—which left open the possibility that he would decline it, thus embarrassing Grant). Convinced that the reformers would be outwitted by professional politicians solely seeking revenge against Grant, Charles Francis Adams responded coolly to Wells's plea that someone be authorized to act for him at the convention with a dismissive letter that was shared with the press—although the careful reader would note that the letter did not preclude his candidacy altogether. Henry chose to follow his father's example and remain away from Cincinnati and his "old political friends." In part, this was due to his depression over his declining influence in the movement; he also may well have grasped the futility of an independent candidacy for the presidency. Perhaps he realized all too well the success of Grant's campaign for reelection and sought to prevent his father from becoming a sacrificial lamb to the unrealistic aspirations of reformers. Clover, "desperately ambitious," took more interest in her future father-in-law's political fortunes than did her husband-to-be, as did Henry's elder brothers.[18]

So the reformers traveled to Cincinnati without Henry Adams, jettisoning principles as they went. Free trade was the first issue to go out the window. Horace Greeley had demanded its abandonment as his price for joining the Liberal Republicans. Staunch advocates of free trade like White, Wells, and Schurz submitted to this decision, just as the administration cut the ground out from under their feet by reducing the tariff. At the convention, the reformers confronted many disgruntled politicians whose commitment to reform was limited to ejecting the occupant of the presidential chair. Schurz's keynote address asserted that the Liberal movement was above the "old tricks of the political trade" in its attempt to achieve a political revolution: "Therefore, away with the cry, 'Anybody to beat Grant'; a cry too paltry, too unworthy of the great enterprise in which we are engaged." But anyone looking out at the delegates from the speaker's rostrum must have wondered what united them aside from a desire to defeat Grant. Free traders mingled with protectionists; civil service reformers sat next to frustrated spoilsmen, both anxious for office; civil rights spokesmen (what few there were) chatted with advocates for sectional reconciliation and the abandonment of Reconstruction; New England patricians discussed the platform with Western agrarian radicals.[19]

Nevertheless, reformers appeared to have the convention under control. They filled the various committees with their men, named their spokesman Schurz permanent chairman, and, conscious of the conditions of Greeley's support, quelled attempts by hard-core free traders to include a stand against protection on the platform. As balloting started, it looked as if Clover Hooper's wish to become the daughter-in-law of a president of the United States would come a step closer to realization. At the end of the fifth ballot, Charles Frances Adams, with 309 votes, needed only 48 more to capture a majority of the convention and the nomination. Only Greeley, with 258 votes, stood a chance of stopping Adams. To this day, no one can readily explain what happened next. As the sixth ballot got underway, delegates began chanting Greeley's name. Henry Demarest Lloyd recalled how "hoary-haired, hard-eyed politicians, who had not in twenty years felt a noble impulse, mounted their chairs and with faces suffused with a seraphic fervor, blistered their throats hurraying for the great and good Horace Greeley." Delegations announced that they were changing their votes. Greeley's numbers crept closer to the magic number of 357. Schurz, sensing disaster, announced that the roll call was invalid, but the New York delegation hooted him down. To his astonishment, Horace Greeley—a foe of the Democratic party, a rabid protectionist, and an advocate of civil service reform only when he found himself on the outs with the Grant administration—was the nominee of the Liberal Republicans.[20]

Greeley's victory was not the surprise some later observers would make it out to be. Senator Lyman Trumbull of Illinois—the initial favorite of free traders such as Wells, White, and Schurz—had lost support to Adams and to his fellow Illinoisan, Associate Supreme Court Justice David Davis. Davis's candidacy aroused the staunch opposition of White, Samuel Bowles, and two other editors, Murat Halstead of the *Cincinnati Commercial* and Henry Watterson of the *Louisville Courier-Journal*. Calling themselves "the Quadrilateral" (after an Austrian defensive position in the Alps), the four editors scrambled to stop Davis. Searching for allies, they turned to another newspaperman, Whitelaw Reid of the *New York Tribune*—Greeley's paper. White hoped to revive Trumbull's candidacy; Watterson and Bowles favored Adams; Halstead would accept either man. Editorials issued by the five newspapers made it clear that Davis was unacceptable because of his Democratic roots; they succeeded in sidetracking the justice's candidacy. However, Trumbull's chances had already peaked, leaving the contest between Adams and Greeley. The triumph of the latter was due in part to the editor's popularity, in part to Missouri Senator B. Gratz Brown's opposition to Adams, and in part to the failure of "the Quadrilateral" to take Greeley's candidacy seriously until it was too late. The supposed leaders of reform had lost touch with the delegates; Adams may have inspired the editors, but the frigid diplomat left a majority of the delegates cold.[21]

Henry Adams was amused by the result. "My father narrowly escaped being the next President," he told Gaskell, "but has come out of the fight very sound and strong." He was relieved by the defeat, for he had feared an "exasperating election" had his father won the nomination. Greeley was "likely to be not only disgraced but beaten." He moaned, "If the Gods insist on making Mr. Greeley our President, I give up."[22] He declined joining in the attack on Grant; instead, he got married.

During the next several months, as Henry and Clover honeymooned in Europe and Egypt, the political campaign in America ground to its inevitable conclusion. Grant had retained much of his popularity with the people. Given a choice between Grant and Greeley, many reformers, including Charles Francis Adams, Jr., chose the general. Charles Francis Adams, Sr.'s triumph at the Geneva Tribunal redounded to the credit of the incumbent; John Quincy Adams II accepted the vice presidential nomination of the splinter "Straight-Out Democrats," suggesting his disgust with both major candidates. As if to illustrate the collapse of Liberal Republicanism, the *North American Review*, in the absence of its editor, judged Grant's administration "a fair one . . . in some respects, extraordinarily good and effective," and endorsed the president for reelection. On November 8, 1872, Grant won reelection. Liberal Republicanism had been defeated. Henry Adams, who had once stood in the front rank, had long since deserted. He was in Florence, Italy, on election day.[23]

In August 1873, Henry Adams, having spent a year abroad, prepared to return to America. The collapse of the Liberal Republican movement and Grant's overwhelming victory at the polls appeared to shut off any hope for independent reformers. Adams, dismissing whatever thoughts remained of a career in politics, contemplated a career as an historian. Aware that Boston was "running dry of literary authorities," he saw an opportunity for someone "who has the ability" to gain prominence: "With it, comes social dignity, European reputation, and a foreign mission to close."[24] It was not political success, but it might have to do.

Settling into a new home on Marlborough Street, just south of the Charles River, Adams resumed his teaching duties at Harvard. He was bored by the routine nature of his position and found precious relief in the knowledge that he would not be burdened with editing the *North American Review* for several months. Lecturing for twelve hours a week to a group of restless undergraduates in three classes, he often found himself at work for ten hours a day, not returning home until dusk. The schedule left little time for socializing or independent work. Even a trip to his old haunts in Washington in February 1874 failed to revive his frustrated ambitions. To Gaskell he rationalized that it was all for the best: "The more I see of official life here, the less I wish to enter it." Disingeniously, he added, "This was always my feeling, and it always grows stronger." But he could not resist jabbing away at politicians, smugly asserting that "it gives one a lofty sense of one's own importance to be able to smile contemptuously on men in high place." He sneered at the "barbaric simplicity" of America's "feeble" politicians. The government was "not so much corrupt as incompetent, enough to make one a howling dervish for life." Rather than attempt to improve this state of affairs, Adams preferred "to laugh at the whole concern."[25] Having failed to gain power, he disparaged those who had. He had to deny that he had even contemplated pursuing the career he had set his heart on. Only by maintaining that he no longer cared for political position and influence could he conceal his failure to obtain them.

But events during Grant's second administration rekindled Henry's hopes of overthrowing the machine. Republican congressmen, including Adams's friend Garfield, had to fend off charges of bribery in the Credit Mobilier scandal. Garfield was also suspected of influence peddling in awarding sidewalk paving contracts. Just as damaging to the Grand Old Party's reputation was the celebrated Salary Grab, a bill passed in the waning moments of the Forty-second Congress awarding legislators retroactive pay increases. The Panic of 1873 swiftly developed into a serious depression, creating new sources of dissatisfaction with the ruling party. Most importantly, Reconstruction was proving a political disaster. Southern Republicans, white and black alike, were being beaten down by the concerted efforts of Democrats to "redeem" the South at any cost, while their Northern counterparts retreated in the face of widespread voter apathy over the fate of the freedman. Democratic triumphs in the 1874 elections, securing that party's majority control of the House of Representatives for the first time since 1858, exposed the weakness of the Republican position.[26]

Affairs in Massachusetts also alarmed Adams and his fellow reformers. In 1874, the Bay State had been rocked by Benjamin Butler's battle to have William A. Simmons, a loyal subordinate, installed as collector of customs in Boston. With the prime source of federal patronage in the state in his hands, Butler might well assume control of the state Republican party, a notion which many Massachusetts Republicans found revolting. Drowned out by reformers' shrieks of dismay was the fact that the present collector, Thomas Russell, was also loyal to Butler, although less reliable. Butler was bent not so much upon expanding his base as retaining what he already had. Nor was the protest related to Simmons's ability to administer his post: even the *Springfield Republican* admitted his skill. His opponents never could bring themselves to admit that what they wanted was someone more attuned to their interest than to Butler's. The rhetoric of good versus evil and the cries of "Butlerism" obscured what was in fact a typical patronage struggle; if anything, the reformers' protest suggested that they sensed Butler was vulnerable to an attack, for Grant's loyalty to him was political, not personal. Simmons won confirmation; two weeks later, Charles Sumner died. Although he had been estranged from many of his former allies in recent years, reformers were saddened by his death. As they followed Sumner's casket to Mount Auburn Cemetery, men such as pallbearer Charles Francis Adams, Sr., must have wondered whether it was time to bury reform as well.[27]

Other reformers saw Sumner's death as a call to battle. They were rallied by Carl Schurz's eulogy, which passed over the Massachusetts senator's steadfast support of civil rights (a cause Schurz had backed away from in recent years) to present Sumner as a leading light in civil service reform and an example of high-minded honesty in politics. The implication was clear: to honor Sumner, reformers must stop Ben Butler before he destroyed all the respectability remaining in Massachusetts. Henry Cabot Lodge, a graduate student of Henry Adams, joined with Moorfield Storey and Brooks Adams to form the "Commonwealth Club" to promote the "purification of politics," as Lodge put it. These young men were not about to see their future spoiled by a repulsive hulk with frog-like eyes who took open joy in ridiculing the aristocratic pretensions and white kid gloves of the Massachusetts elite. Unable to fathom Butler's popularity among the constituents he served so well, these aristocrats attributed his power to wire-pulling and behind-the-scenes conspiracies. They spent much of their time at 91 Marlborough Street, listening to Henry Adams hold forth over tea on the proper course for independents to pursue.[28]

The selection of Sumner's successor presented Massachusetts reformers with an opportunity to reestablish their position. They pushed forward Charles Francis Adams, Sr., as the ideal candidate to assume Sumner's seat, uniting Democrats and anti-Butler Republicans. Henry Adams held out little hope that his father would triumph over the Butler machine. "As my side is commonly defeated in politics," he told Gaskell, "I prefer not to take sides at all, but to laugh at the whole concern"—a statement which revealed more about Adams and his political attitudes than he cared to show. However, Butler's man, Henry L. Dawes, was unable to turn his purchased support of Simmons into a Senate seat. Perhaps Butlerism was not quite as powerful as reformers had made it out to be. Instead, Governor William B. Washburn got the nod, largely due to the intervention of Vice President Henry Wilson, who charged that Adams's election would be both a product and a cause of Republican division. The elder Adams may have lost, but so did Butler. But to Henry Adams, his father's defeat obscured this larger truth. "Politics are contemptible to the last degree and are growing more and more sordid and aimless," he grimly concluded.[29]

Defeat only spurred Henry's brothers Charles and Brooks—the latter, four years out of Harvard—to redouble their efforts to expose the collapse of republican government under Grant. Henry allowed them to express their opinions in the pages of the *North American Review* after he resumed control in 1874. Charles, who had called upon his fellow reformers to "lay down the future faith boldly and loudly,—show the country in fact that we yet live," examined financial policy in the wake of the depression, assailing proposals for inflation as leaving "a lasting stigma upon the honesty and good faith of the American people, both casting and authorizing the gravest doubts on their much-vaunted capacity for self-government." In "The Platform of the New Party," Brooks Adams urged reformers to "return to a study of those principles which lie at the foundation of government." Party organizations had succeeded in removing "every man of large experience and tried ability" from political life. They conducted "an organized attack on ability, integrity, and education" in their quest for power. As a result, the country was "wildly drifting"; unless the press alerted people to "the level of the emergency," the republic was doomed. Instead of offering an analysis of recent events, the Adams brothers merely recited the familiar litany of corrupt party organizations and the need for reform. But an audience fresh from Credit Mobilier and the Salary Grab might be more receptive to the message.[30]

Even in the role of book reviewer, Henry Adams could not always resist striking a blow at the president. Hermann von Holst's *Administration of Andrew Jackson* offered one such opportunity. In translating von Holst for his American readers, Adams chose passages about Jackson, the man who had defeated John Quincy Adams's bid for reelection as president in 1828, which could also apply to Grant. Jackson "was still wholly incapable of raising himself from any point of view to the elevation of a great man"; he "showed no controlling genius in pointing out and opening new paths for his nation"; his administration "systematically undermined the public sense of law, and lowered the respect of the people for their government." Such prose made it clear why Henry's grandfather had been horrified by the idea of Harvard's bestowing an honorary degree on Old Hickory. Jackson's rise to power was evidence that "the people have begun to exchange the *leadership* of a small number of statesmen and politicians of the higher class for the *rule* of an ever more colossally growing swarm of politicians of all classes down to the political bar-keeper and the common thief in the protecting garb of the demagogue." Politics had become "a profession in which mediocrity in an ever-descending scale held sway, and moral laxity was the rule if not the requisite."[31] What had commenced in Jackson's time was now reaching its full fruition in the age of Grant.

Inspired by events, Adams began to toy with the idea of reentering politics. He followed the 1874 elections closely, reporting to Gaskell that his allies "appear to be gaining ground" as administration Republicans suffered defeat, with Butler among the fallen. The political scene seemed promising to a reformer. Adams was also wondering whether he would ever make his mark on the world. He was entering "the yawning gulf of middle-age . . . balder, duller, more pedantic, and more lazy than ever." Even his "fits of wrath and rebellion against the weaknesses and shortcomings of mankind" were now subdued, "though grumbling has become my favorite occupation," he reported to Gaskell. One reason for his discontent was that he found Boston society stifling. "I care little whether we succeed or not in getting into power," he told Lodge, "but I care a great deal to prevent myself from becoming what of all things I despise, a Boston prig (the intellectual prig is the most odious of all)." To an old English friend he described what he meant by a "prig": "They cram themselves with second-hand facts and theories till they bust, and then they lecture at Harvard College and think they are the aristocracy of intellect and are doing true heroic work by exploding themselves all over a younger generation." He despaired, "Are we never to produce one man who can do something himself?" His greatest fear was to ask the question of himself. Politics offered a way to prove himself worthy of his name while lifting him out of boredom.[32]

During the winter of 1874–1875, Adams slipped back into the political reform movement. Its prospects for success looked brighter; moreover, Henry's father remained a favorite of reform Republicans, who once more were pushing him for the Senate with an even better chance of success. Henry was determined not to be left behind. He first contemplated joining a syndicate to purchase the *Boston Daily Advertiser* to serve as the mouthpiece of reform, but the deal fell through. In January 1875, he attended a rally at Faneuil Hall, organized by Charles, Brooks, and his prize student Henry Cabot Lodge, to protest Grant's use of federal troops in the organization of the Louisiana legislature. The meeting was a true family affair, with John Quincy Adams II decrying military interference in the operations of civil government. That politics in Louisiana was rarely civil and that the use of force was not unusual, as suggested by several massacres of blacks and white Republicans, was besides the point. So was the fact that it had been Louisiana Democrats who had initially called upon federal soldiers to maintain order to secure their attempted coup d'état in organizing the state legislature by force and fraud. Facts were of little importance when it came to attacking Grant. "We mashed about with no end of noise," Adams exulted. Even his father's failure to secure a Senate seat—this time it was Dawes who claimed the prize, again in part because Republican leaders saw an Adams candidacy as death to party unity—did not discourage him. A trip to Washington the following month sharpened his desire to try politics once more. Lame-duck Republicans, bemoaning their fate, were pointing angry fingers at the White House. "The President is detested by everyone," Adams gloated. "All the most important men of both parties unite in denouncing him as a most objectionable person and a very dangerous one. Society talks about him as a great blackguard and mean intriguer." Inspired, Adams turned wholeheartedly to the task of mounting a reform movement for 1876. Soon he found himself in "no end of political intrigues" as he embarked on a "single-handed" effort to overthrow the caucus system. "I am losing my own self-respect in this underhand work of pulling wire," he told Gaskell, "but someone must do it and I am amused by it."[33]

Guiding Adams's activities was a clear conception of the task before him. Party organizations were at the root of political trouble. To attack the party system, Adams returned to his argument that reformers had to arouse public interest. He frequently railed against the failure of the people to take decisive and effective action at the polls. Yet Adams had been guilty of the same sins. On the eve of the 1874 elections, he delighted in telling Lodge, "I am not registered and so can't vote. Someone has sent my poll-tax bill, but it's not paid, and I'm not going to town to pay it."[34] Only when Adams began to sniff a possible victory in 1876 did he rouse himself. Once again he sought to place himself at the head of the movement, for followership held no charms for him. For all his talk of acting behind the scenes, he wanted to be at center stage.

Adams took a proprietary interest in the independent movement, bragging to Gaskell about "my new party." He took the lead in organizing a testimonial dinner at New York in honor of Carl Schurz, now out of the Senate. The dinner, replete with pronouncements of reformers' virtue, stirred the interest of several newspapers, who declared that it was the start of another third-party movement. These reports assumed too much too soon, although an informal network was set up with Lodge as secretary. Yet, even as Adams spoke of success, he also began to prepare excuses in case of failure. He speculated to Gaskell that his new party might meet "eternal ridicule through some new absurd failure" or subside "into nothing for sheer feebleness." Even if the reformers "effected a brilliant coup, brought in our man as President, and the rulers of forty million people, in no case can I come in for any part of the plunder," for his father and brothers "block my path fatally."[35] He seemed unable to cope with the idea of success; failure was so familiar that it was comfortable.

Adams's almost flippant assessment of the political situation obscured the fact that many people thought some form of realignment possible. In 1868, some observers had claimed that Grant's election would signal a political transformation; others anticipated a realignment after the ratification of the 15th Amendment, arguing that it marked the end of the mission of the Republican party. The catastrophic defeat suffered by the Democrats in 1872 seemed yet another opportunity to reassess partisan identities. Differences over monetary policy and patronage had strained Republican unity during Grant's second term, as had increasing dissatisfaction with the Grant administration among some party leaders. Democrats had used the issues of corruption and reform to great advantage in their electoral comeback in 1874; many Republicans began to echo the same themes in order to deprive their opponents of a winning issue. Nor was talk of third parties was limited to Adams and his fellow reformers: Greenbackers and Prohibitionists began to make their voices heard. It was unclear exactly what might occur, but in such uncertainly lurked the prospect of realignment.

The reformers, who had now styled themselves Independents, looked to the Ohio gubernatorial race of 1875—a traditional bellwether of the political climate—as a test of their strength. They differed over what course to follow, an ominous sign of the fragile unity of the movement. Many Independents, including Adams, wanted Schurz to speak on behalf of Republican candidate Rutherford B. Hayes, defeat the "inflation" wing of the Democratic Party, and exhibit the power of the Independent movement. Schurz preferred to steer clear of the election and force the major parties to come to the reformers. But repeated requests from Charles Francis Adams, Jr., Henry Cabot Lodge, and other reformers brought Schurz back from a European trip, and he took to the hustings to shred Democratic "rag money."[36]

Hayes barely won the election, with a 5,000-vote margin in a total vote that exceeded 500,000. The Independents, convinced that Schurz had made the difference, congratulated themselves on the result. They may have been right for the wrong reasons. Schurz's participation may have helped Hayes with German-born Protestant voters, many of whom might sense in Hayes's emphasis on public schooling a nativist attack that transcended anti-Catholicism. Indeed, Hayes's candidacy in itself might have won over those Ohio reformers and dissident Republicans dissatisfied by Grant, for Hayes, once a staunch Grant man, had kept his distance in recent years. It had been the Independents, led by Henry's brother Charles, who had called Schurz back with a somewhat different objective in mind. Evident in the Independents' correspondence with Schurz was less of an embrace of Hayes than a fear that the election of Democratic candidate William Allen would mark a victory for inflationist monetary policies, which Independents deplored. They seemed worried at least as much about what might happen in Democratic ranks on the eve of the 1876 contest as in the future of the Republican party. They hoped to use Schurz's appeal with German Protestant voters to counteract inflationist policies.[37]

Henry Adams was willing to overlook the real sources of Schurz's strength with the electorate in focusing instead on the import of the results of the contest. He argued the election showed that Independents "hold the balance of power and gain strength." But a closer look at his reasoning reveals that he was more interested in increasing the leverage of Independents than in advancing Republican chances in 1876. His comment that "Tilden may be our man" suggests he was more interested in defeating Democratic candidate William Allen because of his inflationist views. This would encourage Democrats to nominate for president a hard money man, like Tilden, who was acceptable to Adams and friends, thus making credible an Independent threat to bolt the Republican ranks at a time when a small swing in a tightly contested electorate was of importance. Plainly relieved by Hayes's victory, he mistakenly concluded that "every man in that five thousand is one of us"—when it was more to the point that these voters had served his purposes. Nevertheless, the future looked bright. "You will hear more of this next year," Adams told Gaskell. "We will play for high stakes and have nothing to lose."[38]

Henry Adams held high hopes as 1876 began. In Washington, the Grant administration was weathering rough seas, with the ship of state springing leaks right and left and running aground on the shoals of corruption. Everywhere the beleaguered president turned, he saw trusted associates swamped and many swept away by a torrent of charges. Orville E. Babcock, Grant's private secretary, was implicated in the Whiskey Ring, a conspiracy to defraud revenue collections on alcohol. While a jury acquitted him of criminal charges, not all observers were persuaded of his innocence. Secretary of War William W. Belknap resigned in disgrace after an investigation by a House committee revealed that his current and former wives—who were sisters—had received kickbacks for sutler appointments. The investigation also revealed improprieties by Orvil Grant, the president's brother. Other cabinet secretaries and administration appointees also braved inquiries. The flurry of revelations calmed Adams's fears that Grant might be tempted to seek another term. Henry, along with his fellow Independents, could now consider strategies and candidates.

Secretary of the Treasury Benjamin Bristow appeared to be a logical choice for president. Although nominally a member of the administration, he had become the darling of the Independents for his relentless investigation of the Whiskey Ring. When Bristow uncovered evidence linking Babcock to the St. Louis ring, Bristow's stock as a presidential candidate rose sharply. The pleasure of the Independents increased when Grant, justifiably convinced that Bristow and his aides were aiming for the White House, began to return fire by accusing the secretary of promoting his personal ambitions instead of justice. Liking Bristow because of the enemies he had made, Adams and Lodge looked upon him as their best hope.[39]

Bristow's emergence as a suitable candidate rescued Adams from an embarrassing situation. Schurz, maintaining that the name of Adams held special magic in America's centennial year, had proposed to push Charles Francis Adams before the electorate once more. Henry Adams knew that this would not do. At sixty-nine, the elder Adams was edging towards senility, as even he admitted. The defeat for the Senate seat in 1875 suggested that he would have problems winning in his own state. Many critics agreed with the cruel description of Adams as "that lonely political Selkirk whose cold family lies around him like seals on the Island of Juan Fernandez." Unwilling to face his father's humiliating defeat, Henry declared his support of Bristow. At the same time, he made plans to shape the course of the campaign, organizing buyers to purchase the *Boston Post* as a Independent organ.[40]

Bristow would have to beat out several other Republicans. Among the names most prominently mentioned was the former speaker of the house, James G. Blaine. Before long, reformers would have great cause to object to Blaine's nomination; at the moment, however, many reformers still found him attractive. Far more objectionable were Roscoe Conkling, senator from New York, and his colleague Oliver P. Morton from Indiana—two men who had been among Grant's most steadfast supporters. It was unclear how much influence reformers could have with such men. An assortment of favorite sons, led by Rutherford B. Hayes, rounded out the choices. The picture was much clearer on the Democratic side. Samuel J. Tilden remained the front-runner, supported by, among others, David A. Wells, under the banner of "Tilden and Reform"—a reminder of Tilden's well-publicized role in attacking Boss Tweed. Hard money and reform seemed to have won the day in the Democratic ranks. The stage was set for Independents to assert their influence. Should the Republicans nominate someone not to their liking, reformers could find a warm home in the Democratic camp.[41]

Despite what appeared to be an ideal situation, Henry Adams detected fundamental weaknesses in the position of the Independents. While "we have unquestionably the power to say that any given man shall not be President," Adams realized that "we are not able to say that any given man shall be President." To Schurz he wrote that they would have to abandon any thoughts of forcing a candidate, like his father, on either party: "It would be the experience of '72 in a new shape, and successful or not it would do no permanent good but rather permanent harm." Bristow was the obvious candidate, as the man "who comes nearest to our standard." But Bristow refused to openly consider an Independent candidacy until the Republican convention took place at Cincinnati, and Adams doubted that Bristow would break with the party. "Further," he explained to Schurz, "nothing is more certain than that Mr. Bristow cannot be nominated"—especially in light of the hostility toward him displayed by other Republicans.[42]

Arguing that "the essential part of any policy must be to hold our friends together," Adams saw signs of disunity everywhere. Some reformers were working within Republican ranks for Bristow; several had jumped across to the Democratic party, intent on nominating Tilden; yet another group contemplated independent action and a third party. Only by uniting behind a single plan could reformers hope to influence the upcoming election. Adams suggested that the Independents announce prior to the Republican convention that they would assemble one week after the nomination "to decide whether we will support the republican candidate or nominate a candidate of our own." Meanwhile, they should quietly "work earnestly for Bristow." These tactics made sense. If, by a miracle, Bristow actually won at Cincinnati, the meeting "will merely confirm their action," Adams reasoned. Otherwise, the Independents must accept "the serious responsibility" of nominating their own candidate on the grounds of "resistance to caucus dictation." Such an act might lead to a Democratic victory in the fall contest, but it would be but a prelude to a political realignment and the reorganization of parties. He gallantly offered "to sacrifice my father for such an object, if necessary," adding that Charles Francis Adams had used Martin Van Buren and the Free Soil Party for the same purpose back in 1848.[43]

Adams's proposal was based on some sound assumptions. He accepted the weakness of the Independent cause. Even as Babcock's trial approached its climax, he noted that "the general lethargy about everything" undercut an independent movement that depended on active discontent to flourish. "We are not strong nor united enough to attack in face," he told Schurz. "The public is not ready to support us." The best chance lay in sitting back to await the Republican convention: "If we can make the public at large feel in advance that they are certain of having an alternative . . . we shall sap the foundations of party discipline beforehand without exposing ourselves to any possible attack." Such tactics would also allow those reformers who preferred working for Bristow's nomination as a Republican to coexist peacefully with third-party advocates, since any public move toward a third party would await the results of the Cincinnati convention. Finally, it would keep Schurz a part of the plan, for he seemed to waver between advocating Charles Francis Adams's independent candidacy as a grand gesture and seeking a way to return to Republican ranks under an acceptable candidate.[44]

In contrast to his sober analysis of the state and prospects of the Independent movement, Adams's conception of the ends of the movement were tailored to his own idiosyncratic preferences. To his mind, the best chance for Independent success could succeed best if they acted independently of the existing parties by forming their own party. Although the Democrats might well gain power in the short term, in the long term, he argued, an Independent third party would revolutionize American politics—although exactly how remained rather vague. Adams wanted to wield the Independent movement as a sword with which he could slay his personal dragon, party organizations: "To attack the caucus system is . . . the end and aim of all my political desires. To that object and to that object only do I care to contribute." It was the "rottenest, most odious and most vulnerable part of our body politic. It is the caucus system we want to attack. By making use of it, we lose our own footing." All other schemes were "mere make-shifts." Having already given up all but the slightest hope for electoral victory in 1876, Adams was satisfied with merely making "a point . . . against party organizations." That independent action would destroy any chance of achieving reform in the foreseeable future was beside the point. After all, Adams argued, reform was impossible until a third-party movement resulted either in reforming the Republicans or displacing them.[45]

In adopting this position, Adams had abandoned his previous strategy, grounded in the nomination of a hard money Democrat—perhaps Tilden—of forcing the Republican party to select a candidate conducive to Independent concerns or face its defection to the Democratic party. Such a strategy depended upon Independent unity; it was becoming more apparent that Independents were not unified over which course to pursue. Adams's professed willingness to support Bristow was a sop to Schurz, for Adams doubted that Bristow would secure the nomination, and he was sure that Bristow was too much the loyal party member to accept an independent candidacy. "We must have a man who cares nothing for party or he will betray us," he declared, unaware that his words had far wider application than Bristow alone. Now Adams was willing to make the grand gesture. Convinced that the Democratic party was corrupt beyond redemption, even with Tilden, he hoped that the Independents' separate candidacy would lead to Tilden's victory and political deadlock. Seeking to recapture power, Republicans would have to court the Independents. Political necessity, Adams reasoned, would lead to reform. How realistic this was as a scenario was open to question. It was also irrelevant. Events were moving beyond Adams's control, and in fact Adams never really had control of events—he simply had the ear of Carl Schurz.[46]

Nor was it clear that Schurz was indeed listening. His previous interest in an independent candidacy had dissipated when he realized that it would be no more than a grand gesture. Accepting Tilden's nomination as probable, Schurz knew that while Democrats were always willing to use him, they would not welcome him into their ranks as an equal. All that remained for him, therefore, was a choice between trying to influence Republicans to nominate a candidate acceptable to him, pursue the futile hopes of an independent candidacy, or to stay on the sidelines. He found Bristow acceptable, but he was also intrigued when a letter from Rutherford B. Hayes's private secretary set forth the Ohio governor's reform credentials. There was one final consideration. Like Adams, Schurz wanted to be at the center of the action. He would embrace the Independent movement only if it followed him. Unlike Adams, however, Schurz had a following. Politicians respected his influence with German voters, although it was much exaggerated, since most German Catholics were Democrats. Schurz chose not to share this reality. Perhaps he might convince a Republican candidate inclined to appeal to reformers that he was the foremost representative of their cause, and thus gain influence and perhaps office. Both Schurz and Adams adopted strategies in line with their ambitions; the problem was that their ambitions differed, although they shared the common characteristic of advancing their own prospects.

To Schurz, then, Adams's insistence on holding a meeting of reformers after the Republican convention would not do. Adams wanted to hold the threat of a separate Independent candidacy over the heads of Republican delegates as they traveled to Cincinnati, hoping to induce them to accept Bristow. Schurz preferred to meet before the Republican convention, to make an open declaration of Independent aims; he also hoped to identify himself as the leader of the Independents for the benefit of prospective Republican nominees. With the experience of 1872 behind him, perhaps he knew better than Adams the chances for preserving Independent unity; in that instance, unity did not survive a specific choice. To caucus Independents after the Cincinnati convention might well reveal once more their disunity. After all, the very nature of Independent psychology made it almost impossible for them to act together as a group.

Schurz won out. He issued a call for "a free conference" of Independents at New York on May 15, 1876. Adams recognized his defeat. "We have now no leader nor organization," he grumbled to David A. Wells. The course of Bristow's supporters in pushing his candidacy within the Republican party was "cutting his and our throats." Nor was he pleased with Schurz's plan, doubting whether the conference would be "very weighty in character and influence." The Independents were not united over policy aims, and an indecisive result might well shatter the movement, which was already none too powerful in his eyes. "We are too weak to do more than profit by our enemy's blunders," Adams told Lodge. "If the enemy make no blunders, we are powerless and should do nothing. What is the use of exhibiting our feebleness?" Lacking confidence in the ability of reformers to mobilize public opinion, and frustrated with Schurz's assumption of leadership, Adams prepared to retreat into his accustomed role of critical outsider. Instead of attending the May 15 meeting, he relaxed at his summer home, leaving Lodge to keep him posted.[47]

At 3:15 P.M. on May 15, Lodge gaveled the Fifth Avenue Hotel meeting to order. He then read off a list of the delegates present, an impressive collection of professional men and patricians—though an unfriendly news-paperman preferred to characterize the assemblage as "men who had failed in literature and in life." Wells and Charles Francis Adams, Jr., were in the audience. Charles made a speech to the gathering and, with his customary modesty, proclaimed later, "It hit the mark and hard so that for a few hours I enjoyed the intoxication of oratory." The meeting appointed a committee headed by Schurz to draw up a list of resolutions, then adjourned for the night. The next day Schurz read the resolutions, which called on the major parties to nominate proven reformers or risk the loss of Independent sup-port. All notions of a third-party ticket were set aside—a fact made pain-fully clear when a motion to support Charles Francis Adams, Sr., for president met with silence.[48]

As Henry Adams predicted, the meeting decided little. The reformers still had to await the result of the Republican convention before they could act. At best, Schurz had identified himself as the spokesman of the group, which might serve his interests if not those of other Independents. Politi-cians scoffed at the descriptions of the meeting as public-spirited and com-posed of "the saving element in American politics," noting that these accounts were published in Independent papers. "Oh, they have reenacted the moral law and the Ten Commandments for a platform, and have demanded an angel of light for President," commented one Tammany ward leader. These cynical remarks perhaps went too far, for the reformers, as Adams had al-ready suggested, might have some success in denying certain foes a nomi-nation by promising to bolt in such a case. While Adams appreciated this, he still insisted that only truly independent action in the form of a third party would achieve lasting change. Despite his absence, the Adamses had made their mark. The *New York World* said that they were "certainly the *enfants terribles* of American politics."[49]

James G. Blaine, the front runner for the Republican nomination, al-most gave Adams the blunder he had been waiting for. In April, allegations appeared in several newspapers suggesting that Blaine had engaged in some dubious dealings with railroad stocks. Many of those reformers who had once leaned toward him now drew away in horror. Only a fortnight before the Republicans were to gather at Cincinnati, Blaine's oft-rumored dubious dealings in railroad stocks became the stuff of headlines when James Mulligan told a House subcommittee investigating the matter that he had in his pos-session letters from Blaine which revealed less than proper transactions in-volving the Little Rock and Fort Smith Railroad. As Adams saw it, "Blaine's nomination would now be a stroke of luck for us." He only regretted that these allegations had come to light before the convention, giving the Re-publicans the chance to nominate someone else. Desperate, Blaine moved quickly to save the situation. On June 5, he rose from his seat in the House and, in a melodramatic speech, asserted his innocence. While many applauded the speech as the vindication of a statesman, Henry Adams was not fooled. The speech, he thought, "matches for impudence and far exceeds in insolence" the testimony of the Reverend Henry Ward Beecher in the celebrated Beecher-Tilton adultery affair. Of course, these revelations could only help Bristow's candidacy. But Adams, who deep down did not want or expect Bristow's nomination, preferred to throw up his hands: "What a mess it all is! And how glad I am that I have not got to go to Cincinnati." He would sit and wait.[50]

The news from Cincinnati put a quick end to Independent unity. Having done their best to disavow Grant, many Republicans were not inclined to conduct an entire campaign devoted to defending Blaine's record. Bristow's supporters, unable to secure victory for their own man, were so determined to deny Blaine the top spot that they made a strange alliance with Grant's lieutenants Roscoe Conkling and Oliver P. Morton to defeat the man from Maine by promoting Rutherford B. Hayes, the winner of the 1875 gubernatorial race in Ohio. The impact of the Independents on the proceedings was minimal at best. They had not stopped Blaine; the Mulligan letters, Roscoe Conkling, and Oliver P. Morton had. Nevertheless, Hayes's nomination would seem to have been something of a victory for the Independents, for neither Blaine, Conkling, or Morton secured the nomination, while Hayes was inclined to reform. Henry Adams, however, did not share this assessment. He had always spoken against Hayes's candidacy, in part because he realized that Hayes appealed to reformers and thus imperiled Independent unity. Having counted on either supporting Bristow or battling Blaine, Independents instead had to look at someone Adams described as "a third rate nonentity, whose only recommendation is that he is obnoxious to no one." He now conceded that talk of a third party—his objective all along as a prerequisite for real change—was dead.[51]

Prospects for a realignment of parties, however slim, now faded. Schurz, true to form, hurried to Hayes's side, prodding the nominee to stress reform themes in his letter of acceptance. Other reformers, including Cox, welcomed Hayes's nomination as marking a new departure in the Republican party. Wells remained with Tilden. Adams grimaced at such maneuvers; his reaction suggests that he had wanted to go to "smashing things" with a third party. He begged Lodge to "try and preserve the organization," but his cry for unity was muffled by the stampede of Independents to the major parties. To his disgust, the movement "dissolved like a summer cloud," leaving him, as he sarcastically remaked, "smiling at the ruins."[52]

Adams threw in his lot with Democratic candidate Samuel Tilden, nominated by his party late in June. Tilden was a proven reformer in his eyes. "I too fought with Erie! And shall I now reject the leader who then led me to triumph!" he trumpeted, recalling their joint opposition to Jay Gould. There was little more than this emotional tie, for Adams candidly admitted that Tilden's stands on specie resumption and free trade were balanced by Hayes's avowal of civil service reform and his pledge of justice to all—including whites—in the South. He believed that Tilden was a more skilled leader and a more sincere reformer than Hayes—both questionable assumptions—leaving him little choice but to support the New Yorker: "Indeed after chattering for years about voting for the best man without regard to party, I cannot well do otherwise." Recalling his previous remarks about the corrupt nature of the Democrats, he modified his previous sentiments by expressing the hope that a Tilden victory would give the Democrats "some principles and some brains, and so force the Republicans to a higher level." To add to the excitement, several months later Massachusetts Democrats nominated Adams's father for governor. But Henry's interests, as usual, were limited. "Both parties are impossibly corrupt and the public thoroughly indifferent," he explained to Gaskell. The talk of buying a newspaper ceased. Adopting his characteristic pose of resignation, he concluded: "Others therefore may rush into the fray. I shall read history."[53]

Even as he enlisted under Tilden's banner, Adams criticized his fellow Independents for dashing for cover beneath the major parties like "discreetly clad clergymen caught out in a thunderstorm without any umbrellas." Schurz had outrun the pack in his haste to help Hayes. Adams bitterly called him a "mere will-o'-the wisp" and sarcastically hoped that Schurz would be rewarded with a cabinet office. He observed that his colleagues were also vulnerable to "the torrent of partisanship" and that the Independent movement was merely a "rope of sand." Disgusted, he sat back to watch the campaign unfold, scornfully noting how "on each side the old issues and the old forces stand without pretense of reform and idiotically pound at each other and at everyone who does not get out of their way." He expressed his lack of interest over which reformers supported each candidate, for, as he told Lodge, they would "crack . . . heads reciprocally." He dismissed his own preference for Tilden, noting that "the tendency to blackguard the Adamses generally" had become an American political tradition, along with parades and torchlight rallies: "As we shall catch it equally whether we vote for Hayes or Tilden or not at all, we can afford to grin at it."[54]

Adams grew so apathetic that he confided to Lodge that he would "shut my mouth on politics." This inspired promise lasted three days at most, but in despair he claimed that "politics have ceased to interest me." Not only had his conception of a "part of the center" been aborted, but his bid to exercise political influence had failed once more: "I am satisfied that the machine can't be smashed this time. As I feared, we have ourselves saved it by a foolish attempt to run it, which we never shall succeed in." Had Lodge, who had worked tirelessly for the movement, been malicious, he could have replied that it was doubly hard to run the machine if one expected to do it from a seashore cottage north of Boston. No doubt Adams was not the only one cheered by his decision "to leave this greatest of American problem to shrewder heads than mine."[55]

As the Independent movement dissipated, so did Henry Adams's political ambitions. Having asserted that he was at the forefront of a new movement to unite men of intelligence, breeding, and ability, he discovered that few of his fellow reformers shared his vision or ambition. Fuming at the inability of his peers to understand that party organizations obstructed reform, he decided to express his disgust in the October number of the *North American Review*. "Of course I must have my little say," he told Gaskell, as he prepared to deliver another blow at democracy. The issue would be "a historical monument" to the death of republican institutions at the hands of political parties. It would also be the last monument constructed by Adams within the pages of the *Review*, for he planned "to avail myself of a trifling disagreement with the publishers to throw off that load also and get rid of my editorial duties leaving my monument behind me." The publishers, afraid that Adams's increasingly strident political views would alienate potential clients, told him to tone down his opinions or else. Adams chose to retire.[56]

Adams carefully planned his farewell. Despite his preoccupation with reading galley proofs of a set of essays written by the members of his graduate seminar, including himself, and with being "buried in avalanches of State Papers . . . such gay reading," he gave close attention to the content of his last issue. He would salute Grantism with a pulverizing barrage of criticism. An article on Reconstruction would present the case for the restoration of "home rule" to white Southerners. General William B. Hazen promised to plumb the depths of corruption in the War Department's handling of post traderships under the disgraced Belknap. And Adams eagerly awaited Henry Van Ness Boynton's article on the "Whisky Ring," for Boynton was a loyal supporter of Bristow who had already demonstrated a sharp partisan pen in attacking William T. Sherman's memoirs.[57]

Boynton did not disappoint, turning in an unabashed defense of Bristow's behavior. However, Adams wanted to make the "political moral"—"that in the struggle for reform the country must expect to have both party organizations against it"—clear to the reader. He urged Lodge to prod Boynton to "add another page" stating "*in the strongest possible language*" that reform must strike "at the root of party organizations themselves and cut off *all* their sources of political corruption." Such an addition would "make this article tally with the tone of the number." Boynton followed the advice, to some extent, in calling for a purer form of politics and civil service reform. But Adams, unable to restrain himself to merely pointing the cannon, chose to fire the loudest charge himself. In the aftermath of the Hayes nomination, he revealed to Lodge that "my brother Charles and I plan to concoct a political article together." Since this issue would be his last, he felt no need to hold back any more. Having failed to persuade his fellow reformers to do it his way in the past, he proposed a final lecture on reform politics. "The 'Independents' in the Canvass" was to be his last declaration of political principles. It was the feature article of the October issue. Although it was unsigned, any discerning reader knew that it was the handiwork of Charles and Henry Adams.[58]

The authors offered a survey of the political terrain that made clear their disgust. The Republican party had once contained "a very considerable preponderance of the political virtue and intelligence, and of the disinterested public spirit of the community." With the party's initial tasks of preserving the Union and abolishing slavery accomplished, however, these men had given way to men "who never knew what a principle was." The Democratic party provided an equally grim sight: "Into it had drifted the great mass of the political ignorance, corruption, and venality of the free States" which rendered it "utterly unable . . . to originate a policy or to conduct a respectable opposition." Only Republican ineptitude and corruption had allowed it to survive. Neither party was the proper home for high-minded gentlemen with notions of reform.[59]

To the Adams brothers, Reconstruction was a complete disaster. Republicans had clearly "overstepped the bounds of moderation" in undertaking a policy based on "preconceived theories which were wholly at variance with actual facts." Never having been south of Virginia, a state that had escaped much of Reconstruction, the Adamses chose to rely on the accounts of white Southerners as the "actual facts." They supported the efforts of Southern Democrats "to throw off the odious rule of the enfranchised Africans." After all, they gravely asserted, it was "indisputable fact that peace and quiet and good-will between the races" had been achieved in "redeemed" states. The "sensible" black (assuming there were any) "should pray . . . to be let alone by his 'protectors' at Washington," who were "the most dangerous enemies the freedmen have had." Following the recommendations of white Southerners, Democrats, and many fellow reformers, the Adamses hoped that blacks would be allowed "as quietly and speedily" as possible to resume their "natural relations" with Southern white society. In support of this aim, they asserted that the "position and prospects" of blacks in redeemed states "are infinitely preferable" to their situation in states still under Republican control.[60]

Such comments on Reconstruction reflected how far the Adams family had drifted from the days of John Quincy Adams—although perhaps the family's interest in antislavery had never quite been the deep commitment that others made it out to be, and had never included a heartfelt concern for the fate of the slaves. The Adams brothers' assessment was little more than a brief for white supremacy and Redemption, revealing deep-seated racism. They showed no interest in terrorism against blacks and their white allies either as an act of inhumanity or as a violation of law and order. Indeed, they did not care. Not all reformers shared this apathy, but it was a sad fact that many of them did. In their minds, Reconstruction simply got in the way of more important issues. In fact, one of the prime examples of the corruption of the Grant administration in their eyes was its Reconstruction policy. It violated scientific law because it was based upon the assumption that blacks deserved an equal opportunity to advance in society and to participate in politics—the former was a fancy, and the latter was a crime in light of black inferiority. It threatened representative government and federalism because it resulted in the expansion of federal powers and the use of force to put down disorder—although the behavior of white Southerners had provided the necessity for both. It was not reform; it was corruption—suggesting the limited sense in which they employed these terms. And, in any case, Reconstruction would soon be over—in part because of the apathy of Northern whites such as the brothers Adams.

Henry and Charles preferred to discuss the "living questions" at stake: civil service, the currency, and tariff reform. The major parties failed to satisfy the requirements of reformers. The Republicans had not enacted their platform professions in favor of specie resumption, civil service reform, and tariff reduction. President Grant, the Adamses pointed out, was not solely to blame for these failings, for Congress had broken down Grant's "weak" attempts at reform. Surprising as this statement may seem coming from any Adams, Henry and Charles designed it to counter delusions that without Grant, the Republicans would naturally become the reformer's party once more. The Democrats were little better, offering only the slightest hope for tariff reduction. Both platforms were "unadulterated rubbish"; no discerning citizen should "attach the slightest weight to them."[61]

Since national politics was bankrupt, men who refused to consider political life as a job were naturally drawn to the Independent movement. The May 15 meeting was "the first important act of the campaign," attended by "men who cared little for office and who were deeply dissatisfied with existing political conditions." The Adamses asserted that these men "had behind them a large constituency," although the authors wisely offered no proof. Lacking a common program, the movement collapsed in the face of the major party nominations, "which made outside action practically impossible." The authors mocked the speed with which Independents, in rushing to choose sides, had destroyed any chance of united action. They failed to consider that such behavior gave the lie to their characterization of the

Fifth Avenue Conference as a gathering of noble public-spirited men "who cared little for office." Perhaps the Independent movement was unable to act in unity precisely because it was composed of men who prided themselves on their independence.[62]

The Independent movement had committed suicide. The Adams brothers dismissed the death as inevitable and chose instead to instruct the "Independent Voter" on how to behave, both in the immediate contest and in the future, by establishing guidelines of conduct. The "Independent Voter" had to dismiss campaign rhetoric as claptrap. He had to "hold parties to a rigid and absolute adherence to their professions; and when they fall short of those professions, he must do what he can to defeat them, regardless of consequences." How he was to "hold parties to a rigid and absolute adherence to their professions" while ignoring party rhetoric and meaningless platforms, the two major sources of party professions, the authors did not say. One should vote for men with known political beliefs tested in public office—an indication that the dark horse Hayes did not deserve reformers' votes, although in fact Hayes was a three-time governor and former congressman whose beliefs were well-known.[63]

In the long run, Independents had to remain outside of party organizations to achieve their goals. They had to support the candidate and party which "offers the best chance for obtaining reform." Obviously Henry had won out over Charles on this point. No more insurgent movements; no more worry about "battling it out within the party." The argument made a virtue out of the reformers' inability to play the game by refusing to play it.

And what were the goals of Independents? The Adamses graciously outlined a comprehensive agenda of reform for all to follow. All government officials below cabinet level "shall hold their appointments during good behavior," ending the patronage system. An immediate return to specie payments would put an end to a fluctuating financial system which "tends to shake the foundations of public morals." Tighter administration and revision of the internal revenue laws would cut off "the most scandalous and the vilest" source of party support. Finally, the concept of protection embodied in the tariff system must be abandoned.[64]

Henry and Charles Adams were aware that not all reformers shared these aims. They reminded their readers that the true goal of reform was "not currency reform, not revenue reform, not administrative reform, but all these only so far as they tend to result in political reform." To individual reformers who might quibble over details, the authors dogmatically declared that "if one part of the old system goes, all must go, and the reform movement will either be fruitless or it will carry out its principles to the end." The Independents should be intent on "purifying the political practice." Underlying this visionary and somewhat vague goal was the realization that reformers were often divided over specific reforms. A general goal might preserve unity.[65]

Offering the means to achieve this overarching objective, the authors sounded Henry Adams's favorite theme. Reformers must pledge eternal "resistance to the corruptions of our political system" perpetuated by greedy political parties. Parties were the source of the problem. Their search for self-preservation and power fomented corruption. They had distorted the intent of the Constitution. Reformers had to "cut up these evils by the roots." The now-familiar indictment followed. The Senate was "the fortress of party organization and the focus of party intrigue." The nation needed a president willing to do battle with the Senate, although such a struggle might "shake our political system to its center." The contest would entail "many years of incessant struggle, and probably more than one serious political crisis." But it had to be done. Unless the juggernaut of corruption propelled by political parties was halted, "our political system must break down and some new experiment must be substituted in its place." Americans had to be "ready to go back to the early practice of the government" before parties had shorn the nation of its dignity. It would be a battle worthy of the Founding Fathers.[66]

Thus, Charles and Henry Adams advocated the election of Samuel J. Tilden, but for somewhat perverse reasons. Hayes appeared naive and unaware of the difficulty of the task before him. If elected, he had to look to men like Blaine and Conkling for support; otherwise, he would be a president without a party and would ultimately fail. Tilden's election, on the other hand, would ensure the eventual triumph of reform principles. A Democratic president pitted against a Republican Senate would surely ignite the long-awaited battle over control of the patronage. Reformers could rest content if Tilden's entire term were spent reducing the Senate "to its proper constitutional functions"—a declaration that recalled Henry Adams's recommended agenda for Ulysses S. Grant back in 1869. In opposition for the first time in nearly two decades, the Republican party would inevitably pass through a "preliminary hardening and solidifying of opinion" that would create a party determined to pursue reform. Since this change was inevitable, the authors spared themselves from explaining how it would occur. They did not consider that while the Democratic party had been out of power for sixteen years, it had not adopted reform. Sooner or later, the Republicans would regain power and repair the republic. It all seemed so simple.[67]

"The 'Independents' in the Canvass" is instructive as a measure of what Henry Adams had—and had not—learned about American politics. He had lost faith in party platforms and campaign promises. Political amateurs were not up to the task: that had to be left to the experienced hands of reform-minded professional politicians. But the consistency of Adams's beliefs was striking. He continued to dismiss Reconstruction as irrelevant, although the issue had played a major role in American politics and would continue to do so even after the end of federal intervention. That it was relevant was also evident to large numbers of blacks and whites whose lives hinged on its outcome, but then Henry Adams had no time and even less concern for them. He spoke of the "large constituency" which reformers represented, but where was it on election day? Whom did reformers represent but themselves? His traditional hatred of the Senate and of political parties was still there, as were his three policy concerns of civil service, tariff, and currency reform. All Adams could show for eight years of political education was to say that while reform was potentially strong politically, divisions among reformers crippled it as an effective issue. The only solution he could offer Independents was to act as a united bloc. Since both parties were corrupt, and would become more so if reformers followed his advice and withdrew from party ranks, this was a weak reed indeed.

Still more revealing is the article's discussion of the presidency. Intended to demonstrate Hayes's naiveté, it revealed that an element of realism had crept into Adams's thought. A president was not, "as so many seem to suppose, an autocrat ruling the nation . . . by his own supreme will." He was "merely" the chief executive, "with very limited powers, who must look somewhere for support, if his administration is not to result in ignominious failure." More specifically, a president "has got to have a party behind him, or fail." He had to be willing to distribute offices (especially cabinet posts) among the party leaders to gain their support. To undertake a reform of the civil service in the face of this fact was "no trifling task."[68]

Perhaps brother Charles wrote this section, for it would be difficult to attribute these insights to Henry Adams. After all, Henry had tried and convicted Grant as a weak president for turning to his party for support in exchange for patronage while lending civil service reform only half-hearted support. It is difficult to reconcile Henry's emphasis on the limited power of the presidency, designed to highlight Hayes's credulity about the possibility of reform, with his criticism of Grant's decision to work within those limits, even if it were toward ends which Henry did not approve. Perhaps the very exaggeration rooted in partisanship that Henry deplored in others explains his treatment of Grant; perhaps it was the fact that he had come to hate Grant as the embodiment of all that he despised in American politics, and as the major obstacle to Henry's own political future. If so, the political education Adams received was a most flawed one, not least because it had failed to force him to engage in a little bit of honest introspection.

With this article, Henry Adams bade politics farewell. For all his talk about reform being a long and bitter fight, he had had enough of it. An

Adams was accustomed to leading a movement; otherwise, he must leave it. The fiasco of 1876 merely confirmed his feelings of helplessness and despair. No matter which candidate was declared the winner, reform had suffered another staggering defeat. Hayes's triumph, while it brought to power men like Schurz and Evarts, was so tainted that Adams could not give the new administration more "than a silent and temporary sympathy." It merely illustrated "the way politics work: always unsatisfactorily." Instead of transforming the political system, the reformers had been absorbed by it. The nominations of Hayes and Tilden might please Independents, but they also destroyed any notion of true reform through the overthrow of the existing system, a goal Adams had sought to achieve with the establishment of a third party.[69]

Politics were not the only thing Adams found disappointing. Boston continued to bore him: "There is no society worth the name, no wit, no intellectual energy or competition, no clash of minds or of schools, no interests, no masculine self-assertion or ambition." He was equally frustrated by his teaching career, a pale substitute for political office. Stripped of his editorship of the *North American Review*, he did not look forward to putting all his energies into teaching, for the "grind at the University wheel" held no charms for him. He took to being "foul and abusive" in hopes of driving students out of his classes. Tired with "mere railing at the idiocies of a university education," he finally quit.[70]

Resigned to political failure, Henry Adams sought to rationalize it. He claimed he disliked the life of a politician; in any case, he was too principled (and too cranky) to engage in political bargaining. Besides, he told Gaskell, he was now convinced that "literature offers higher prizes than politics." It was time to try history instead. He planned to return to Washington, but not as a politician. With Evarts installed as secretary of state under Hayes, Adams had free access, not to political power, but to the archives of the State Department. It would have to suffice.[71]

CHAPTER SIX

FAILURE

As far as he had a function in life, it was as stable-
companion to statesmen, whether they liked it or not.
The Education of Henry Adams

"To me, politics have been the single uncompensated disappointment of life—pure waste of energy and moral," Henry Adams concluded in 1888. Of course, he had failed to obtain office, but it was never clear that he sought it. He was far more disappointed by his failure to exercise influence on policy and politics, especially in his endeavor to elevate the conduct and purposes of American politics by restoring control of the government to an educated elite. His high ideals of elite management of American life had come to naught; he was left to find what little solace he could as a caustic Mugwump, often wishing success to whichever party appeared the more earnest in its desire to complete the destruction of the republic.[1]

In a letter to Henry Cabot Lodge, himself an aspiring Massachusetts Republican, Adams tried to dissuade him from running for Congress by claiming that politics destroyed one's integrity. In the process, he revealed his own disillusionment. He had never known "a young man go into politics who was not the worse for it." Honest men "became disappointed and bitter," while dishonest men "lose self-respect" in their pursuit of power. Public service, he concluded in typical Adams family fashion, should be viewed as "a disagreeable necessity. The satisfaction should consist in getting out of it."[2]

Yet Adams did not heed his own admonition. He was reluctant to let go of reform politics. In the 1880s he became a stockholder in the *New York Evening Post*, a reform organ run by E. L. Godkin, Carl Schurz, and Horace White. For several years, he tried to advise Godkin on editorial policy without result. When Grover Cleveland disappointed reformers by appointing New York politico Daniel Manning to head the Treasury Department in 1885, Adams, insisting once more that the Treasury was the key post in any administration, criticized Godkin for approving the selection. Godkin merrily went his own way, and Adams was left alone to declare, "Independents are not fools. They have borne many bitter disappointments, and can bear one more." The old yearnings manifested themselves in other ways as well. In 1881, Adams confided to Godkin that "if I were ten years younger, I would write some political sketches" for the *Evening Post*; his jest after Garfield's death that he would go to Washington "to try for an office under the new man," preferably in the diplomatic service, sounded all too much like a revival of his own frustrated ambitions. Adams's advice to Lodge, given two months later, revealed that his failure still rankled. If he could not succeed, no one else should try.[3]

Adams remained bitter over his frustrated ambition for the rest of his life. "When I think of the formulas of our youth," he wrote Gaskell in 1894, "when I look at my old set of John Stuart Mill,—and suddenly recall that I am actually a member of the Cobden Club,—I feel that somewhere there is the biggest kind of a joke, if I could only see it." He held most politicians in contempt. "I always feel a very active sentiment of personal antipathy to politicians," he explained to one of his old English friends, "and rarely fail to tell them so." ("This results in winning their cordial aversion to a surprising degree," he acknowledged.) He scorned the success of others: "I always thought political power the most barren of all forms of success," he asserted in a letter to Wayne MacVeagh, Garfield's attorney general. He scoffed at reformers who remained in the fight. They "lie and manoeuvre just like candidates for office," he told Godkin in 1881.[4] Politics corrupted all who engaged in it, or so it seemed. Adams's escape was all the more miraculous because he had so dearly wanted power.

Writing to his brother Charles in 1903, Adams expressed surprise that they and their peers had not done better in life: "We started ahead of everybody. I suspect the loss of our best four years in the war had something to do with it. The infernal ten-year reaction must have thrown out a number more." His own shortcomings were particularly disturbing. Although "we were educated politically," the Adams brothers had failed to exercise political power. Even as Theodore Roosevelt sat in the White House, Adams concluded, "Reform proved a total loss."[5]

But Adams, displaying the morbid side of the family heritage, could not simply bury his disappointed political ambitions. Like a coroner, he wanted to know the reasons for their demise. He could not escape the fact that he had failed. Even when he looked out of the window of his house on Lafayette Square toward the White House, he found his view blocked by the statue of the supposed originator of the spoils system, that old family foe, Andrew Jackson. But he could not let go of his interest in politics, either. In part, Adams's career as a historian, novelist, and author of the *Education* was an attempt to understand his failure by setting it in a broader context. In his work he sought to explore the relationships between private ethics and public life, between knowledge and power, as he tried to discern the direction of American democracy.[6]

In *The Life of Albert Gallatin* (1879), Adams used his subject to illustrate both the promise of elite rule and the fate of the public-spirited, disinterested man of intellect and learning in American politics. Gallatin "aimed at providing for and guiding the moral and material of a new era,—a fresh race of men." Adams envied Gallatin's "good fortune" at entering "public life at a time when both parties believed that principles were at stake." Such an environment enabled Gallatin to seize the leadership of the Jeffersonian Republicans "by the sheer force of ability and character, without ostentation and without the tricks of popularity." Gallatin and his fellow Republicans ultimately failed to prevent the advent of corruption, poisoning the ideal republic they hoped to establish, "due chiefly to the fact that they put too high an estimate upon human nature." Adams explained that Gallatin soon resigned himself to the inevitable. By 1815, Gallatin's "statesmanship had become, what practical statesmanship always has and must become, a mere struggle to deal with concrete facts at the cost of philosophic and *a priori* principles." He "knew better how to accept defeat and adapt himself to circumstances, how to abandon theory and to move with his generation."[7]

As Adams penned these words, he must have reflected on how Gallatin's decision compared with his own choice to withdraw from politics rather than make compromises. Adams could have been looking in the mirror when he described Gallatin's appearance: "the shrewd and slightly humorous expression of the mouth; the most fluent and agreeable talker of his time was still the most laborious analyzer and silent observer; the consciousness of personal superiority was more strongly apparent than ever, but the man had lost control over events and his confidence in results; he had become a critic, and, however genial and conscientious his criticism might be, he had a deeper sense of isolation. . . ."[8]

Adams made no secret of his admiration for Gallatin. He told Samuel J. Tilden that the biography "was a labor of love": "For combination of ability, integrity, knowledge, unselfishness, and social fitness Mr. Gallatin has no equal. He was the most fully and perfectly equipped statesman we can show." To Lodge he explained that "the moral of his life lies a little deeper than party politics." Gallatin was a symbol of the "inevitable isolation and disillusionment of a really strong mind—one that combines force with elevation." Adams doubtless thought this description fit himself as well. Some twenty years later, Adams recalled that he had shown Gallatin "a respect and devotion that I never thought proper to show my own kith."[9]

If *Gallatin* showed Henry Adams as he wanted to be remembered, his

John Randolph (1882) showed him as many would remember him. Most critics of *Randolph* point to it as a veiled attacked on the South and on an old antagonist of the Adams family. However, the reader is also struck by the basic similarities between author and subject. Like Adams, Randolph "had an immense family connection, which gave him confidence and a sense of power, from his birth surrounded by a society in itself an education." The Virginian's mind "was restless and uneasy, prone to contradiction and attached to paradox." Here appeared to be a young man of intelligence and ability, born into a society that he could one day expect to lead. Unfortunately for Randolph, he "was born just as the downward plunge began, and every moment made the outlook drearier and more awful."[10]

Unaware of the fate in store for him, Randolph prepared himself to guide the course of the young republic. He sided with the Jeffersonian Republicans in their struggle to overthrow the Federalist oligarchy. Adams observed "how solemnly these young reformers of 1800 believed in themselves and in their reforms," no doubt remembering his own yesterdays. When Randolph perceived that his party was violating its precepts in practice, he went into open opposition, becoming a doomsayer. His tactics were legendary; he could "pour out a continuous stream of vituperation in well-chosen language and with sparkling illustration." The book's final sentence spoke to both men's political careers: "Time misspent, and faculties misemployed, and senses jaded by labor or impaired by excess, cannot be recalled."[11]

Adams had originally planned to complete his trilogy of American politicians with a study of Aaron Burr for the *American Statesmen Series.* While Adams thought that Randolph was "the type of a political charlatan who had something in him," Burr was "the type of a political charlatan pure and simple, a very Jim Crow of melodramatic wind-bags. I have something to say of both types." Gallatin, Randolph, and Burr provided three perspectives from which to view the impact of party on American politics. Men of principle must either compromise their ideals, as Gallatin had done, or become ineffectual, carping critics, as Randolph had. Only men like Burr could thrive in a world of murky morals which rewarded pragmatism, not abstract principle. John T. Morse, editor of the series, turned down the Burr manuscript on the grounds that Burr did not merit inclusion in a series celebrating successful American politicians. "Houghton declines to print Aaron because Aaron wasn't a 'Statesman,'" Adams grumbled to John Hay. "He should live awhile at Washington and know our *real* statesmen."[12] Eventually, Adams decided to forgo publishing his Burr sketch, although he probably used it in writing his *History.*

Closer to home, Adams's first novel, *Democracy* (1880), examined the state of American politics after the Civil War. The central theme of the novel, embodied in one sentence, is uttered by Madeleine Lee, the novel's protagonist as well as Adams's alter ego: "I must know whether America is right or wrong." In search of the answer, the widowed Mrs. Lee travels to Washington to observe and understand American politics from the vantage point of—where else?—a house on Lafayette Square. There, she meets Senator Silas P. Ratcliffe, the "Prairie Giant of Peonia"—a figure taken to represent James G. Blaine with a dash of Roscoe Conkling and a sprinkling of images of half a dozen other senators. He is intent on taking hold of his party and its new president, who is known as the "Hoosier Quarryman" (the "Galena Tanner"?), "a noble type of man, perhaps the very noblest that had appeared to adorn the country since the incomparable Washington"— a description much like the one of Ulysses S. Grant in the *Education*. In fact, Ratcliffe becomes—what else?—secretary of the treasury under the new president. Mrs. Lee finds herself attracted to Ratcliffe, for reasons that have as much to do with the power he possesses as with his personal qualities. She is about to marry him when she discovers that he had once received a bribe in exchange for his approval of a subsidy to a steamship company. Faced with Ratcliffe's corruption, she turns down his offer of marriage and flees to the Nile, where the Adamses had honeymooned in 1872.[13]

Throughout *Democracy*, Adams ridiculed American politics. The Senate "was a place where people went to recite speeches," and one naively assumed that "the speeches were useful and had a purpose. . . . This is a very common conception of Congress; many Congressmen share it." Senators had "a boundless and guileless thirst for flattery" and were filled with assurances of their innate superiority. The American politician, as represented by Ratcliffe, had no sense of ethics or morals: he "talked about virtue and vice as a man who is color-blind talks about red and green." After all, was not "democracy, rightly understood, . . . the government of the people, by the people, for the benefit of senators?" Even reformers were fit subjects for Adams's abuse, as represented by Congressman C. C. French, "who aspired to act the part of the educated gentleman in politics and to verify the public tone." French possessed "an unfortunately conceited manner" and made "playful but ungainly attempts at wit" in society. "Rather wealthy, rather clever, rather well-educated, rather honest and rather vulgar," French, like Adams, was "always bubbling with the latest political gossip."[14]

But there was a more serious side to *Democracy*, embodied in an exchange between Mrs. Lee and Senator Ratcliffe over civil service reform. Ratcliffe challenged Mrs. Lee to ask other senators "what chance there is for your Reforms so long as the American citizen is what he is." At one point, Mrs. Lee asked him, "Are we forever to be at the mercy of thieves and ruffians? Is a responsible government impossible in a democracy?" Ratcliffe's reply is revealing and instructive. "No representative government can long be much better or much worse than the society it represents," he answered. "Purify society and you purify the government. But try to purify the government artificially and you only aggravate failure." As this exchange suggests, Adams had turned his attention to the social basis of American democracy. *Democracy* argued that American democracy, while giving free rein to the material instincts of Americans, did not elevate their morals.[15]

"The antics of Presidents and Senators had been amusing—so amusing that she had nearly been persuaded to take part in them": thus Adams, through Mrs. Lee, looked back at his political career. Mrs. Lee had come to Washington for one purpose: "What she wanted was POWER." But she could not abandon her principles. Ratcliffe had told her, "In politics we cannot keep our hands clean." She (and Adams) decided in favor of clean hands, but only after some thought: she did not break off with Ratcliffe after he revealed to her his role in altering election returns in his state during the Civil War, a sign of the war's impact upon public morals. In the end, however, Madeleine Lee confessed: "The idea of my purifying politics is absurd."[16]

As with his political biographies, Adams used *Democracy* to explore the problem of morality in political life. When one of the book's characters inquired about the progress of Madeleine Lee's political education, she responded, "I have got so far as to lose the distinction between right and wrong. Isn't that the first step in politics?" This time, Adams moved beyond this level of analysis to explore the dilemma of the reformer in politics. Ratcliffe explained the dilemma most clearly in a conversation with Mrs. Lee:

"And yet you are a hard critic, Mrs. Lee. If your thoughts are what you say, your words are not. You judge with the judgment of abstract principles, and you wield the bolts of divine justice. You look on and condemn, but you refuse to acquit. When I come to you on the verge of what is likely to be the fatal plunge of my life, and ask you only for some clue to the moral principle that ought to guide men, you look on and say that virtue is its own reward. And you do not even say where virtue lies. . . . Duty is duty, for you as well as for me. I have a right to the help of all pure minds. You have no right to refuse it. How *can* you reject your own responsibility and hold me to mine?"

This was one of the virtues of *Democracy*. If Adams ended by terming politicians one of the "criminal classes," he still made an honest effort to understand the politician's point of view. If it was not exactly Olympian detachment, it was an improvement.[17]

That Adams chose a woman as his central figure was no accident, either. Women could neither run for office nor vote—and were thus denied participation in electoral politics. But women could advise, as both Madeleine Lee and Henry Adams sought to do. Both sought an education in politics by going to Washington, and both abandoned the enterprise—although at least Mrs. Lee spurned an offer of marriage to the system, while no one popped a similar question to Adams, the unrequited suitor for influence in government. Moreover, by playing on prevailing images of women as the incorruptible, arbiters of morality, Adams sharpened his portrayal of American politics as immoral and corrupt.

If *Democracy* was the story of Adams's political career, its reception epitomized it. The novel's success was due to his pointed sarcasm and acid characterizations of Washington life, not to his message about the fate of American democracy. He amused and shocked his readers once more, but the impact, as always, was temporary. The guessing game over the identities of the characters and the author merely made manifest Adams's failure to do more than entertain his readers. He could not make them reflect over the fate of the republic. All he evoked were giggles and disgust. In more recent years, the novel has enjoyed a resurgence in popularity among scholars, who accept Adams's perspective and content themselves with looking over his shoulder, rarely pausing to number themselves as part of the society that Adams chose to examine.[18]

Adams returned to a historical approach with the *History of the United States during the Administrations of Thomas Jefferson and James Madison*. It located the beginning of the end with Thomas Jefferson's ascent to the presidency—an idea especially appealing to an Adams. Jefferson and his followers failed to shape the growth of the republic because they violated their principles freely in domestic policy while blindly embracing them in foreign policy. That the republic had survived Jefferson and Madison was due not to their farsighted statesmanship but to material advantages which compensated for their incompetency. The lesson was inescapable. Social and economic development would proceed apace, regardless of attempts by government to control and guide it. The republic would fall victim to its own inability to govern itself. "What object, besides physical content, must a democratic continent aspire to attain?" he asked in the last chapter. If Adams could not understand the progress of evolution from President Washington to President Grant, he found the course of devolution from President Jefferson to President Grant all too clear.[19]

Finally, there is *The Education of Henry Adams*. Replete with irony and paradox, the *Education* has provided much food for thought, including the bitter taste of Adams's political failure. Adams reserves his strongest sarcasm for his discussion of American politics, one of the most vivid themes in the work. He claimed that the great failure of the American policy was its inability to create "a working political system" suited to the needs of the Gilded Age. The Constitution had collapsed, "and with it the eighteenth-century fabric of a priori, or moral, principles. Politicians had tacitly given it up. Grant's administration marked the avowal." Men wasted their time "on expedients to piece out—to patch—or, in vulgar language, to tinker—the political machine as often as it broke down." Inevitably, the present system would become "the clumsiest—the most inefficient." The republic of the Founding Fathers was dead.[20]

And Ulysses S. Grant—the savior of the Union—had destroyed it. "A great soldier might be a baby politician," Adams concluded. The president was "a defiance of first principles." He upset Darwinism: "He should have been extinct for the ages." His administration "outraged every rule of ordinary decency, . . . wrecked men by the thousands, but profited few." Worst of all, said Adams, Grant "had shipwrecked his career." Despite this overwhelming indictment of Grant and his times, Adams still felt compelled to offer an explanation for his failure to gain influence. Anticipating the question of why he never held office, Adams "preferred to answer simply that no President had ever invited him to fill one." Besides, he "saw no office that he wanted," and reasoned that "he was likely to be a more useful citizen without office." This was playing with the reader, for Adams had not sought office so much as he desired to exercise influence over those who held office. He denied his ambition even as he damned Grant for thwarting it. Forced to choose, he claimed, between his moral principles and his interests, he went with principle. He then waited for the reader to applaud.[21]

This begs the question. Why blame Grant—or anyone or anything—for stifling Henry Adams's career if Adams cared so little for politics? Adams could neither come to terms with his own ambition nor take any real responsibility for his failure. The *Education* becomes a form of special pleading. While Adams continually claimed in the work that he was a failure, he suggested that it was not his fault, that he had not really failed. Measured by any other standards than his own, his life was indeed a success. But he himself preferred to argue that it was a failure beyond his control to salvage. Time and again, when Adams had to make a decision—joining the army, going to Harvard in 1870—he asserted that the choice was made for him by others, just as John Quincy Adams had once forced him to go to school against his will. In short, Henry Adams refused to take responsibility for his own life and his own failure.

The *Education* revealed far more about Henry Adams's disappointment with his world than it did about the world in which he was disappointed. In the process, it produced a distorted picture disguised as a balanced perspective on the politics of post-Civil-War America. To be sure, here and there appeared insights into the need to find new ways to govern in a time of change, but Adams failed to offer a sustained analysis of the problems presented by the emerging order. Instead, he embarked on a pseudo-scientific discussion about laws and science, force and energy, knowledge and ignorance, in rambling passages which his admirers have mistaken for profundity. That these impersonal and uncontrollable forces would have appeared to relieve Grant and his contemporaries of responsibility for the fate of the republic never occurred to him; if it had, we would have been deprived of the entertainment provided by his most quotable descriptions. As Robert Dawidoff has put it, "*The Education* always has it Adams's own way; that is what autobiography is for."[22]

That the *Education* had provided an accurate rendering of events even Adams was prepared to deny. "I have no scruple, in my own theories, about handling my material in the view of a climax, and for artistic purposes, the climax must always tend to tragedy," he said.[23] He read too much significance into his own experiences, transforming them into cosmic symbols where none existed. He was either unwilling or unable to accept personal responsibility for his fate. Rather, he preferred to blame in turn his "education" for rendering him unfit for the world, and the world for falling away from the model for which his education had prepared him. It is not an appealing picture.

Failure was the central theme of Henry Adams's life. He railed at humankind's inability to reconcile science and art, reason and faith, material improvement and spiritual fulfillment. He judged both his society and himself failures. While these themes have intrigued Adams scholars, few have given serious thought to the nature of Adams's failure in politics. Rather, both Adams's prime proponents and critics, mostly intellectuals and scholars themselves, divide into two camps: those who take Adams's side bemoan the lack of intellect in the American polity and society, while those who criticize him often simply accept that absence as a fact of life and ridicule Adams's failure to accept reality. In either case, these commentators usually accept Adams's basic premise about the nature of American political life. By setting the terms of the debate in the *Education*, Adams had already taken the first trick. "The more educated Americans become, the more they read Henry Adams; the more educated they become, the more they see things as he told them they would," Dawidoff observes. "The more readers Henry Adams has, the more things become like they seemed to him."[24]

To define Adams's political failure solely in terms of his failure to obtain political office is to miss the point. Adams's political ambitions transcended mere office. His aim was to establish an elite of talent and education to guide the nation. To frame the issue in these terms makes Adams's failure significant beyond himself. It raises the question of why the United States did not develop a governing elite based on intellect who could resolve the problems of an emerging industrial order. As Adams himself put it in 1869: "The great problem of every system of Government has been to place administration and legislation in the hands of the best men. We have tried our formula and found that it has failed in consequence of its clashing with our other fundamental principle that one man is as good as another."[25] Grant's presidency did nothing to alter Adams's analysis.

In Adams's case, one can ask what he proposed to do had he succeeded in obtaining power and position. Civil service reform, free trade, and specie resumption might have become a reality. But would these in themselves have rescued the republic? Or was Adams more interested in forming a new American state, an act which would make clear his affinity with his ancestors? If so, he never pursued this task systematically, and he offered an analysis of present institutions more critical than constructive. He wanted to repair the machinery of government but was at a loss to say what that machinery would do. Alert to the threat of industrial capitalism to the ideals of democracy, he never thought seriously about how government should respond. All he could offer was the hope that the elite would somehow handle it. The fundamental changes he came to advocate demanded more, and Adams was not equal to the task of offering a blueprint for the future. Instead, he contented himself with the notion that people were losing control of their world, and the situation would result in a general smash up.

Adams could do little more than dream of gaining power, given his refusal to play the political game wholeheartedly. Historians who blame him for not adjusting to political reality often err in understanding their subject. Adams certainly was no political innocent. He was quite capable of pulling strings when he had friends in power. His suggestions for Independent strategy in 1876 demonstrate that he was realistic in much of his analysis of the political situation, however vague his own goals were. But he could not bring himself to work within the system precisely because he was trying to change it. He wanted power on his own terms. "His job was to figure out what he would best do for America; America's part was to let him," Dawidoff notes. "How America would use, recognize, accept, reward, welcome, and secure the talent of this supremely and confidently, intellectually and artistically, gifted son was the acid test of regime."[26]

At times Adams sought to excuse his inability to secure power and influence in national politics by claiming that the combined impact of the Civil War and Grant's administration barred people like himself from effective participation in politics—an explanation which has attained some popularity among historians as well. According to this interpretation, men of mind and refined taste found themselves trampled by the mass of vulgar, slimy politicos rushing to get in line at the Great Barbecue. Filled as it was with corruption and bad manners, this world of wheel and deal was no place for a gentleman. In the *Education* Adams reinforced this image of a world run amuck. Explaining why he had done so little by 1868, he assured his readers that the "defeat was not due to him, nor yet to any superiority of his rivals. He had been unfairly forced out of the track, and must get back into it as best he could." After all, "No one had yet regained the lost ground of the war." If he had failed to make a name for himself in Grant's Washington, it was not his own fault: "none of Adams's generation profited by public activity. . . . No editor, no political writer, and no public administrator achieved enough good reputation to preserve his memory for twenty years." He concluded that "all Washington . . . conspired to drive away every young man who happened to be there, or tried to approach. Not one young man of promise remained in the Government service. All drifted into opposition. The Government did not want them in Washington."[27]

Perhaps Adams was expecting a little too much of himself. After all, then as now, very few people became powers in Washington during their thirties. Certainly several of Adams's contemporaries—John Hay, Henry Cabot Lodge, and Oliver Wendell Holmes, Jr., to name but three—played important roles in national politics later on. Three of Adams's Washington associates—David A. Wells, Francis A. Walker, and James A. Garfield—left their mark on the Gilded Age. So, for that matter, did Henry's brother Charles and Moorfield Storey. These men had frequently used the war as a stepping-stone to political power. And Massachusetts origins did not automatically disqualify anyone from positions under President Grant. Godkin noted a month after Grant entered the White House, "Massachusetts has been so heavily drawn upon already that I suppose there is no chance for anybody else from the State." Both Charles Francis Adams Sr. and Jr. enjoyed appointments under Grant. Henry Adams's statement begs contradiction; it is not fair to assail Grant's Washington, as R. P. Blackmur did, for "its inability to furnish a free field for intelligent political action." For, as Blackmur suggested, "Power was what Adams wanted, but on his own terms; the terms of his training."[28] These terms proved impossible to meet; and why meet them, anyway?

If one of the dominant themes of the *Education* is the story of Adams's failure in political life, a close reading of the work reveals that Adams did not hold himself accountable for his failure. He constantly claimed that, of all his contemporaries, he appeared to be the best prepared to succeed, yet success always eluded him. His articles on Grant's administration promised to make him "a political authority," for "with his sources of information, and his social intimacies at Washington, he could not help saying something that would command attention." This did not depend on his gaining a wide readership, as he well knew: "The difference is slight, to the influence of an author, whether he is read by five hundred readers, or by five hundred thousand; if he can select the five hundred, he reaches the five hundred thousand." His articles would have been "more effective than all the speeches in Congress or reports to the President that could be crammed into the Government presses." What, then, prevented success? Adams argued that it was partly due to fate. At crucial points in his life, fate intervened in the form of war, progress, family, or friends, and dragged him away from his destiny. Adams seems to have been hopelessly adrift in his world, unable to influence events or outcome in any meaningful way. In the end, he became the manikin mentioned in the author's preface, without ego, without a will of its own. As Adams himself suggested, however, perhaps that manikin "must be treated as though it had life. Who knows? Possibly it had!"[29]

Henry Adams's personality and his approach to politics were the main causes of his failure in American politics. He appealed to the elite, not to the voting public that elected politicians to office. In fact, he had nothing to offer most voters. He had to depend on his ability to influence policy-makers to gain political success. However, his personality and political style served to throttle whatever chance he had of making a positive impact. His descriptions of public figures, while wonderful as political satire, served only to amuse his readers and alienate the very people he needed to influence—like Ulysses S. Grant—and to distract people from his analysis. Even reform journals like the *Nation* and the *Springfield Republican* took exception to his prickly prose. His arrogance merely reinforced this tendency. Manifestly unfit by temperament and physique to thrive in electoral politics, he had to depend upon his pen and personality for influence with men in government. Both poisoned his efforts. "The arrogance and aggressiveness with which Henry Adams pitted himself against the conditions of the regime and the age keep him interesting," notes Dawidoff. Nevertheless, as Dawidoff observes, those very characteristics suggest why Adams's own age found him less interesting: "Adams really was detached from American life, not merely philosophically but actually. . . . Was he more committed to reform or to unpopularity?"[30]

Adams's talents as a political leader were a curious mixture of insight and ineptitude. His ambivalence over political means created contradictions. He urged reformers to rouse public opinion in the pages of an elitist journal with a small circulation. He wrote that reformers should be willing to engage in the pushing and shoving surrounding the distribution of patronage, but he kept his own hands to himself. Calling on his comrades for active participation in unified efforts, he stayed away from both the Cincinnati Convention of 1872 and the New York meeting of Independents four years later, and he was not very active in presidential campaigns. Carl Schurz may have had him in mind when he remarked in 1882 that some of his fellow reformers backed away "from the actual battle after having made all sorts of strategic movements to bring it on." Endorsing decisiveness and involvement as essential to political success, Adams was himself indecisive. He let events and outsiders make decisions for him. He would not choose his own fate.[31]

Such erratic behavior dissipated much of his political effectiveness, and he did not have much to spare. His tendency to exaggerate his importance blinded him to his weak position. With a naiveté as charming as it is astounding, Adams assumed that political influence was his for the asking. Oliver Wendell Holmes, Jr., contended that Adams expected political office "to be handed to him on a silver platter." At Harvard, students and faculty alike snickered over the story that Adams could always be found at his office—waiting for the news that he had been nominated for the presidency. Like his ancestors, Adams itched for office—although probably with less intensity—as a sign of influence. Unlike them, he did not get it. He made himself embarrassingly available, but even close friends like Wells, Walker, and Cox offered nothing. The only offer he did receive—the mission to Costa Rica in 1882—was so minor as to be humiliating to the descendant of three ministers to England.[32]

Despite his intense desire to be an insider, Adams often sensed that his sensibilities condemned him to the observer's role. In his writings he often pictured himself as an outsider who could do little more than comment on the world around him. In his 1869 article "Men and Things in Washington," he posed as a European diplomat and compared the "prodigious charade" of politics to a play. At a time when professional politicians characterized reformers as effeminate, Adams used a woman, Madeleine Lee, as his personal vehicle in *Democracy*, dramatizing his own sensibilities through a character barred by her sex from holding political office. Madeleine and Adams both could only try to influence officeholders. By the time he wrote the *Education*, Henry Adams had resigned himself to the fact that while no one "held better cards, . . . he never got to the point of playing the game at all; he lost himself in the study of it, watching the errors of the players."[33]

Adams's political philosophy was little more than warmed-over classical republican theories of political institutions as propounded by his ancestors. His concern with uncontrolled power, corruption, strict adherence to the law and the Constitution, separation of powers, fear of patronage and its effect—all were central to republican thought. Adams was acutely conscious of his responsibility to continue the efforts of his forefathers to save republicanism. He did in fact develop some useful insights into the problems of Gilded Age America—most notably a concern with the impact of industrial and corporate growth on American society and its political institutions—but he never addressed this issue in his political writings beyond noting that the original conception of republicanism might prove too frail to withstand the revolutionary changes challenging its survival.

But Adams never developed these insights. He never set forth the foundations of a new American state. Instead, he seemed more interested in recovering the original republic. By exposing corruption, to "build by slow degrees this deep foundation of moral conviction," Adams could "bequest the result to posterity as a result not inferior to that of the Republic's founders"—an aim "high enough to satisfy the ambition of one generation." But by 1870, he was beginning to doubt whether anyone could accomplish the task. The collapse of checks and balances, the end of separation of powers, all left "little doubt that the great political problem of all ages cannot, at least in a community like that of the future America, be solved by the theory of the American Constitution." The collapse of political reform as an independent political movement over the subsequent six years confirmed his fears. By 1906 he concluded that "the system of 1789 had broken down. . . . The moral law had expired—like the Constitution."[34]

Adams was trapped by his frame of reference. He could not understand political change except in terms of the collapse of the republican ideal. While he was exposed to nineteenth-century political thought, Adams viewed Mill and Tocqueville as merely providing an updated version of classical republicanism, Adams style. In his political writings, he never addressed the problem beyond predicting that republicanism would probably prove too frail to withstand the challenge of industrial and technological change. Later he would build the *Education* around the theme of the failure of his attempts at education to keep up with the pace of change. That book, along with "The Rule of Phase Applied to History" (1909) and "A Letter to American Teachers of History" (1910), represented his attempt to grapple with change—an attempt to understand it by reducing it to a set of laws and mathematical formulas, replacing political theory based on moral absolutes with a "scientific" method of inquiry. However confused some of Adams's writings during this period may seem to modern readers, they suggest that at last he was trying to break fresh ground in his own way. This represented a step forward from his jeremiads of the 1870s bewailing the end of the republic. They also stand in marked contrast to his later analyses of American politics, which ranged from the insightful to the fantastic (and often fatalistic) and occasionally partook of the absolutely bizarre ramblings which some have mistaken for true genius.

Ironically, in his quest to rid the republic of the corrupting impact of the patronage system, Henry Adams alienated the one man most sympathetic to his goal of removing political intrigue from the governing process:

Ulysses S. Grant. Had Adams but known that Grant despised "mere trading politicians" and was predisposed towards reform, he could have assisted Grant's efforts. It was no accident that Grant was the first president to call for civil service reform. Here, one would think, was just the man Henry Adams wanted in the White House. What drove Grant and men like Adams apart was a basic clash in personality as well as policy. For Grant soon tired of the condescending behavior of reformers. He found them hypocritical in their attitudes towards patronage, unrealistic about politics, and unreasonable in their criticism of him. The "wild and astounding declarations" of reformers convinced him that there was "a good deal of cant about civil service reform, which throws doubt upon the sincerity of the movement." He declared that "the most troublesome men in public life are those over-righteous people who see no motives in other people's actions but evil motives, who believe all public life is corrupt, and nothing is well done unless they do it themselves." In a rare display of sarcasm, Grant concluded: "They are narrow-headed men, their two eyes so close together that they can look out of the same gimlet-hole without winking." Doubtless he appreciated the joke of one correspondent, who offered that the Adams family resembled a potato, because the best part was underground.[35]

Theodore Roosevelt, who first met Henry Adams while attending Harvard, also complained that political reformers' efforts were counterproductive when they engaged in hyperbole and sarcasm in presenting their arguments. As a result, readers tended to dismiss reformers' assertions of corruption and incompetency. "The longer I have been in public life, and the more zealous I have grown in movements of reform," he wrote Owen Wister, "the greater the horror I have come to feel for the exaggeration which so often defeats its own object." As an example, he cited Adams's *Democracy*: "I eagerly welcome the assault on what is evil; but I think that it hinders instead of helping the effort to secure something like a moral regeneration if we get the picture completely out of perspective by slurring over some facts and overemphasizing others." In 1905, Roosevelt reread *Democracy*, "that novel which made a great furor among the educated incompetents and the pessimists generally about twenty-five years ago." He told Henry Cabot Lodge that while it "had a superficial and utter cleverness, . . . it was essentially false, essentially mean and base." Although Roosevelt did not know who wrote *Democracy* (he guessed that E. L. Godkin and Clover Adams were involved, a very near miss), he thought "poorly" of the author.[36]

Roosevelt recalled that once he, too, had little respect for Republican politicos. "I suppose that this was because while at Harvard and for a year or two afterwards I moved in what might be called Mugwump circles," he told William D. Foulke. When he "got out into the world of men and . . .

120

took part in the rough and tumble of life where great deeds are actually done," Roosevelt became skeptical of his former friends, a feeling which later evolved into scorn after he was denounced by many Mugwumps for joining Lodge in support of James G. Blaine's presidential bid in 1884. People like Carl Schurz and Charles Sumner, two of Henry Adams's flawed idols, "came from among the classes that write; and the people who feel superior to others, and who also have the literary habit, are apt to persuade themselves and others that there really is such superiority." Roosevelt classed Henry Adams among these "heroes only of the cloister and the parlor," terming him, along with Henry James, as "charming men, but exceedingly undesirable companions," especially because of "the tone of satirical cynicism which they admired." Ironically, James himself agreed with Roosevelt's assessment of Adams. In the short story "Pandora," he based the character Mr. Bonnycastle on Adams: he "was not in politics, though politics were much in him"; it seemed that for him "the only way to enjoy the great Republic would be to burn one's standards and warm one's self at the blaze."[37]

Adams's personality, political philosophy, and perception of politics, then, explain much of his failure in politics. All were shaped in part by the fact that he was an Adams. Even his personality seemed part of the legacy. "Thanks entirely to our family-habit of writing," Henry once confessed to Brooks, "we exist in the public mind only as a typical expression of disagreeable qualities. Our dogmatism is certainly odious, but it was not extravagant till we made it a record." Holmes noted that while Adams and his brothers possessed "great talents," they also had "a gift of turning all life to ashes, that does not do justice to their own good points." One of Adams's graduate students discounted Adams's argumentative nature by saying that he was "disputatious by family inheritance." More importantly, his family heritage defined his duties and obligations, set the standards for success, and dictated how one was to attain these goals. As Henry Cabot Lodge remarked, "a biographer of any one of the fourth generation might well make his theme a study in heredity."[38]

Henry Adams embraced the family heritage and strove to accommodate his personal preferences to it. He molded a career for himself as a gentleman who, as a man of letters and as a politically active citizen, would guide the development of American culture, politics, and society. Unfortunately for him, the family heritage was really a family myth, a creation of the mind rather than a description of reality. The principles of duty, selflessness, public service, and ethical statesmanship were ideals one aspired to attain, rather than an accurate description of Adams's forefathers' behavior and motives. John Adams had agonized over the tension between these principles and his own personal ambitions and preferences. His descendants inherited the tension as well as the principles, with the added pressure that they saw their ancestors in the light of the myth, not the reality. As Lodge reminded readers of Charles Francis Adams, Jr.'s autobiography, "It must not be forgotten that this remarkable heritage brought to those who received it burdens as well as honor." Perhaps Henry's brother, John Quincy Adams II, put it better when he complained of being "absolutely beaten over the head with ancestry."[39]

Henry Adams felt great pressure to conform to these standards. Striving to create an identity for himself within the family tradition became an emotionally traumatic for him. By 1868 he thought he had succeeded at last in finding his true place in American life. But events during Grant's administration destroyed Adams's plans for personal success. Convinced that he had a role in the regeneration of republicanism, Adams discovered that there was no place for him in Ulysses S. Grant's America. He blamed Grant for that fact. To the end of his life, he raged about Grant to anyone who would listen. "I never could understand him, and never shall," he complained to James H. Wilson, a former friend of Grant who had also soured on the general; "How the deuce he ever rose to be a corporal beats my knowledge of human nature." His ambitions defeated, his career discarded, Adams lapsed back into his bouts of depression and pessimism. Events during the 1880s, especially Clover's suicide in 1885, completed his decline into self-pity. Only by understanding how Adams viewed Grant—as the incarnation of everything that had thwarted his career—can we understand why Adams went after Grant with such passion in *The Education of Henry Adams*.[40]

The source of Henry Adams's failure in politics lay within the man, not his times. His flaws obscured some useful traits and a superb intellect. His failure in politics paved the way for his later and greater successes. Yet, for all those achievements, Adams always remembered that he had not done what he had set out to do.

ABBREVIATIONS

ABA	Abigail Brooks Adams
AP	Adams Family Papers, Massachusetts Historical Society
BA	Brooks Adams
CA2	Charles Francis Adams, Jr.
CFA	Charles Francis Adams, Sr.
CMG	Charles Milnes Gaskell
Cycle	*A Cycle of Adams Letters, 1861–1865*, 2 vols., ed. Worthington C. Ford (Boston, 1920)
Education	*The Education of Henry Adams*, ed. Ernest Samuels (New York, 1973)
HBA	Henry Brooks Adams
HCL	Henry Cabot Lodge
JQA2	John Quincy Adams II
LHA	*The Letters of Henry Adams*, 6 vols., ed. J. C. Levenson, Ernest Samuels, Charles Vandersee, and Viola Hopkins Winner (Cambridge, Mass., 1982–1988)

NOTES

PREFACE

1. HBA to CA2, November 10, 1911, *LHA* 6:480.
2. HBA to CA2, November 10, 1911, *LHA* 6:480; *Education*, 266.
3. HBA to Henry James, May 6, 1908, *LHA* 6:136.
4. Ernest Samuels, *The Young Henry Adams* (Cambridge, Mass., 1948), viii–ix.
5. R. P. Blackmur, *Henry Adams* (New York, 1980), 7; Earl N. Harbert, *The Force So Much Closer Home: Henry Adams and the Adams Family* (New York, 1977); John J. Conder, *A Formula of His Own: Henry Adams's Literary Experiment* (Chicago, 1970); HBA to Elizabeth Cameron, February 6–13, 1891, *LHA* 3:408; Edward Chalfant, *Both Sides of the Ocean: A Biography of Henry Adams, His First Life, 1838–1862* (Hamden, Conn., 1982) and *Better in Darkness: A Biography of Henry Adams, His Second Life, 1862–1891* (Hamden, Conn., 1994).
6. Ari Hoogenboom, *Outlawing the Spoils: A History of the Civil Service Reform Movement, 1865–1883* (Urbana, 1961); John G. Sproat, *"The Best Men": Liberal Reformers in the Gilded Age* (New York, 1968).
7. William H. Jordy, *Henry Adams: Scientific Historian* (New Haven, 1952), 261, 265.
8. William Dusinberre, *Henry Adams: The Myth of Failure* (Charlottesville, 1980).
9. *Education*, 317.
10. *Education*, 16.

CHAPTER 1: THE EDUCATION OF AN ADAMS

1. *Education*, 4.
2. *Education*, 36.
3. *Education*, 26; CFA to HBA, October 28, 1858, AP; CFA to CA2, November 8, 1861, *Cycle* 1:67–69.
4. Martin Duberman, *Charles Francis Adams, 1807–1886* (Stanford, 1960), 23; *Education*, 6, 31, 35; HBA to CA2, November 3, 1858, *LHA* 1:5; Charles Francis Adams, Jr., *Charles Francis Adams, 1835–1915: An Autobi-*

ography (Boston, 1916), 12; Paul C. Nagel, *Descent from Glory: Four Generations of the John Adams Family* (New York, 1983), 217; Jack Shepherd, *Cannibals of the Heart: A Personal Biography of Louisa Catherine and John Quincy Adams* (New York, 1980), 397. The letters that Louisa Adams received from Mexico were written by Robert Buchanan, an officer in the 4th U.S. Infantry and a family relation. In one of history's little ironies, in the same regiment was a young lieutenant who served as regimental quartermaster. The two officers did not get along, and in 1854, Buchanan secured the young officer's resignation. The young officer was Ulysses S. Grant.

5. Edward C. Kirkland, *Charles Francis Adams, Jr., 1835–1915: The Patrician at Bay* (Cambridge, Mass., 1965), 33.

6. *Education*, 14–16.

7. Shepherd, *Cannibals of the Heart*, 96, 312–21, 340–43 (Charles Francis Adams cited on page 343); Duberman, *Adams*, 32–33, 52. Alcoholism ran rampant in the Adams family, a fact that perhaps explains why Henry was reluctant to make much of rumors concerning Grant's drinking habits. That Adams was not only aware of such charges but may have heard them from Buchanan himself is suggested by a passage in the *Education* (264). Buchanan remained in contact with the Adams family throughout the Civil War. See CA2 to ABA, January 20, 1863, *Cycle* 1:234–35.

8. Charles Francis Adams, Jr., *Charles Francis Adams* (Boston, 1900), 93–95. In *Patricide in the House Divided: A Psychological Interpretation of Lincoln and His Age* (New York, 1979), George B. Forgie suggests that the Civil War generation suffered from the imposing legacy left by the Founders.

9. HBA to CA2, February 28, 1867, *LHA* 1:521; *Education*, 3, 14–16.

10. *Education*, 29–51 passim; Charles Francis Adams, Jr., *Autobiography*, 32.

11. Samuels, *The Young Henry Adams*, 10. Samuels dismisses Adams's pessimism about his college years in chap. 4 of the *Education* ("Harvard College"), but Adams makes it clear that his greatest successes at Harvard took place outside the classroom.

12. *The Young Henry Adams*, 12–16, 34–37; Chalfant, *Both Sides of the Ocean*, 72.

13. *The Young Henry Adams*, 48–51.

14. The ploy of a "European excursion" as a way to buy time and create distance was not unique to Adams. See, for example, Howard M. Feinstein, *Becoming William James* (Ithaca, 1984), chap. 13; and Melvin Kalfus, *Frederick Law Olmsted: The Passion of a Public Artist* (New York, 1990), chap. 7.

15. *Education*, 70–71; Charles Francis Adams, Jr., *Autobiography*, 19; CFA to HBA, November 25, 1858, and CFA to Sumner, October 3, 1858, AP. Adams traveled from Quincy to New York, where he boarded a steamer for Liverpool (see Chalfant, *Both Sides of the Ocean*, 101).

16. CFA to HBA, October 25, 1858; December 26, 1858; and January 29, 1859, AP.

17. CA2 to HBA, October 9, 1858, and December 9–23, 1858, AP.

18. See Nagel, *Descent from Glory*, 215–17.

19. *Education*, 75–77; HBA to CA2, November 3–7, 1858, and December 17–18, 1858, *LHA* 1:2–11; HBA to Charles Sumner, December 22, 1858, *LHA* 1:12; Samuels, *Henry Adams*, (Cambridge, Mass., 1989), 32–33.

20. HBA to CA2, November 3–7, 1858, and January 18, 1859, *LHA* 1:5, 13–16.

21. HBA to CA2, January 18, 1859, and March 13, 1859, *LHA* 1:14–15, 28.

22. HBA to CA2, December 17–18, 1858, and March 13, 1859, *LHA* 1:6–11, 26–28.

23. CFA to HBA, November 25, 1858; July 18, 1859; August 18, 1859; and December 15, 1859, AP; HBA to CA2, May 9, 1860, *LHA* 1:140. Charles Francis Adams seems to have forgotten about his correspondence with his own father some thirty years before, when he complained that Old Man Eloquent's letters "are degenerating into sermons" (see Duberman, *Adams*, 29–30).

24. HBA to CA2, June 7, 1859; July 3–4, 1859; and November 23, 1859, *LHA* 1:45, 52, 65.

25. CA2 to HBA, December 19–23, 1858; January 15, 1859; and November 3, 1859, AP.

26. CA2 to HBA, January 15, 1859, AP; HBA to CA2, February 9, 1859, and November 23, 1859, *LHA* 1:20, 22–24, 65–66.

27. Duberman, *Adams*, 218; HBA to ABA, March 10, 1860, *LHA* 1:100; HBA to CA2, March 26, 1860, *LHA* 1:105.

28. HBA to CA2, March 26, 1860, *LHA* 1:106; Chalfant, *Both Sides of the Ocean*, 141, 146–76.

29. Samuels, *The Young Henry Adams*, 72; HBA to CA2, June 15, 1860, *LHA* 1:177.

30. For accounts of the crisis, see Roy Nichols, *The Disruption of the American Democracy* (New York, 1948); Allan Nevins, *The Emergence of Lincoln: Prologue to Civil War, 1859–1861* (New York, 1950); and David M. Potter, *The Impending Crisis* (New York, 1976).

31. HBA to CA2, November 23, 1859, *LHA* 1:67.

32. HBA to CA2, March 26, 1860, and HBA to ABA, May 6, 1860, *LHA* 1:106, 137.

33. HBA to CA2, March 26, 1860, and HBA to ABA, May 6, 1860, *LHA* 1:106, 137.
34. HBA to ABA, February 13 and 20, 1860, and HBA to CA2, May 19, 1860, *LHA* 1:91, 92, 149.
35. HBA to ABA, July 1, 1860, *LHA* 1:180.
36. Duberman, *Adams*, 223.
37. HBA to CA2, December 9–13, 18–20, and 26, 1860, *LHA* 1:204, 205, 208, 213.
38. HBA to CA2, December 9–13 and 18, 1860, and January 2, 1861, *LHA* 1:204–210, 217. See also Potter, *The Impending Crisis*, 533–34, and Daniel Crofts, *Reluctant Confederates: Upper South Unionists in the Secession Crisis* (Chapel Hill, 1989), 204–5, 234, 238–43.
39. HBA to CA2, January 17, 1861, *LHA* 1:222.
40. HBA to CA2, January 2 and 24–28, 1861, and February 5, 8, and 13, 1861, *LHA* 1:217, 226–27, 229–31.
41. HBA to CA2, December 18, 1860, and January 2 and 8, 1861, *LHA* 1:208, 217, 219.
42. HBA to CA2, January 2, 11, and 24–28, 1861, *LHA* 1:217, 220, 225.
43. HBA to CA2, February 8 and 13, 1861, *LHA* 1:229–32.
44. *Education*, 107.
45. Duberman, *Adams*, 256–58; Samuels, *The Young Henry Adams*, 93–96.
46. *Adams*, 256–58.
47. HBA to Sumner, March 22, 1861, *LHA* 1:232–33.
48. Duberman, *Adams*, 256–58; Samuels, *The Young Henry Adams*, 93–96.
49. Oliver Wendell Holmes, Jr., cited in George M. Fredrickson, *The Inner Civil War: Northern Intellectuals and the Crisis of the Union* (New York, 1965), 219; William Dean Howells, cited in Daniel Aaron, *The Unwritten War: American Writers and the Civil War* (New York, 1973), 122.
50. HBA to CA2, May 16, 1861, and June 10, 1861, *LHA* 1:236–40.
51. HBA to CA2, August 5, 1861, *LHA* 1:246–48; *Education*, 129.
52. HBA to CA2, July 26, 1861, and September 20, 1861, *LHA* 1:245–46, 253–54; CA2 to HBA, August 23, 1861, *Cycle* 1:28–30.
53. CA2 to CFA, June 10, 1861, *Cycle* 1:10–11.
54. HBA to CA2, December 28, 1861, *LHA* 1:266–68; CA2 to HBA, January [?], 1862, *Cycle* 1:102.
55. HBA to CA2, October 5, 1861, and December 13, 1861, *LHA* 1:254–55, 265–66. Chalfant, *Both Sides of the Ocean*, part 3, contains the most detailed analysis of these dispatches, although Chalfant's claim for Adams's influence in resolving the *Trent* affair is surely exaggerated and, in any case, unsupported.
56. HBA to CA2, January 10 and 22, 1862, *LHA* 1:268–71; HBA to Henry J. Raymond, January 24, 1862, *LHA* 1:271–73; Samuels, *The Young Henry*

Adams, 116; Chalfant, *Better in Darkness*, 22.

57. HBA to CA2, February 14, 1862, and November 21, 1862, *LHA* 1:281–83, 314–16.

58. HBA to CA2, December 28, 1861; March 15, 1862; and April 11, 1862, *LHA* 1:266–68, 284–86, 289–92.

CHAPTER 2: A NATIONAL SET OF MEN

1. *Education*, 137.

2. HBA to Frederick W. Seward, January 30, 1862, *LHA* 1:275; HBA to CA2, January 23, 1863, *LHA* 1:327.

3. *Education*, 138–44; HBA to CA2, February 20, 1863, and March 6 and 20, 1863, *LHA* 1:331–33, 336.

4. HBA to CA2, January 30, 1863, and March 20, 1863, *LHA* 1:328, 336.

5. HBA to CA2, February 13, 1863, *LHA* 1:329–30; HBA to John Gorham Palfrey, March 27, 1863, *LHA* 1:340.

6. HBA to CA2, February 13, 1863, *LHA* 1:329–30; John Stuart Mill, cited in Samuels, *The Young Henry Adams*, 137. In the *Education* (126), Adams gives the reader the impression that he met Mill nearly a year earlier; his contemporary correspondence seems a surer guide to dating the encounter.

7. Charles Vandersee, "The Political Attitudes of Henry Adams" (Ph.D. diss., UCLA, 1964), 31–32; Alan S. Kahan, *Aristocratic Liberalism: The Social and Political Thought of Jacob Burckhardt, John Stuart Mill, and Alexis de Tocqueville* (New York, 1992). Again, Adams in the *Education* (192) gives a rather jaundiced recollection of Reeve and followers of Mill and Tocqueville in general.

8. Samuels, *The Young Henry Adams*, 164; HBA to HCL, June 25, 1874, *LHA* 2:194. Samuels suggests (134) that Herbert Spencer influenced Adams's thought in the 1860s, but the Englishman is not mentioned in his writings until the 1870s, and then in such a way as to suggest that Adams had not previously perused his works. It seems probable that while Adams may have been attracted to notions of laws of development, he was more interested in how to manipulate those laws, as suggested by Comte. Adams's skeptical view of Darwin's theory was, of course, most memorably expressed in the *Education* (266): "The progress of evolution from President Washington to President Grant, was alone evidence enough to upset Darwin."

9. Samuels, *The Young Henry Adams*, 137. See also John Quincy Adams, entry for November 11, 1831, in *The Diary of John Quincy Adams, 1794–1845*, ed. Allan Nevins (New York, 1951 [1928]), 424; and James T. Schleifer, *The Making of Tocqueville's "Democracy in America"* (Chapel Hill, 1980), 49, 56, 65, 102.

10. J. C. Levenson, *The Mind and Art of Henry Adams* (Boston, 1957), 18–19; David Contosta, *Henry Adams and the American Experiment* (Boston, 1980), 32–34.

11. HBA to CA2, May 1, 1863, *LHA* 1:347–50.

12. HBA to CA2, October 16, 1863, *LHA* 1:399–400; Dusinberre, *Henry Adams: The Myth of Failure*, 42–53.

13. *Henry Adams: The Myth of Failure*, 35; HBA to Palfrey, February 12, 1862, and May 29, 1863, *LHA* 1:279–80, 357–59; HBA to CA2, June 25, 1863, *LHA* 1:364–66.

14. HBA to CA2, February 13, 1863, and October 23, 1863, *LHA* 1:329, 401–2; Henry Watterson, *"Marse Henry": An Autobiography*, 2 vols. (New York, 1919), 2:34; Samuels, *The Young Henry Adams*, 121.

15. HBA to CA2, November 13, 1863, *LHA* 1:406; Samuels, *The Young Henry Adams*, 127.

16. HBA to CA2, November 21, 1862, *LHA* 1:315.

17. HBA to CA2, May 22, 1862, *LHA* 1:300–1.

18. Mill, cited in Aaron, *The Unwritten War*, 102; HBA to CA2, May 22, 1862, *LHA* 1:300–1; HBA to CA2, July 17, 1863, *LHA* 1:371.

19. HBA to CA2, January 9, 1863; May 8, 1863; and July 23, 1863, *LHA* 1:324, 351, 375.

20. HBA to CA2, May 10, 1865, *LHA* 1:494.

21. For Adams's wartime desires for a harsh peace, see HBA to CA2, May 16, 1862, and July 14, 1865, *LHA* 1:299, 498; HBA to Palfrey, August 23, 1866, *LHA* 1:509; HBA to CA2, March 1, 1867, and April 3, 1867, *LHA* 1:524, 527–28.

22. HBA to CA2, July 14, 1865, *LHA* 1:498; *Education*, 42.

23. "British Finance in 1816" (*North American Review*, April 1867) and "The Bank of England Restriction" (*North American Review*, October 1867) are readily available in Charles F. Adams, Jr., and Henry Adams, *Chapters of Erie and Other Essays* (Boston, 1871); HBA to Charles Eliot Norton, February 28, 1867, *LHA* 1:522.

24. HBA to CA2, April 3, 1867, *LHA* 1:528; *Education*, 252.

25. On Massachusetts Republicanism, see Dale Baum, *The Civil War Party System: The Case of Massachusetts, 1848–1876* (Chapel Hill, 1984), and Eric McKitrick, *Andrew Johnson and Reconstruction* (Chicago, 1960), 215–37.

26. Baum, *The Civil War Party System*, 107–8; HBA to CA2, May 8, 1867, *LHA* 1:533.

27. *The Civil War Party System*, 107–8; HBA to CA2, May 8, 1867, *LHA* 1:533; HBA to Palfrey, August 23, 1866, *LHA* 1:509–10.

28. HBA to Edward Atkinson, October 5, 1868, *LHA* 2:3. On the Butler-Dana contest, see William B. Hixson, *Moorfield Storey and the Abolition-*

ist Tradition (New York, 1972), 16–19; David Montgomery, *Beyond Equality: Labor and the Radical Republicans, 1862–1872* (New York, 1967), 360–68; and Paul Goodman, "The Politics of Industrialism: Massachusetts, 1830–1870," in *Uprooted Americans: Essays to Honor Oscar Handlin,* ed. Richard L. Bushman et al. (Boston, 1979), 161–208.

29. HBA to CA2, May 8, 1867; November 16, 1867; and December 24, 1867, *LHA* 1:532–34, 557, 562.
30. HBA to CA2, November 16, 1867, *LHA* 1:557.
31. Benjamin Moran, in *The Journal of Benjamin Moran, 1857–1865,* 2 vols., ed. Sarah Agnes Wallace and Frances Elma Gillespie (Chicago, 1949), 2:1125, 1166–67, 1269; Samuels, *The Young Henry Adams,* 150; Otto Friedrich, *Clover* (New York, 1979), 167–68.
32. HBA to CA2, February 13, 1863; October 30, 1863; December 11, 1863; May 10, 1865; December 21, 1866; and May 8, 1867, *LHA* 1:330, 402–3, 414, 495, 514–16, 533; Dusinberre, *Henry Adams: The Myth of Failure,* 16, 38; CA2 to HBA, January [?], 1862, and January 23, 1862, *Cycle* 1:102, 237–39; Harold Dean Cater, *Henry Adams and His Friends* (Cambridge, Mass., 1947), cxvi n. 170; CA2 to JQA2, February 19, 1863, AP.
33. HBA to Palfrey, August 23, 1866, *LHA* 1:508–9; HBA to CA2, October 22, 1867, *LHA* 1:555.
34. HBA to CA2, March 15, 1862, *LHA* 1:285.
35. HBA to CA2, December 24, 1867, *LHA* 1:561–62.

CHAPTER 3: THE ROAD TO WASHINGTON

1. HBA to CMG, September 25, 1868, *LHA* 2:2; *Education,* 237–41; Samuels, *Henry Adams* (Cambridge, Mass., 1989), 77.
2. HBA to Atkinson, October 5, 1868, *LHA* 2:3; HBA to CMG, November 5, 1868, *LHA* 2:5; *Education,* 244–45.
3. HBA to CMG, November 25, 1868, *LHA* 2:5–6; *Education,* 245–46.
4. CA2 to CFA, May 29, 1864, *Cycle* 2:133–34; Charles Coleman, *The Election of 1868* (New York, 1933), 330; CFA to HBA, December 23, 1868, *LHA* 2:16 n. 1.
5. HBA to CMG, November 5, 1868, *LHA* 2:5; HBA to CA2, November 23, 1868, *LHA* 2:9.
6. *Education,* 249–50; HBA, "The Argument in the Legal Tender Cases," *Nation,* December 17, 1869.
7. HBA to David A. Wells, January [12], 1869, *LHA* 2:11; HBA to CA2, December 13, 1868, *LHA* 2:10.
8. On Garfield, see Allan Peskin, *Garfield* (Kent, Ohio, 1978), 246, 260–66.
9. HBA, "American Finance, 1865–1869," *Edinburgh Review* 79 (April 1869): 504–33; *Nation,* May 6, 1869; Chalfant, *Better in Darkness,* 159.

10. HBA to CA2, January 27, 1869, *LHA* 2:14.
11. *Education*, 251–52; Chalfant, *Better in Darkness*, 157.
12. Mark A. DeWolfe Howe, *Portrait of an Independent: Moorfield Storey, 1845–1929* (Boston, 1932), 124–29.
13. *Portrait of an Independent*, 124–29.
14. For the fullest statement of this position, see Geoffrey Blodgett, "Reform Thought and the Genteel Tradition," in *The Gilded Age*, ed. H. Wayne Morgan, 2d ed. (Syracuse, 1970), 55–76. Blodgett has offered a sympathetic defense of the politics of the era in "A New Look at the Gilded Age: Politics in a Cultural Context," which appears in *Victorian America*, ed. Daniel Walker Howe (Philadelphia, 1976), 95–108. Blodgett modified his description of this first cadre of reformers in 1980, admitting that the leaders of reform were "a relatively diffuse and scattered group of prominent individuals." See Blodgett, "The Mugwump Reputation, 1870 to the Present," *Journal of American History* 66 (March 1980): 867–87. Blodgett cites the Adams brothers as representative of this first group. Blodgett's comments about this first generation of reform leadership often overlook his own point that the second generation of so-called Mugwumps was far more purposeful and offered a more coherent perspective of American politics than did the reformers of the 1870s. To treat the reformers of the 1870s as a coherent group—and to present Henry Adams as their representative—distorts significant differences and minimizes Adams's personal responsibility for his fate in politics. Adams should be understood, first and foremost, on his own merits, especially since so many people, including Blodgett, draw upon his example to illustrate their points. For an illustration of this tendency, see William E. Nelson, *The Roots of American Bureaucracy* (Cambridge, Mass., 1982), which cites Adams and accepts his comments.
15. George F. Hoar, *Autobiography of Seventy Years*, 2 vols. (New York, 1904), 1:246; *Nation*, March 4, 1869.
16. *Education*, 262.
17. CFA, Diary, December 1868–March 1869 passim, AP.
18. HBA to CA2, December 13, 1868; January 22, 1869; February 3 and 23, 1869, *LHA* 2:10, 13, 17, 20; HBA to John Bright, February 3, 1869, *LHA* 2:18.
19. HBA to CA2, January 22, 1869, *LHA* 2:20.
20. HBA to CA2, January 27, 1869, and June 22, 1869, *LHA* 2:14, 39.
21. Henry Brooks Adams, "The Session," *North American Review* 58 (April 1869): 610–40; repr. in *The Great Secession Winter of 1860–61 and Other Essays*, ed. George Hochfield (New York, 1958), 63–93, at 64–65.
22. "The Session," in *The Great Secession Winter*, 65–67, 70.

23. "The Session," 70–71.
24. "The Session," 70–74.
25. HBA to Atkinson, February 1, 1869, *LHA* 2:15; HBA to Palfrey, February 19, 1869, *LHA* 2:19.
26. CFA to HBA, January 6 and 20, 1869, and February 3, 1869, AP.
27. For an account of Grant's first days in office, see William S. McFeely, *Grant: A Biography* (New York, 1981), 287–97.
28. William B. Hesseltine, *Ulysses S. Grant: Politician* (New York, 1935), and David H. Donald, *Charles Sumner and the Rights of Man* (New York, 1974), cover these events fairly well. See also Boutwell's *Reminiscences of Sixty Years in Public Affairs*, 2 vols. (New York, 1968 [1902]); Grant's previous offer of office is recounted therein (2:204). On Boutwell and Harvard, see Samuels, *The Young Henry Adams*, 11.
29. Adams, "The Session," in *The Great Secession Winter*, 68; HBA to CA2, March 11, 1869, *LHA* 2:21.
30. *Education*, 262: Blodgett, "Reform Thought and the Genteel Tradition," in *The Gilded Age*, 65; HBA to CA2, May 3, 1869, *LHA* 2:28.
31. HBA to CA2, March 29, 1869, *LHA* 2:22; HBA to CMG, March 30, 1869, *LHA* 2:23.
32. HBA to Bright, February 3, 1869, and May 30, 1869, *LHA* 2:17–18, 33–35; Chalfant, *Better in Darkness*, 160–61, 171–72, 177–79. Chalfant's speculation on the impact of these letters seems to me overwrought.
33. HBA to CMG, April 19, 1869, *LHA* 2:25; HBA to CA2, April 29, 1869, *LHA* 2:26.
34. HBA to CMG, April 19, 1869, *LHA* 2:25.
35. HBA to CA2, May 17, 1869, *LHA* 2:30; HBA to CMG, May 17, 1869, *LHA* 2:31–32; *Nation*, May 6, 1869; *Springfield Republican*, May 1, 1869; CFA to HBA, May 5, 1869, AP; Samuels, *Henry Adams*, 81–82.
36. HBA to CA2, May 3 and 7, 1869, *LHA* 2:27, 28; HBA to CMG, May 17, 1869, *LHA* 2:32.
37. HBA to CA2, May 21, 1869, *LHA* 2:33.
38. HBA to CMG, June 20, 1869, *LHA* 2:37.
39. HBA to CMG, June 20, 1869, *LHA* 2:37; HBA to Bright, May 30, 1969, *LHA* 2:35.
40. HBA to CMG, July 11, 1869, *LHA* 2:41; James A. Garfield to Mrs. Garfield, July 8, 1869, Garfield Papers, Library of Congress.

CHAPTER 4: A POWER IN THE LAND

1. *New York Times*, April 21, 1869.
2. HBA to CMG, August 27, 1869, *LHA* 2:42–43.
3. Henry Brooks Adams, "Civil Service Reform," *North American Review* 59 (October 1869): 443–75; repr. in *The Great Secession Winter*, 95–128.

Ronald M. Peters's *The Massachusetts Constitution of 1780: A Social Compact* (Amherst, Mass., 1978) is the most recent study of the document.

4. Adams, "Civil Service Reform," in *The Great Secession Winter*, 101–5.
5. "Civil Service Reform," 98.
6. "Civil Service Reform," 99–104.
7. "Civil Service Reform," 113.
8. "Civil Service Reform," 110–11.
9. "Civil Service Reform," 113, 126–28.
10. "Civil Service Reform," 113, 126–28; HBA to CMG, May 17, 1869, and August 27, 1869, *LHA* 2:31–32, 42; HBA to CA2, September 4, 1867, *LHA* 1:550.
11. Adams, "Civil Service Reform," in *The Great Secession Winter*, 106.
12. "Civil Service Reform," 111.
13. Hoogenboom, *Outlawing the Spoils*, 68–69; Richard E. Welch, Jr., *George Frisbie Hoar and the Half-Breed Republicans* (Cambridge, Mass., 1971), 35.
14. Zoltan Haraszti, *John Adams and the Prophets of Progress* (Cambridge, Mass., 1952), 27–28; Adams, "Civil Service Reform," in *The Great Secession Winter*, 128.
15. *New York Tribune*, October 26, 1869; *Nation*, November 11, 1869; *Springfield Republican*, October 27, 1869.
16. *Springfield Republican*, October 27, 1869.
17. HBA to Jacob D. Cox, November 8, 1869, *LHA* 2:50–51; Hoogenboom, *Outlawing the Spoils*, 67.
18. HBA to Cox, November 8, 1869, *LHA* 2:50–51. Cox responded ten days later, telling Adams that he read the piece "with great satisfaction" (Cox to HBA, November 18, 1869, AP).
19. HBA to CMG, October 5, 1869, and December 7–13, 1869, *LHA* 2:47, 56.
20. Hoogenboom, *Outlawing the Spoils*, 65–72.
21. Claude M. Fuess, *Carl Schurz, Reformer* (New York, 1932), 160; Hans L. Trefousse, *Carl Schurz: A Biography* (Knoxville, 1982), 182–85; HBA to Carl Schurz, October 27, 1870, *LHA* 2:86; Hoogenboom, *Outlawing the Spoils*, 60; Schurz to William Grosvenor, March 29, 1869, Schurz Papers, Library of Congress; Allan Nevins, *Hamilton Fish: The Inner History of the Grant Administration* (New York, 1937), 119.
22. On Garfield's career during this period, see Peskin, *Garfield*, chaps. 15–17.
23. Hoogenboom, *Outlawing the Spoils*, 70–72.
24. HBA to CMG, December 7, 1869, *LHA* 2:54.
25. Peskin, *Garfield*, 310–12; HBA to Garfield, December 30, 1869, *LHA* 2:59; HBA to CMG, March 7, 1870, *LHA* 2:66.

26. The most substantial account of this affair is Kenneth D. Ackerman's *The Gold Ring: Jim Fisk, Jay Gould, and Black Friday, 1869* (New York, 1988), although Ackerman does not always handle evidence with care, and his account of Grant's involvement rests all too much on the testimony of Gould, Fisk, and Corbin. Far less satisfactory—indeed, unacceptable—are Edward Chalfant's fanciful speculations in *Better in Darkness*, chaps. 9–11 and the accompanying notes. A close look at Chalfant's footnotes and sources reveals that his most important allegations—that Abel Corbin arranged for the death of newspaper editor Henry J. Raymond to insure access to the columns of the *New York Times*, that Julia Dent Grant accepted government bonds and assisted the conspirators, and that the president himself became involved (and that Henry Adams learned but concealed all of the above)—reflect the author's own feelings about Grant rather than the results of his research, as suggested by the lack of evidence to support his creatively reasoned contentions.

27. *Nation*, March 3, 1870.

28. [Henry Brooks Adams], "The New York Gold Conspiracy," *Westminster Review* 94 (October 1870): 411–36; repr. in *The Great Secession Winter of 1860–61 and Other Essays*, ed. George Hochfield (New York, 1958), 159–89. Later, Adams would suggest that Grant was more deeply involved, though he failed to offer more than a few pointed aspersions (see *Education*, 270–72). This subsequent account was shaped by Adams's desire to make a different point about the scandal than he had offered in the "New York Gold Conspiracy." Previously he had wanted to attack Gould, Fisk, and the threat of corporate power; now he wanted to shift the focus onto incompetence if not malfeasance in governance as personified by Grant.

29. Adams, "New York Gold Conspiracy," in *The Great Secession Winter*, 188–89.

30. HBA to Palfrey, May 29, 1863, *LHA* 1:357–59.

31. HBA to CMG, March 7, 1870, *LHA* 2:66; *Education*, 286–87.

32. [Henry Brooks Adams], "Men and Things in Washington," *Nation*, November 25, 1869.

33. HBA to CMG, June 20, 1869; November 23, 1869; and December 7–13, 1869, *LHA* 2:38, 52, 53–56.

34. HBA to CMG, December 7–13, 1869, *LHA* 2:56; *Education*, 262–65.

35. HBA to CMG, December 7–13, 1869, *LHA* 2:53–56. There is no record of Grant's reaction to this sole visit to the White House by Adams, although in October 1870, the president made clear his negative sentiments in a letter to Badeau. See Ulysses S. Grant to Adam Badeau, October 23, 1870, in Adam Badeau, *Grant in Peace: From Appomattox to*

Mount McGregor (Hartford, 1887), 472.

36. HBA to CMG, November 23, 1869, *LHA* 2:52; *Education*, 262–65.

37. HBA to CMG, March 28, 1870, *LHA* 2:67.

38. Irwin Unger, *The Greenback Era: A Social and Political History of American Finance, 1865–1879* (Princeton, 1965), 172–78; HBA, "The Arguments in the Legal Tender Case," *Nation*, December 17, 1868; "The Reopening of the Legal-Tender Case," *Nation*, April 7, 1870; *Education*, 249–50, 256–57; HBA to CMG, March 7, 1870, *LHA* 2:66.

39. HBA, "The Senate and the Executive," *Nation*, January 6, 1870; James Ford Rhodes, *History of the United States, 1850–1877*, 7 vols. (New York, 1892–1906), 6:378.

40. *Education*, 274–76. For two accounts of the roots of the Grant-Fish-Sumner feud, see Donald, *Sumner and the Rights of Man*, 408–10, 454–58; and Adrian Cook, *The Alabama Claims: American Politics and Anglo-American Relations, 1865–1872* (Ithaca, 1975), 103–23. The *Nation* picked up on Grant's comment about Motley's hair in its January 19, 1871 issue; Adams had leaked the statement to Godkin.

41. *Education*, 274–76; McFeely, *Grant*, 336–37.

42. It is fair to infer that Henry Adams's later recollections of his impression of Sumner might well have been influenced by his brother Charles's essay on the Treaty of Washington. See Charles Francis Adams, Jr., *Lee at Appomattox and Other Essays* (Freeport, N.Y., 1970 [1902]), chap. 2.

43. HBA to CMG, February 20, 1870, and March 28–April 3, 1870, *LHA* 2:64, 67–68.

44. HBA to CMG, March 7, 1870, and March 28–April 3, 1870, *LHA* 2: 65–68; Chalfant, *Better in Darkness*, 204; *Nation*, March 10, 1870, and May 5, 1870.

45. HBA to CMG, March 7, 1870, *LHA* 2:65–66; *Education*, 277–79.

46. Henry Brooks Adams, "The Legal Tender Act," *North American Review* 60 (April 1870): 299–327; *Nation*, May 12, 1870; *New York Tribune*, April 21, 1870; HBA to CMG, April 29, 1870, *LHA* 2:69.

47. William S. Robinson, *Warrington's Pen Portraits* (Boston, 1877), 419–20; Harold Davis, ed., "From the Diaries of a Diplomat: James S. Pike," *New England Quarterly* 14 (1941): 108.

48. Henry Brooks Adams, "The Session, 1869–1870," *North American Review* 61 (July 1870): 29–62; repr. in *The Great Secession Winter*, 191–222.

49. "The Session, 1869–1870," in *The Great Secession Winter*, 193–96.

50. "The Session," 196–97.

51. "The Session," 196–99.

52. "The Session," 196–99.

53. "The Session," 219–22.

54. "The Session," 219–22. See also George Hochfield, *Henry Adams: An Introduction and Interpretation* (New York, 1962), 1–10; and Stephen Skowronek, *Building a New American State: The Expansion of National Administrative Capacities, 1877–1920* (Cambridge, England, 1982), 1–162.

55. *Springfield Republican*, August 8, 1870; *Nation*, August 11, 1870; *New York Tribune*, August 9, 1870; Chalfant, *Better in Darkness*, 216.

56. Timothy O. Howe, *Wisconsin State Journal*, October 8, 1870.

57. HBA to CMG, December 19, 1870, *LHA* 2:95; *Springfield Republican*, May 1, 1869.

58. Timothy O. Howe to Grace Howe, December 9, 1870, Timothy O. Howe Papers, Wisconsin State Historical Society; Adam Badeau, *Grant in Peace*, 472.

59. HBA to Charles W. Eliot, July 3, 1870, *LHA* 2:72; *Education*, 287–90.

60. HBA, "Mr. Dawes—President Grant—General Butler," *Nation*, February 10, 1870; James Russell Lowell cited in Louis A. Coolidge, *Ulysses S. Grant* (Boston, 1917), 284.

61. John Russell Young, *Around the World with General Grant*, 2 vols. (New York, 1879), 2:262–66.

62. McFeely, *Grant*, 366–68; Nevins, *Hamilton Fish*, 358–72 (Grant/Fish exchange on 372).

63. HBA to CMG, August 4, 1870, *LHA* 2:77; *Education*, 292–94.

64. HBA to CMG, September 29, 1870, *LHA* 2:82.

65. Hesseltine, *Ulysses S. Grant*, 217; Hamlin Garland, *Ulysses S. Grant: His Life and Character* (New York, 1989), 427; *New York Herald*, November 5, 1870.

66. HBA to CMG, October 25, 1870, *LHA* 2:84.

67. HBA to Cox, October 31, 1870, *LHA* 2:86.

CHAPTER 5: FROM FIGHT TO FLIGHT

1. HBA to CMG, September 29, 1870, and November 11, 1870, *LHA* 2:81, 89; HBA to Wells, October 25, 1870, *LHA* 2:85.

2. HBA to CMG, November 18, 1870, *LHA* 2:89.

3. HBA to Cox, October 31, 1870, and November 11, 1870, *LHA* 2:86, 87–88; HBA to CMG, November 19, 1870, *LHA* 2:89; HBA to Schurz, October 27, 1870, *LHA* 2:86.

4. HBA to CMG, November 19, 1870, *LHA* 2:90; HBA to Cox, November 28, 1870, *LHA* 2:91–92.

5. HBA to Cox, November 28, 1870, *LHA* 2:91–92; Kirkland, *Charles Francis Adams, Jr.*, 160–61; CA2, Diary, November 22, 1870, AP; *New York Evening Mail*, January 3, 1871, in the scrapbooks in the Ulysses S. Grant Papers, Library of Congress.

6. See Hesseltine, *Ulysses S. Grant*, 220–37.
7. HBA to Cox, December 8, 1870, *LHA* 2:93; Garfield to Burke Hinsdale, February 22, 1871, Garfield Papers, Library of Congress.
8. HBA to Cox, December 8, 1870, *LHA* 2:92–93.
9. HBA to Norton, January 13, 1871, *LHA* 2:97; HBA to Wells, January 17, 1871, *LHA* 2:98.
10. Hoogenboom, *Outlawing the Spoils*, 86–88; Donald, *Sumner and the Rights of Man*, 490–93; Earle D. Ross, *The Liberal Republican Movement* (New York, 1919), 42.
11. HBA to Schurz, April 25, 1871, and May 16 and 24, 1871, *LHA* 2:107–9, 111; *Nation*, January 26, 1871; HBA to CMG, June 20, 1871, *LHA* 2:112.
12. For the most incisive and comprehensive investigation of the political role of the press, see Mark Wahlgren Summers, *The Press Gang: Newspapers and Politics, 1865–1878* (Chapel Hill, 1994).
13. HBA to Schurz, April 25, 1871, *LHA* 2:108; HBA to CMG, June 20, 1871, *LHA* 2:111–12.
14. Samuels, *The Young Henry Adams*, 222–25; Chalfant, *Better in Darkness*, 239–42. Chalfant (240–43) makes far too much of the inclusion of "The New York Gold Conspiracy" and its impact on the Grant administration and President Grant. Coming as it did after Adams's open break with the administration, the revelation of his authorship of "The New York Gold Conspiracy," if anything, reduced the article's impact, for now it was evident that the author numbered himself among the president's critics.
15. Duberman, *Charles Francis Adams*, 342–44.
16. HBA to CMG, December 14, 1871, and April 27, 1872, *LHA* 2:122–23, 135; HBA to Cox, September 30, 1871, *LHA* 2:116; HBA to Samuel J. Tilden, November 9, 1871, *LHA* 2:120.
17. HBA to CMG, October 2 and 23, 1871; November 13, 1871; December 14, 1871; and April 27, 1872, *LHA* 2:117–19, 121–23, 134; Dusinberre, *Henry Adams: The Myth of Failure*, 67.
18. HBA to CMG, April 27, 1872, *LHA* 2:135; Duberman, *Charles Francis Adams*, 358–61; Chalfant, *Better in Darkness*, 262–65.
19. Ross's *The Liberal Republican Movement* remains the best account of the convention, but see also Matthew T. Downey's "Horace Greeley and the Politicians: The Liberal Republican Convention in 1872," *Journal of American History* 53 (March 1967): 727–50; James G. Smart's "Whitelaw Reid and the Nomination of Horace Greeley," *Mid-America* 49 (October 1967): 227; and Richard A. Gerber's "The Liberal Republican Movement of 1872 in Historiographical Perspective, *Journal of American History* 62 (June 1975): 40–73. Joseph Logsdon's *Horace White*:

Nineteenth Century Liberal (Westport, Conn., 1971), 211–13, covers the abandonment of free trade. Most perceptive is the discussion offered by Mark Wahlgren Summers in *The Era of Good Stealings* (New York, 1993), 215–26.

20. William Gillette, *Retreat from Reconstruction, 1869–1879* (Baton Rouge, 1979), 61–63.

21. On the convention itself, in addition to the sources cited in note 19 above, see Donald W. Curl, *Murat Halstead and the Cincinnati Commercial* (Boca Raton, 1980), 62–69, and Summers, *The Press Gang*, 244–46.

22. HBA to CMG, April 27, 1872, and May 30, 1872, *LHA* 2:135, 137; HBA to Whitelaw Reid, May 15, 1872, *LHA* 2:136.

23. "The Campaign of 1872," *North American Review* 65 (October 1872):401–22; see also Chalfant, *Better in Darkness*, 270, 740 n. 36, although Chalfant's argument that Charles Francis Adams, Jr., wrote the article seems difficult to sustain in light of its content, which is favorable to Grant.

24. HBA to HCL, June 2, 1872, *LHA* 2:134.

25. HBA to CMG, October 26, 1873; February 13, 1874; and March 26, 1874, *LHA* 2:180, 188, 190. Perhaps Adams took some satisfaction in awarding the lowest grade in an English history class to Ulysses S. Grant, Jr. See John Y. Simon, "Ulysses S. Grant and Civil Service Reform," *Hayes Historical Journal* 4 (Spring 1984): 13.

26. For Grant's second-term struggles, see Gillette, *Retreat from Reconstruction*; Hesseltine, *Ulysses S. Grant*; Nevins, *Hamilton Fish*; and McFeely, *Grant*.

27. Duberman, *Charles Francis Adams*, 388–90; Donald, *Sumner and the Rights of Man*, 3–12, 581–87. In *The Era of Good Stealings* (247–49), Summers offers a most insightful revisionist assessment of the Simmons fight—one which I follow for the most part. See also Baum, *The Civil War Party System*, 188–89.

28. Stow Persons, *The Decline of American Gentility* (New York, 1973), 161; Sproat, *"The Best Men,"* 90; John A. Garraty, *Henry Cabot Lodge: A Biography* (New York, 1953), 45; Summers, *The Era of Good Stealings*, vii–viii, 175–77.

29. Duberman, *Charles Francis Adams*, 389–90; Baum, *The Civil War Party System*, 189–90; HBA to CMG, March 26, 1874, and June 22, 1874, *LHA* 2:190, 193–94.

30. Charles Francis Adams, Jr., "The Currency Debate of 1873–74," *North American Review* 119 (July 1874): 111–20, 129–46; Brooks Adams, "The Platform of the New Party," ibid., 33–60.

31. The review is found in *Sketches for the North American Review*, ed. Edward Chalfant (Hamden, Conn., 1986), 139–46.

32. HBA to CMG, October 31, 1874, and May 24, 1875, *LHA* 2:211, 225–26; HBA to HCL, May 26, 1875, *LHA* 2:227; HBA to Sir Robert Cunliffe, August 31, 1875, *LHA* 2:235. See also Charles Vandersee, "The Pursuit of Culture in Adams' *Democracy*," *American Quarterly* 19 (Summer 1967): 239–48.

33. HBA to HCL, December 30, 1874, *LHA* 2:215; HBA to CMG, February 15, 1875, *LHA* 2:217; *Springfield Republican*, January 14–16, 1875; Duberman, *Charles Francis Adams*, 390; Baum, *The Civil War Party System*, 199–200. Even Judge Hoar, Henry's old pal, preferred Dawes to the elder Adams.

34. HBA to HCL, October 31, 1874, *LHA* 2:212.

35. HBA to CMG, May 24, 1875, *LHA* 2:225–26; HBA to Schurz, April 12, 1875, *LHA* 2:222.

36. Fuess, *Carl Schurz, Reformer*, 216–18; Trefousse, *Carl Schurz: A Biography*, 225.

37. Trefousse, *Carl Schurz: A Biography*, 225.

38. HBA to CMG, October 4–15, 1875, *LHA* 2:238

39. HBA to CMG, February 9, 1876, *LHA* 2:247. On Bristow, see Ross A. Webb, *Benjamin Helm Bristow* (Lexington, Ky., 1969).

40. HBA to CMG, May 24, 1876, *LHA* 2:225–26; HBA to Schurz, February 14, 1876, and March 6, 1876, *LHA* 2:249–51, 261; HBA to Francis A. Walker, February 29, 1876, *LHA* 2:259–60; Summers, *The Press Gang*, 244.

41. Keith Ian Polakoff, *The Politics of Inertia: The Election of 1876 and the End of Reconstruction* (Baton Rouge, 1973), chaps. 2 and 3.

42. HBA to Schurz, February 14, 1876, *LHA* 2:249–51; HBA to CMG, February 9, 1876, *LHA* 2:247.

43. HBA to Schurz, February 14, 1876, *LHA* 2:249–51.

44. HBA to Schurz, February 14, 1876, *LHA* 2:249–51.

45. HBA to Schurz, February 14, 1876, *LHA* 2:249–51.

46. Adams's letter of February 14, 1876, to Schurz is the clearest statement of Adams's political perspective at this time. His letters of February 15 and 17, 1876, to Henry Cabot Lodge (*LHA* 2: 253–53) offer his clearest view on Bristow.

47. HBA to HCL, February 27, 1876, and May 15, 1876, *LHA* 2:257–58, 267; HBA to Wells, March 20, 1876, *LHA* 2:262.

48. *New York World*, May 16, 1876; Kirkland, *Charles Francis Adams, Jr.*, 163.

49. Fuess, *Carl Schurz, Reformer*, 222–23; Trefousse, *Carl Schurz: A Biography*, 227–28, *New York World*, May 16, 1876.

50. HBA to HCL, June 4 and 7, 1876, *LHA* 2:272–73; Summers, *The Press Gang*, 290–94.

51. HBA to HCL, June 4, 1876, and HBA to CMG, June 14, 1876, *LHA* 2:272, 274–77.
52. HBA to CMG, June 14, 1876, and September 8, 1876, *LHA* 2:276, 292–93; HBA to HCL, June 7, 1876, *LHA* 2:273.
53. HBA to HCL, June 30, 1876, and August 5, 1876, *LHA* 2:280–81, 285; HBA to Wells, July 15, 1876, *LHA* 2:282.
54. HBA to HCL, August 5 and 31, and September 4, 1876, *LHA* 2:285, 297–99; Henry and Charles Francis Adams, "The 'Independents' in the Canvass," *North American Review* 73 (October 1876): 426–67; repr. in *The Great Secession Winter,* 291–332, at 296.
55. HBA to HCL, June 21 and 24, 1876, *LHA* 2:278–79.
56. HBA to CMG, September 9, 1876, *LHA* 2:292–93.
57. HBA to HCL, June 12, 1876, *LHA* 2:274. Hazen never did complete his article; ironically, according to William T. Sherman, it was Orville Babcock, a featured player in the Whiskey Ring scandal, who had supplied Boynton with material for his attack on Sherman's *Memoirs.* See Lloyd Lewis, *Sherman: Fighting Prophet* (New York, 1932), 617. Sherman's suspicion is confirmed by letters in the Orville E. Babcock Papers at the Newberry Library in Chicago.
58. HBA to HCL, June 12, 1876, and August 25, 1876, *LHA* 2:274, 288. In *Better in Darkness* (327–28), Chalfant suggests that Charles alone wrote the piece, ignoring the fact that it follows Henry's notions and that Henry himself once said it was Charles "to whom I generally leave the duty of declaring our joint opinion" (HBA to Schurz, February 14, 1876, *LHA* 2:249).
59. Adams and Adams, "'Independents' in the Canvass," in *The Great Secession Winter,* 291–92.
60. "'Independents' in the Canvass," 293–303.
61. "'Independents' in the Canvass," 304–6.
62. "'Independents' in the Canvass," 294–96.
63. "'Independents' in the Canvass," 304–7.
64. "'Independents' in the Canvass," 326–30.
65. "'Independents' in the Canvass," 326.
66. "'Independents' in the Canvass," 327–31.
67. "'Independents' in the Canvass," 323–34.
68. "'Independents' in the Canvass," 312–13.
69. HBA to CMG, April 14, 1877, *LHA* 2:302–3.
70. HBA to CMG, June 14, 1876, and September 8, 1876, *LHA* 2:275–76, 292–93. As Mark Summers points out in *The Era of Good Stealings,* the reformers in fact had enjoyed a success in terms of the nomination of Hayes and Tilden; Adams's complaint was that it was the system which needed changing, not the candidates.
71. HBA to CMG, April 14, 1877, *LHA* 2:302–3.

CHAPTER 6: FAILURE

1. HBA to Cunliffe, December 16, 1888, *LHA* 3:160.
2. HBA to HCL, November 15, 1881, *LHA* 2:444.
3. HBA to E. L. Godkin, September 19, 1881, and February 23 and 27, 1885, *LHA* 2:434–35, 576–77.
4. HBA to CMG, September 27, 1894, *LHA* 4:215–16; HBA to Sir John Clark, March 6, 1881, *LHA* 2:420; HBA to Wayne MacVeagh, September 25, 1881, *LHA* 2:436–37; HBA to Godkin, September 26, 1881, *LHA* 2:437–38.
5. HBA to CA2, December 8, 1903, *LHA* 5:529.
6. Ernest Samuels, *Henry Adams: The Middle Years* (Cambridge, Mass., 1958), 168. For a somewhat different interpretation of the relationship between Adams as historian and Adams as examiner of American republicanism, see Russell L. Hanson and W. Richard Merriman, "Henry Adams and the Decline of the Republican Tradition," *American Transcendental Quarterly* 4 (September 1990): 161–83.
7. Henry Adams, *The Life of Albert Gallatin* (New York, 1943 [1879]), 154, 491–92, 560.
8. *The Life of Albert Gallatin*, 301–2.
9. HBA to HCL, October 6, 1879, *LHA* 2:376; HBA to Tilden, January 24, 1883, *LHA* 2:491; HBA to Elizabeth Cameron, April 17, 1899, *LHA* 4:710.
10. Henry Adams, *John Randolph* (Boston, 1882), 5, 11, 14.
11. *John Randolph*, 47, 172, 306.
12. HBA to John T. Morse, Jr., April 9, 1881, *LHA* 2:424; HBA to John Hay, October 8, 1882, *LHA* 2:475.
13. Henry Adams, *Democracy* (1880), in *Novels, Mont Saint Michel, The Education*, ed. Ernest and Jayne N. Samuels (New York, 1983), 14, 39, 81–82. For a different perspective, see B. H. Gilley, "*Democracy*: Henry Adams and the Role of the Political Leader," *Biography* 14 (Fall 1991): 349–65.
14. Adams, *Democracy*, 11–12, 17, 18, 21–22, 174.
15. *Democracy*, 33, 37.
16. *Democracy*, 8, 168, 178.
17. *Democracy*, 88–89, 99.
18. See Samuels, *Henry Adams: The Middle Years*, 84–104.
19. Henry Adams, *History of the United States during the Administrations of Thomas Jefferson and James Madison*, ed. Earl N. Harbert (New York, 1986), 1345.
20. *Education*, 280–81.
21. *Education*, 262, 266, 280, 322, 333.
22. Robert Dawidoff, *The Genteel Tradition and the Sacred Rage: High Cul-

ture vs. Democracy in Adams, James, and Santayana (Chapel Hill, 1992), 50.

23. HBA to BA, February 18, 1909, *LHA* 6:229.

24. Dawidoff, *The Genteel Tradition and the Sacred Rage*, 34.

25. HBA to Palfrey, February 19, 1869, *LHA* 2:19.

26. Dawidoff, *The Genteel Tradition and the Sacred Rage*, 41.

27. *Education*, 238, 241, 295–96.

28. Godkin to Norton, April 15, 1869, in *The Gilded Age Letters of E. L. Godkin*, ed. William M. Armstrong (Albany, N.Y., 1974), 135–36; Blackmur, *Henry Adams*, 5–7.

29. *Education*, xxx, 258–59.

30. Dawidoff, *The Genteel Tradition and the Sacred Rage*, 36, 52.

31. Blodgett, "Reform Thought and the Genteel Tradition," in *The Gilded Age*, 57.

32. Ernest Samuels, *Henry Adams: The Major Phase* (Cambridge, Mass., 1964), 193; Jack Shepherd, *The Adams Chronicles* (Boston, 1975), xiii; Jordy, *Henry Adams: Scientific Historian*, 267 n. 36.

33. Melvin Lyon, *Symbol and Idea in Henry Adams* (Lincoln, Nebr., 1970), 144; *Education*, 4. In *No Place of Grace: Antimodernism and the Transformation of American Culture, 1880–1920* (New York, 1981), T. J. Jackson Lears argues that Adams was torn between masculine and feminine values. One might add that his career as a political journalist had served, at least to some degree, to reconcile those values.

34. Adams, "Civil Service Reform," in *The Great Secession Winter*, 128; "The Session, 1869–1870," in *The Great Secession Winter*, 222; *Education*, 280–81.

35. Grant to William T. Sherman, June 21, 1868, William T. Sherman Papers, Library of Congress; John Russell Young, *Around the World with General Grant*, 2 vols. (New York, 1879), 2:264–65, 365; George W. Calif (?) to Grant, January 18, 1875, Ulysses S. Grant Papers, Library of Congress.

36. Theodore Roosevelt to Owen Wister, April 27, 1906, and Roosevelt to HCL, September 2, 1905, in *The Letters of Theodore Roosevelt*, 8 vols., ed. Elting Morrison (Cambridge, Mass., 1951–1954), 5:10, 222.

37. Roosevelt to William D. Foulke, January 4, 1907, in *The Letters of Theodore Roosevelt* 5:539–40; Roosevelt to HCL, January 28, 1909, in *The Letters of Theodore Roosevelt* 6:1490; Samuels, *Henry Adams: The Middle Years*, 168–69; Henry James, "Pandora," *New York Sun*, June 1 and 8, 1884. Adams dismissed TR as "pure act" in the *Education*, classifying him in the same terms as Grant, who found "action . . . the highest stimulant—the instinct of fight" (*Education*, 265, 417).

38. HBA to BA, March 4, 1900, *LHA* 5:100; Oliver Wendell Holmes, Jr., to Sir Frederick Pollock, March 24, 1916, in *The Correspondence of Mr. Justice Holmes and Sir Frederick Pollock*, 2 vols., ed. Mark A. DeWolfe Howe (Cambridge, Mass., 1941), 1:235; J. Lawrence Laughlin, "Some Recollections of Henry Adams," *Scribners Magazine* 69 (1921): 576–85, at 578; Lodge, "Memorial Address," cited in Charles Francis Adams, Jr., *Autobiography*, xv.
39. Lodge, "Memorial Address," xv; Nagel, *Descent from Glory*, 240.
40. HBA to James H. Wilson, May 20, 1884, *LHA* 2:540–41.

BIBLIOGRAPHICAL ESSAY

What follows is a short discussion of works pertinent to this study. Many of these works have contributed to my understanding of Adams and American politics in the years after the American Civil War; others either were published or came to my attention after the manuscript was essentially finished, although I have profited from them.

The primary source for this study is the papers of Henry Adams. A new, six-volume edition of his letters, edited by a team of scholars based at the University of Virginia, is now available: *The Letters of Henry Adams*, ed. J. C. Levenson, Ernest Samuels, Charles Vandersee, and Viola Hopkins Winner (Cambridge, Mass., 1982–1988), is a godsend to Adams scholars. The Massachusetts Historical Society has produced a microfilm edition of Henry Adams's incoming and outgoing correspondence on 33 reels; this pales in comparison to the 608 reels containing the Adams Family Papers, including the diary of Charles Francis Adams and letters among members of Henry's family. A sample of this latter correspondence was reprinted in *A Cycle of Adams Letters, 1861–1865*, 2 vols., ed. Worthington C. Ford (Boston, 1920). Although *The Letters of Mrs. Henry Adams*, ed. Ward Thoron (Boston, 1936), is a rich source of material on Henry's wife, the letters must be used with care, as material has been deleted by the editor.

Adams's own publications provide the other basic source for this study. His articles between 1869 and 1876, with the exception of "American Finance," are reprinted in *The Great Secession Winter of 1860–61 and Other Essays*, edited by George Hochfield (New York, 1958). Edward Chalfant has assembled Adams's *Sketches for the North American Review* (Hamden, Conn., 1986). *The Life of Albert Gallatin* (Philadelphia, 1879) and *John Randolph* (Boston, 1882) are important for the light they shed on Adams's perceptions of his era. The most explicit statement of his views, however, is in his novel *Democracy* (New York, 1880). Adams's authorship of *Democracy* remained a secret for decades after the book's publication, although some people suspected him of having written it. Finally, Adams's *History of the United States* (Boston, 1889–1891) is an extended commentary on both the America of Thomas Jefferson and the America of Henry Adams.

All Adams scholars must come to terms with *The Education of Henry Adams* (Boston, 1918). In this striking volume, Adams presented himself as he chose to be remembered by the public. The *Education* is part autobiography, part novel, part philosophy, and part social commentary, for Adams consciously shaped and distorted the facts of his life to fit larger themes concerning power, education, and knowledge. Most of all, the *Education* is an explication of Henry Adams's personal myth conveyed with a wry and sometimes cynical smile. The historian who uses the *Education* as a source for Adams's life and times must handle the document with especial care and sensitivity. I have quoted it as a description of Adams's actual experiences only when it seems to ring true with other evidence. Adams's portrayal of politics during the Age of Grant is self-serving and seriously warped, although it has deceived many a historian into taking it for gospel truth.

The most thorough study of Adams's life is Ernest Samuels's three-volume biography, of which the first volume, *The Young Henry Adams* (Cambridge, Mass., 1948), covers the first forty years. Samuels's account of Adams's political career is superficial and is based upon the blind acceptance of the Independent/Mugwump perspective as objective reality. Samuels's other volumes, *Henry Adams: The Middle Years* (Cambridge, Mass., 1958) and *Henry Adams: The Major Phase* (Cambridge, Mass., 1964), are far more impressive. Recently, Samuels has prepared a revised and abridged version of the biography, *Henry Adams* (Cambridge, Mass., 1989), but there are no substantial alterations to his earlier account of Adams's political career.

Edward Chalfant's *Both Sides of the Ocean: A Biography of Henry Adams, His First Life, 1838–1862* (Hamden, Conn., 1982) is the first of a projected three-volume biography. This initial volume covers the same ground discussed in chapter 1 of this study. Chalfant's volume reflects prodigious research and contains some suggestive interpretations, but its overall argument is not persuasive, and a few of its interpretations are wrong-headed. Especially questionable are his statements about Adams's role in the *Trent* affair and his presentation of Adams as a prematurely mature young man who was the rock of stability in his family and whose preternatural abilities included conceiving *The Education of Henry Adams* in May 1860. Chalfant's second volume, *Better in Darkness: A Biography of Henry Adams, His Second Life, 1862–1891* (Hamden, Conn., 1994), demonstrates renewed diligence in research about Adams but is marred by the same faults that mark the first volume. Chalfant fails to place Adams in context; his allegations concerning the roles played by members of the Grant family are unsupported by evidence and display a hostility toward the Grants that exceeds even Adams's. Despite a few flashes of insight, Chalfant's portrait of Adams is neither biography or scholarship but a true labor of love that approaches idolatry.

Elizabeth Stevenson's sprightly but somewhat thin *Henry Adams: A Biography* (New York, 1956) portrays Adams as a brash young man. Unfortunately, that is about all she has to say about his political career. William H.

Jordy's *Henry Adams: Scientific Historian* (New Haven, 1952) is a very intelligent study of Adams's public life and his career as a historian. The same cannot be said of Robert A. Hume's *Runaway Star: An Appreciation of Henry Adams* (Ithaca, 1951), at least in its discussion of Adams's political activities.

Several studies of Adams the writer discuss his political career in terms of his early literary efforts. J. C. Levenson's *The Mind and Art of Henry Adams* (Boston, 1957) is one of the better works on Adams, especially in its discussion of Adams's pre-1868 life and his use of satire. Levenson correctly comments that, while most readers know Adams from the *Education*, "the image which they identify with the man is a projection partly of Adams, partly of themselves." George Hochfield's *Henry Adams: An Introduction and Interpretation* (New York, 1962) is refreshing, for Hochfield questions Adams's political aims and his portrait of Grant's Washington, an achievement rare among Adams biographers. In *A Formula of His Own: Henry Adams's Literary Experiment* (Chicago, 1970), John J. Conder provides an interesting evaluation of the *Education* as literature but fails to address how Adams altered reality to suit his formula. James G. Murray in *Henry Adams* (New York, 1974) alternates between perceptive analysis and a tendency to seek the cosmic in Adams's works. Like Levenson, Vern Wagner stresses Adams's love of satire and overstatement in *The Suspension of Henry Adams* (Detroit, 1969). Melvin Lyon's discussion of *Symbol and Idea in Henry Adams* (Lincoln, Nebr., 1970) lends insight into Adams's use of analogy and metaphor. In *Seeing and Being: The Plight of the Participant Observer in Emerson, James, Adams and Faulkner* (Middletown, Conn., 1981), Carolyn Porter correctly understands Adams's prime goal of seeking influence. William Merrill Decker's *The Literary Vocation of Henry Adams* (Chapel Hill, 1990) contains a very interesting chapter on "The Romance and Tragedy of Statesmanship," which draws connections between prose and politics.

In recent years, several new books on Adams have appeared. The best so far is David Contosta's *Henry Adams and the American Experiment* (Boston, 1980). Skillfully combining recent scholarship on the politics of the 1870s with a thoughtful appraisal of Adams's career, Contosta provides an excellent introduction to Adams. However, he blurs Adams's description of Grant's Washington by treating it as if it encompassed the eight years of Grant's presidency, when in reality Adams lived there for just nineteen months. Another absorbing study is *Henry Adams: The Myth of Failure*, by William Dusinberre (Charlottesville, 1980); it contributes an excellent critique of Adams's *History* and underlines the importance of his personal relationships. However, Dusinberre's assertion that Adams desired a literary career is misleading, for Adams's writings make clear that he desired to fuse politics with literature as a gentleman of letters involved in public life as a political journalist and adviser. R. P. Blackmur's *Henry Adams* (New York,

1980) is an exercise in unabashed admiration. Here the problem of a biographer identifying with his subject is especially serious, for Blackmur often imitates Adams's writing style. Robert Dawidoff's *The Genteel Tradition and the Sacred Rage: High Culture vs. Democracy in Adams, James, and Santayana* (Chapel Hill, 1992) stresses the Tocqueville-Adams connection in an insightful essay. Earl N. Harbert's *The Force So Much Closer Home: Henry Adams and the Adams Family* (New York, 1977) is sometimes suggestive; Joanne Jacobson's *Authority and Alliance in the Letters of Henry Adams* (Madison, Wis., 1992) reminds us of the importance of his correspondence in revealing his relationships; Patricia O'Toole's *The Five of Hearts: An Intimate Portrait of Henry Adams and His Friends, 1880–1918* (New York, 1990) covers Adams's later life.

Marian Hooper Adams has also attracted biographers. Otto Friedrich's *Clover* (New York, 1979) teems with chatty asides and gossip; it cites Gore Vidal's *1876* (itself a pale imitation of Adams's *Democracy*) as its primary source for that year's events. Eugenia Kaledin's *The Education of Mrs. Henry Adams* (Philadelphia, 1981) argues that Clover's experiences typified the tensions of American upper-class women. For Henry Adams's platonic affair with Elizabeth Cameron, see Arline Boucher Tehan, *Henry Adams in Love: The Pursuit of Elizabeth Sherman Cameron* (New York, 1983).

The literature on the Adams family is huge. Paul C. Nagel's *Descent from Glory: Four Generations of the John Adams Family* (New York, 1983) is the place to begin. James Truslow Adams's *The Adams Family* (New York, 1930) still has some value, although it is more correctly a collective biography than a study of the family. Peter Shaw's *The Character of John Adams* (Chapel Hill, 1976) is engrossing and incisive portraiture. John Howe's *The Changing Political Thought of John Adams* (Princeton, 1964) and Zoltan Haraszti's *John Adams and the Prophets of Progress* (Cambridge, Mass., 1952) prove quite helpful. On John Quincy and Louisa Catherine Adams, see Jack Shepherd's sensitive *Cannibals of the Heart* (New York, 1980) and David F. Musto's "The Youth of John Quincy Adams," *Proceedings of the American Philosophical Society* 113 (1969): 269–82, an essay which discusses the origins of the Adams family myth. On the matriarchs of the family, see Paul C. Nagel's *The Adams Women: Abigail and Louisa Adams, Their Sisters and Daughters* (New York, 1987). Martin Duberman has produced the definitive biography of Henry's father in *Charles Francis Adams, 1807–1886* (Stanford, 1960). Having delved through Charles Francis Adams's papers, I salute Duberman's courage and question his sanity for undertaking the study. Edward C. Kirkland's *Charles Francis Adams, Jr., 1835–1915: The Patrician at Bay* (Cambridge, Mass., 1965) is the best we have, but it is far from complete; Thomas K. McCraw's *Prophets of Regulation* (Cambridge, Mass., 1984) includes an informative chapter on Charles. No biography exists of John Quincy

Adams II. On Brooks Adams, see *Brooks Adams: Constructive Conservative*, by Thornton Anderson (Ithaca, 1951); and the fuller *Brooks Adams: A Biography*, by Arthur F. Beringause (New York, 1955). Abigail Adams Homans has written an entertaining memoir of her uncles Charles, Henry, and Brooks in *Education by Uncles* (Boston, 1966).

The New England in which Henry Adams grew up has been the subject of several studies. Daniel Walker Howe's *The Unitarian Conscience: Harvard Moral Philosophy, 1805–1861* (Cambridge, Mass., 1970) provides an intellectual backdrop, while Howe's *The Political Culture of the American Whigs* (Chicago, 1979) does the same for the political scene. Ronald Story's *The Forging of An Aristocracy: Harvard and the Boston Upper Class, 1800–1870* (Middletown, Conn., 1980), Martin Green's *The Problem of Boston: Some Readings in Cultural History* (New York, 1966), and E. Digby Baltzell's *Puritan Boston and Quaker Philadelphia: Two Protestant Ethics and the Spirit of Class Authority and Leadership* (New York, 1979) sketch in the social and cultural background.

For Adams's fellow reformers and Liberal Republicans, see Mark A. DeWolfe Howe's *Portrait of an Independent: Moorfield Storey, 1845–1929* (Boston, 1932), Joseph Logsdon's *Horace White: Nineteenth Century Liberal* (Westport, Conn., 1971), Claude M. Fuess's *Carl Schurz, Reformer* (New York, 1932), Hans L. Trefousse's *Carl Schurz: A Biography* (Knoxville, 1982), Donald W. Curl's *Murat Halstead and the Cincinnati Commercial* (Boca Raton, 1980), Norma L. Peterson's *Freedom and Franchise: The Political Career of B. Gratz Brown* (Columbia, Mo., 1965), Gordon Milne's *George William Curtis and the Genteel Tradition* (Bloomington, Ind., 1956), John A. Garraty's *Henry Cabot Lodge: A Biography* (New York, 1953), and William M. Armstrong's *E. L. Godkin* (New York, 1978). Must reading is Mark Wahlgren Summers's spirited *The Press Gang: Newspapers and Politics, 1865–1878* (Chapel Hill, 1994); its accounts of the composition of the news should give pause to those people who cite newspapers uncritically, while its portrait of correspondents as political participants is right on the mark. Ironically, Henry Adams does not appear in Summers's index.

On the civil service reform movement of the 1870s, Ari Hoogenboom's *Outlawing the Spoils: A History of the Civil Service Reform Movement, 1865–1883* (Urbana, 1961) remains the standard work. The political reformers are dissected in John G. Sproat's *"The Best Men": Liberal Reformers in the Gilded Age* (New York, 1968), Earle Dudley Ross's *The Liberal Republican Movement* (New York, 1919), and John Tomsich's *A Genteel Endeavor: American Culture and Politics in the Gilded Age* (Stanford, 1971). Geoffrey Blodgett's "Reform Thought and the Genteel Tradition," a chapter in *The Gilded Age*, ed. H. Wayne Morgan, 2d ed. (Syracuse, 1970), is far more relevant to this study than his *The Gentle Reformers: Massachusetts Democrats in the Cleveland*

Era (Cambridge, Mass., 1966). Economic issues are covered in Walter T. K. Nugent's *Money and American Society, 1865–1880* (New York, 1968) and *The Money Question During Reconstruction* (New York, 1967), Robert P. Sharkey's *Money, Class, and Party: An Economic Study of the Civil War and Reconstruction* (Baltimore, 1959), and Irwin Unger's *The Greenback Era: A Social and Political History of American Finance, 1865–1879* (Princeton, 1965). Two other books of interest are Thomas L. Haskell's *The Emergence of Professional Social Science: The American Social Science Association and the Nineteenth-Century Crisis in Authority* (Urbana, 1977) and Mary O. Furner's *Advocacy & Objectivity: A Crisis in the Professionalization of American Social Science, 1865–1905* (Lexington, Ky., 1975). Alan S. Kahan's *Aristocratic Liberalism: The Social and Political Thought of Jacob Burckhardt, John Stuart Mill, and Alexis de Tocqueville* (New York, 1992) establishes a wider context for these concerns.

On politics during the Grant administration, one should turn to William R. Brock's *Conflict and Transformation: The United States, 1844–1877* (New York, 1973), David H. Donald's *Liberty and Union: The Crisis of Popular Government, 1830–1890* (Boston, 1978), and William Gillette's *Retreat from Reconstruction, 1867–1879* (Baton Rouge, 1979) for overviews. However, no good monograph exists on Grant's presidency. On Grant as president, the best biography remains William B. Hesseltine's *Ulysses S. Grant: Politician* (New York, 1935), which argues that Grant possessed political ability and casts a skeptical eye upon the motives of reformers. William S. McFeely's *Grant: A Biography* (New York, 1981) says virtually nothing about the reformers versus Grant. Good introductions to Grant as a politician are John A. Carpenter's *Ulysses S. Grant* (New York, 1970) and Louis A. Coolidge's *Ulysses S. Grant* (Boston, 1917). Adam Badeau's *Grant in Peace: From Appomattox to Mount McGregor* (Hartford, 1887) and John Russell Young's *Around the World with General Grant*, 2 vols. (New York, 1880) contain Grant's often caustic remarks about reformers. By far the best and most thoughtful study of corruption, politics, and reform in the 1870s is Mark Wahlgren Summers's *The Era of Good Stealings* (New York, 1993).

For members of the Grant administration, see Allan Nevins's *Hamilton Fish: The Inner History of the Grant Administration* (New York, 1937), George S. Boutwell's *Reminiscences of Sixty Years in Public Affairs*, 2 vols. (New York, 1968 {1902}), Jacob D. Cox's "How Judge Hoar Ceased to Be Attorney General," *Atlantic Monthly* 76 (1895): 162–73, and Ross A. Webb's *Benjamin Helm Bristow* (Lexington, Ky., 1969). Charles Sumner has received his due in David H. Donald's *Charles Sumner and the Coming of the Civil War* (New York, 1960) and *Charles Sumner and the Rights of Man* (New York, 1974). Three of Adams's friends in power in Congress have been the subjects of first-rate biographies: *Garfield*, by Allan Peskin (Kent, Ohio, 1978);

George Frisbie Hoar and the Half-Breed Republicans, by Richard E. Welch, Jr. (Cambridge, Mass., 1971); and, as mentioned above, *Carl Schurz: A Biography*, by Trefousse.

Paul Goodman, "The Politics of Industrialism: Massachusetts, 1830–1870," in *Uprooted Americans: Essays to Honor Oscar Handlin*, ed. Richard L. Bushman et al. (Boston, 1979), and Richard H. Abbott, "Massachusetts: Maintaining Hegemony," in *Radical Republicans in the North: State Politics during Reconstruction*, ed. James C. Mohr (Baltimore, 1976), offer surveys of the political scene in the Bay State. Dale Baum's *The Civil War Party System: The Case of Massachusetts, 1848–1876* (Chapel Hill, 1984) focuses on the transitions within Republican ranks during the Grant administration. Stephen Skowronek's *Building a New American State: The Expansion of National Administrative Capacities, 1877–1920* (Cambridge, England, 1982) offers new ways of looking at what reformers wanted to do.

Finally, several works discuss the impact of the Adams and his fellow intellectuals. George M. Frederickson's *The Inner Civil War: Northern Intellectuals and the Crisis of the Union* (New York, 1965) omits Henry Adams in favor of his brother Charles in its discussion of New England's response to the war. Daniel Aaron looks at Henry and the war in *The Unwritten War: American Writers and the Civil War* (New York, 1973) in an exceptional chapter. For an evaluation of Aaron's work, see Lewis P. Simpson's "The Civil War and the Failure of Literary Mind in America," in *The Brazen Face of History: Studies in the Literary Consciousness in America* (Baton Rouge, 1980), chapter 5 (103–14). Robert Kelley's *The Transatlantic Persuasion: The Liberal-Democratic Mind in the Age of Gladstone* (New York, 1969) overlooks the impact of Mill and English liberal radicalism upon American intellectuals. For Anglo-American intellectual and cultural ties, see *Victorian America*, edited by Daniel Walker Howe (Philadelphia, 1975). Far less impressive is the discussion of Adams in John P. Diggins's *The Lost Soul of American Politics: Virtue, Self-Interest, and the Foundations of Liberalism* (New York, 1984), in part because at times Diggins mistakes the writings of Charles Francis Adams, Jr., for those of his brother.

INDEX

DATE DUE

The Library Store   #47-0107